"A wise traveler emerging from a mainstream businessman is an evolution that's huge and takes immense courage. The lessons are learned, little by little, literally on the traveler's feet, and Hickey's story is inspiring. The reader will be stunned by the vitality of the journey, amped not in the least because the writer is well outside the range, often out of sight, of anything hinting at Western culture. This is a great read, and you need to get ready for the ride of your life. It won't be the same as taking your BMW—or even your old, beat-up Chevy—and trading it in for a backpack, setting off on a personal trip around the globe where you face hippopotami in the shallows and your fellow travelers exhausted or high in a hostel or dance to the drums at a wedding few Western eyes have witnessed or deal with a con-man in the back streets of a third world city. It won't be the same. But it's close."

—Clive Matson, writer, teacher and author of
Let the Crazy Child Write!

BOOK 1

BREAKING FREE

*There are days that rumble through
the pages of time waiting to be lived.
Days fantasies are made of.
This was to be one of those days.*

DENIS HICKEY

Published in 2013 by Vingdinger Publishing LLC
Copyright © Denis Hickey 2013

The moral right of the author has been asserted.

ISBN: 978-0-9888588-4-8 (paperback)
ISBN: 978-0-9888588-1-7 (ebook)
LCCN: 2013932578

Front cover design by Paweł Jońca
Interior and back cover design by Jill Ronsley
Maps by Kazimierz Pelczar
Ebook formatting by Sun Editing & Book Design

Websites:
vingdingerpublishing.com,
breakingfree-thebooks.com

Printed and bound in the USA

While this book is a memoir, the names of some people have been
changed to protect their civil rights.

To Ella Hinds

Contents

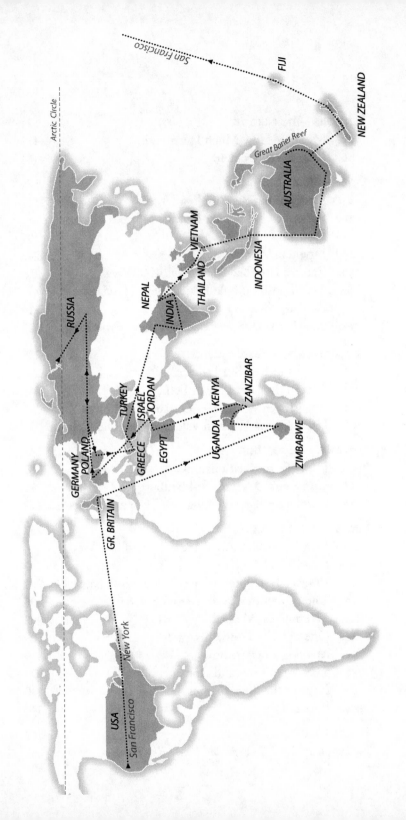

Acknowledgements

I WOULD LIKE TO ACKNOWLEDGE Clive Matson, poet extraor-
dinaire, who, during our twenty-five year friendship, taught me
elements and refinements of writing. Clive helped think this
book through and encouraged me to publish. I would also like to
thank the many students of Clive's who critiqued *Breaking Free*
over the years.

Thanks to my original editor and son-in-law, Tom Hinds, for
his considerable effort and perseverance editing and prodding me
to eliminate some favorite stories because they held up pace or
fit poorly; also for the many words and phrases he conjured up in
his fertile imagination.

To my daughters, Shannon and Chimene, who read and critiqued this book, adding clarity in areas often personal to them,
and to my former wife, Kathleen, who edited and trusted my
point of view. Thanks to my brother Dan for his meticulous and
articulate editing, and to my sister Marilyn and cousin Sharon for
reading and caring. Thanks mom for your faith in me.

My thanks for the stories and friendship of travelers along
the way: to Carmen in Kenya, Sweet Sue in Uganda and among
giants in Egypt, Mark in Dahab. Thanks Christian for providing
a touch of home in Hamburg and for arranging my voyage to
Siberia. To Sasha and Irena in Moscow for their hospitality.

Thanks Malgosia for persevering with me, and for your
thoughts and gentle prodding to gradually move *Breaking Free*
to market.

I owe gratitude to my friend Rich Rourke for supplying willpower and process to break free in the first place, and thanks to

Nicola, Gudren and Eberhart for use of your spectacular house on a Corsican cliff overlooking the Adriatic where I wrote much of this book.

I would like to acknowledge my buddy Frank Zolfo for his positive attitude and command to "get this book published!" My second book in this series, to be published soon, has unforgettable scenes with Frank in a jungle experiencing the difference between $500 and $10 a night lodgings.

Thanks Barney Kirsen for constructing *breakingfree-thebooks.com* website and for his expert help in developing and executing a marketing strategy.

Finally, thanks to Jill Ronsley for providing the final edit of *Breaking Free* which improved the pace significantly, and for her internal book design and back cover. Jill also gave me invaluable advice during the publishing process, and is the sweetest person.

BOARDROOM BLOWOUT

M
Y OLD LIFE ENDED ON the twenty-ninth floor of the Transamerica Pyramid. I was standing with my back to a group of thirty expensively suited men—the managers of a sugar conglomerate headed for bankruptcy, and their high-priced lawyers, bankers, and consultants. They sat around a polished hardwood table in the boardroom of a top San Francisco law firm, neat rows of yellow pads and sharp pencils at the ready. My partner, Larry, and Scott, a junior partner, stood near the head of the table. They had just finished proposing a way to stop the cash hemorrhage in the company's domestic operations.

We were "turnaround experts." We saved struggling companies from going under. But as I began to pontificate on how the international operations could rebound from disaster, I was suddenly paralyzed. The connections between the colorful graphs I was meant to be presenting and their meaning faded from my consciousness. No words came out of my mouth.

At first, I was puzzled. Puzzlement quickly morphed into panic, as the memory cells storing my presentation fizzled, then short-circuited. Trying to make sense of what was happening to me, I desperately searched the graph on screen for anything that might bring me back. But all that came to mind was "I'm fucked!"

The room was quiet. There was nothing to say to these people. I just stood there, my back to them, in silent humiliation, listening to occasional rustling sounds.

Thoughts and images streamed by. Last night with my wife, Kathi, in a Sausalito hotel overlooking the Bay and the city's shimmering skyline. My pride in celebrating our twenty-fifth anniversary. Our toasts to tenacity. But caught in these memories was the queasy uneasiness churning within me lately.

My life was going too fast. Out of control. No time for family or friends, no time to philosophize, no time even to listen to anyone. My laugh was forced, a business tool really, and anger roiled under the surface. When was the last time I'd had a real belly laugh caused by real amusement? And worst was the depressing sense that what I did for a living had no value. My life was ticking away.

How long had I been standing here? It felt like forever.

The graphs in front of me still meant nothing. My panic had passed. I was now merely sheepish. I'd have to say something, sooner or later, but what? Tell a joke maybe?

I took a deep breath, placed the pointer on the rostrum, and turned to face the room: "I guess that's it!" I said, "Any questions?"

The company's portly, young, clean-cut CEO came to my rescue. He spoke as though nothing strange had happened. "Denis, it wasn't quite clear to me whether you felt the European operations ... blah, blah, blah...."

I looked around the table at the expressionless faces of professionals who had just witnessed a meltdown, and then to Larry who gave me a "Whew, I'm glad that's over" look. I answered the CEO's question. The short-circuited wire had somehow mended and my memory had returned. I fielded a couple of follow-up queries and hastily retreated to my place at the table.

Ten torturous minutes later, Scott got up to leave and I jumped at the opportunity to join him. It was either that or continue to scribble hangman's nooses on the yellow pad.

At the elevator, Scott looked at me concerned: "What the fuck was that all about?"

"I don't know. I just lost it."

"What does that mean?"

A tough question! I thought for a moment, and then, fingering my jaw like the perplexed foggy person I was, let loose with the first thing that came to my mind.

"I think it means my life is never going to be the same."

It took the better part of a year to end my old life. I wrapped up the business and went to Esalen, a renowned center of philosophy and psychology in Northern California. I worked in the kitchens, began to learn the simple life, and realized I had to embark on a bigger journey. While my daughters, Shannon and Chimene, graduated from college and Kathi worked on her PhD in psychology, I was organizing a yearlong voyage around the world.

The Arctic Circle was key to direction and timing. I wanted to visit Siberia and to catch a gap in the weather, and a boat heading north, I would need to be there by late July. The rest of the trip, beginning in Africa and ending in an island off New Zealand, accommodated that intention. Can you imagine? Siberia! It sounded like a joke, but there I was arranging an around-the-world ticket with lots of stops, visas, access to money, and inoculations against all sorts of diseases.

Finally in March 1993, I traded my pale yellow Mercedes for a teal-green Eagle Creek backpack, and stepped out of the speeding world into the unknown. No more suits and ties, no more getting up at a prescribed time in the morning, no more filled schedules and calendars. I left California wearing a white panama hat, jeans, a light jacket tied around my waist, and a money belt strapped under my shirt.

I was naive about backpacking and nervous about how I would spend my time. Judgmental and cynical, I was also sophisticated in understanding the workings of organizations and people's minds, and excelled at asking penetrating questions to find the story. I had been a senior manager on the leading edge of technology in five different fields and had restructured troubled companies for the past ten years, but I had a narrow understanding of almost everything else except sports.

As I boarded the plane in San Francisco and waved goodbye to my daughters, I recalled something my grandmother once said to me: "Always remember, Denny, fifty can be the beginning of a new life, rather than the beginning of decline." I was three years shy of fifty.

ZIMBABWE

THE LITTLE BOY

1

HANGING OUT IN AFRICA

THE RUGGED SAVANNAH PASSED SERENELY underneath Air France Flight 504 as it approached Harare Airport in Zimbabwe. From 5,000 feet, I scoured the parched land for foraging wild animals, maybe an elephant or wildebeest. No luck! As the engines groaned in their effort to reduce air speed, I realized I was about to land in *Africa*. Even the sound of the word made me feel younger, reborn. It brought up vivid associations: *wild* and *free*.

When I was a little boy, my family moved from New York City to a slice of property along Senix Creek. The creek flowed with the tides of the Great South Bay in Long Island. Across its often silky water, lay forbidding woods where a great blue heron perched high on the skeletal branch of a ghostly white birch. Yet the woods were enticing. They said, "Come, explore." Squinting into the sun that filtered through the trees on the other side, my siblings and I would row across the creek in an old wooden blue boat.

In my early teens, I bought a used fifteen-horsepower Evinrude outboard motor and fixed it to the boat. When I wasn't in the relentless clutches of my father's "work to be done," I'd whisk away at full throttle down the creek and into the bay, a thin layer of water vibrating at my feet as the boat bounced hard across the waves. Wind rushed refreshingly in my face, my hair flew in all directions, and the smell of salt and seaweed filled my lungs. I felt such an easy and intimate sense of freedom in that old blue boat.

I wasn't a little boy anymore, but I was once again free. Free to speed through the blustery skies and ride whatever exciting waves travel brought. Free for one year to do anything—and be anyone—I wanted.

As the airplane wheels locked in anticipation of landing, I knew it would be a big change from my previously sedentary life. Years of work in upper management had taught me to deal with change with a dispassionate attitude. So I tried to keep cool at the thought of landing in Africa, even though it was passion I was after, but I couldn't quite suppress that little boy's excitement stoked by the thrill of exploration.

I stepped out of the plane into the fresh, hot, still air. It was the kind of stillness found in the eye of a hurricane—where even the insects freeze in the knowledge of what's coming.

About twenty black attendants arrived decked out in contrasting pale blue and sugar white uniforms. For the first time in many years my white Western consciousness was encountering the black mystery of Africa. Meanwhile, workers were slowly arriving to service the two jumbo jets now parked on the tarmac. The enormous planes dwarfed the wooden terminal building we were walking towards. They looked out of place, like two swans that had landed by accident in a children's swimming pool.

But, hey, I was standing tall on African soil.

Inside the terminal a scattering of unhurried people milled about, and the olive-green floor shone with fresh polish. I sauntered over to the exchange booth and handed over a hundred-dollar bill to a round-faced clerk. In exchange she handed me a five-inch wad of Zimbabwe twenties that must have been as old as the airport.

"Do you have any larger bills?" I asked.

"Denominations of fifty will arrive soon," she responded, before shrugging in resignation, "but the government has made this promise every month for two years!"

Welcome to Africa, Denis!

Outside the terminal, a taxi driver carefully laid my spanking new backpack on a bald tire in the trunk of his dilapidated bucket-of-bolts vehicle and opened one of the three functional doors for me. He looked about fifty, with scars that could have been from juvenile acne. Was he legitimate? Would he try to take me to some nefarious places? Sharing the space in my mind with these worries was a recurring happy thought: one day I'd been planning a trip, the next day I was in Africa, as free as the animals I hoped to see.

As we rolled through the flat golden land that folded into infinity, the driver asked in a deep clear voice how I liked President Clinton. I said he was doing fine, and then changed the subject to the man's family. I discover a lot about people by talking about their families. Besides, questions are a comfortable way for me to adapt to any new environment. They keep me in control until I piece together the lay of the land.

He was quite willing to talk, and told me, in a serious tone, that he had ten children, and, counting on his fingers, twenty-one grandchildren.

"Wow! Twenty-one? Are you happy?"

"No!"

He eyeballed me in the mirror, a curious sizing-up look, and then shifted the Fifties-style shaft into third gear.

"Why not?"

"Because," he replied, "it is too expensive to educate children. I drive this taxi twenty-eight years and do not own it."

"I understand the pressure of putting kids through school," I commiserated. "I've done it myself, but only two children. Why did you have so many?"

His web of facial wrinkles became pronounced. "For protection."

"From what?"

He sighed. "Old age, I guess." Outside the golden savannah had turned into suburban sidewalks made of dirt.

The *Lonely Planet* guidebook gave Harare an estimated population of over a million people. The low-rise inner city reminded me of 1940s America—except for the number of people. Bodies were everywhere: walking around, waiting in long lines for jammed buses. Children and babies were ubiquitous—holding hands, bulging inside tummies, peeking their little heads from terry-cloth wraps attached to the moms' backs, their tiny feet dangling at the sides. My first thought was how in the world did mothers with babies on their backs know when the kids had to take a leak, or worse? I doubted the babies wore Pampers.

Like many middle-sized American cities, downtown Harare had lots of streets and shops, a few tall buildings, a sprinkling of shabby beggars, and construction everywhere. But I was struck by the differences: buildings weren't more than fifteen stories high; the streets were all dusty; and nobody was hurrying frantically for an appointment. Sweat came from the glare of the sun, not the pressure of the paper chase. This was exactly the pace I had yearned for.

The driver dropped me off at the two-star Brontë Hotel where I would stay a few nights before decompressing further at a youth hostel. The plan was to stay in cheaper hotels and hostels, while checking into a four-star once a week for a decent meal and bath.

I sat in a trance somewhere between my predictable past and an uncontrolled future. A year on my own with no strings attached. This modest hotel room wasn't for vacation or business. It was the first hotel room of my travels. Now for my first adventure.

Just before I left the States, I met a prestigious doctor in Chicago. When he discovered my plans he insisted I call up his sister. "Be sure to look up Ellie in Harare," he had said. "She and her husband, Randy, will treat you like royalty. Randy's the life of the party type, loves to drink and tell stories."

Ellie offered to pick me up straightaway, but I insisted on waiting for a few days to get my feet wet. She talked disparagingly about the Brontë, as if it was beneath me, so I diverted her criticism by saying that I wanted to sample these kinds of hotels and hostels as part of my experience. In any case, I found the Brontë rather pleasant and clean and looked forward to lounging in the inviting garden.

The next morning, I decided to treat myself to breakfast at a first-class hotel called the Monomotapa, which was a short walk away. I sauntered along a path through the towering palm trees and lush, green lawns of a park bordering the west side of Harare. It was comfortably hot, around eighty-five degrees, with decent humidity and a slight breeze.

A drummer and a guitarist, both sitting cross-legged and wearing sunglasses, entertained a small but growing crowd. The drummer's pink tongue quivered as he strained to hit a higher register, his white teeth like a piano keyboard—with only a few of the notes missing. The drums were made of restaurant-size tomato cans with parched rawhide fastened across the mouth and around the sides. The lids of the cans served as cymbals. Despite their simplicity, the drums blended sweetly with the melody coming from the deep-voiced guitarist, whose head bobbed up and down to the beat as he strummed the chorus of the only English song they sang: "If I said you had a beautiful body, would you hold it against me?"

Ragamuffin little kids played soldiers to the music. They wore cardboard box armor and wielded palm branch swords. They ran about barefoot in tattered shirts and shorts that cried of age. A little girl wobbled on novice legs into the crowd. Her large, round head was out of proportion to her short legs. While her mud-brown eyes were so wide open they could have been tacked to her eyebrows. Two gray scabs nestled amid her stubbled hair and green mucus seeped from her nose to her lips. I wondered about the whereabouts of the mother, but the girl appeared comfortable with what she was doing.

The guitarist switched to the flute and the urchin girl was soon dancing languidly to the music. Then, an energetic six year old boy, with a mischievous grin and a head also dotted with scabs, began to swagger around the outside of the gathered crowd teasing street-vendors who were selling popcorn and candy. Dressed only in faded green shorts with a gaping hole above the left buttock, he decided to skip in front of the musicians, slapping the cymbals and daring them to scold him. Instead, the musicians laughed. In time, one of the vendors gave the boy a lollipop. This unprotected life certainly gave the kids an air of street smarts that contrasted sharply with Western children their age.

At a break in the entertainment, I continued across the park until the city reappeared. I soon reached the semi-circular Monomotapa Hotel on Julius Nyerere Way, named after the former president of Tanzania. Nyerere was renowned as a great statesman, and had befriended Zimbabwe's President Mugabe during his armed struggle against white-only rule in what was then Rhodesia.

Overlooking the city, the Monomotapa's top floor accommodated a swimming pool surrounded by lacy linen-covered dining tables. White people donned sunglasses, smoked cigarettes, and wrote letters. Old whites, young ones, thin ones, and those riddled with fat. The only blacks in sight were the uniformed waiters.

I dined alone with feelings of separation, and at one point recalled an old Star Trek episode featuring two aliens aboard the

Enterprise. Half their bodies were white and half black. They hated each other. Turned out that if your left side was white you were in the ruling class, while right-side-white meant under-privileged. I thought about the particulars that separate us, and how I was a product of those particulars.

It was only later that day, eating beans and eggs at a sidewalk café and starved for conversation, I broke through that sense of separation. I stoked up the courage to say "Hi" to another lone diner, a woman. She looked to be around twenty-six, hazel eyes, sandy-blond, shoulder-length hair, light freckles hatched by the sun, and loose clothes on a pleasant figure. She responded im-mediately with a friendly demeanor and before long we moved our chairs closer—the subtle hook of common heritage pulling us together.

Sara said she lived in a village on the eastern corner of Zimbabwe, and that she was on holiday in Harare. She gave me her background: from Massachusetts, recent Harvard graduate, now working with Zimbabwean women in education and devel-opment. I was amazed at how easy it was to meet her. Striking up a conversation in the States was never so natural.

We decided to hang out together for a while. Sara played guide around the city as we conversed. Occasionally, barefoot beggars wanting money, our watches, or our shoes interrupted us. We passed the main post office and American Express, before stopping outside a hotel housing one of Harare's nightclubs. She asked if I wanted to take a peek since it was open in the daytime. I was game for anything. It was all so new. We climbed three dingy floors, walked down an equally dingy hallway, and entered a cramped, dimly lit room thick with the rawness of body odor and the heavy pulse of dance music. Small groups of black men stood by a bar and sat at cardboard tables drinking bottles of beer and talking.

"Nightclubs are for men in Zimbabwe," Sara whispered in my ear, uncomfortably conscious of stares. "Women who come here are considered prostitutes."

For the short time we stayed, only two other women, both black, joined the crowd. Heads downcast, and knees drawn to-gether, they sat on a wooden bench along the wall without saying a word. They looked humble. I felt safe, but Sara's eyes flitted around nervously while she mopped humidity from her brow. We didn't dally, just killed a beer and left.

Sara joined me for dinner at Guido's, an Italian restaurant that I had discovered near the Brontë. Of course, I pondered the difference in our ages and sex. This was fantasyland with no script. Who knew what was going to happen. Once seated, I leaned into the candle-lit table and asked her about the family with whom she lived.

"Oh, they're probably above average for Zimbabwe. In the sense that the man of the family is educated. His name is Robert." Catching my quizzical look, she added, "Black Africans often have two first names, their African name and a Christian confirmation name. They use the confirmation name in the presence of whites." The candlelight reflected off her greenish-brown eyes.

"Also, we live in a wooden house, not a hut. That's affluence. I sleep in a small room with three of the daughters, eat sadza at least twice a day, and—"

"What's sadza?"

"Sadza? Oh, that's the staple meal in Zimbabwe. Basically, it's maize ground up into what they call mini-meal. At first, I hated it. It's thick and pasty like day-old oatmeal. Now I'm used to it. I even like it.

"Anyway, Robert works for the government as a clerk, and his wife handles the chores around the house. She also farms a small parcel of land and raises the kids."

"What's with the kids and babies? I've never seen so many children. Every female over sixteen seems pregnant."

She pushed out her lower lip, stroked it with her index finger. "Women are valued based on the number of kids they have, especially boys," she answered, her Boston accent singed with a mixture of indignation and acceptance. "Kids take care of you in old age, not like in the United States where you retire and live off a pension. Kids in Africa are the pension plan."

"How about females? Do they go to school?"

"Too expensive! The whole family, including uncles and aunts, scrape up money to send the oldest or brightest boy to school. Not the female. She gets pregnant."

"What about birth control?"

"Shh," she hushed me. "Not so loud! Birth control is not a popular subject here."

"The pension plan?"

"That's the obvious reason. But birth control also threatens the male ego." She wiped red sauce off her lips after wolfing down pasta as if a Zimbabwe speed record was at stake. A pained expression enveloped her face: "It's hard for an American to watch the subservient role women play. It's changing slowly, but like a glacier, not a rolling stone. My job is to educate women about the fundamentals of hygiene and the world they live in, without upsetting husbands or fathers. I have to keep reminding myself that this is their culture."

"What do all these kids do when they grow up? I read that the population is growing at four percent annually." For the first time, I mentally ran the numbers. "Jesus! That means it doubles every fifteen years."

"It's a big problem. Young men leave the village for a job in the city. They live in surrounding shantytowns. The luckier ones send money home to their families. Home means subsistence farming more than anything else. Their farming methods wear out the land and they have regular droughts. Then, too, inflation is high...." The rest of the sentence was replaced by a shake of the head. Through the flickering light, Sara used her knife to play with her napkin. She looked pretty.

"You wind up with a scarcity of food at increasing costs," she was saying, "not enough jobs, and far too many people!"

After dinner, we parted ways. Sara was taking the bus back to her village in the morning. She invited me to visit if I got the chance. It was tempting. It was also tempting to ask her to stay. But I didn't. I guess it was fear of rejection that held me back. I could say it was fidelity, but I'd be lying.

That night at the Brontë, for the first time in ages, I looked intently at my face in the bathroom mirror, wondering if Sara found me attractive. The mirror showed a man with blondish hair, good skin, and nice features, a few extra pounds but in good shape physically. Although I have never been called handsome, I have consistently been called cute and charming.

I thought about visiting Sara, but the opportunity never came up. I guess she was meant to introduce me to Africa and show me that hanging out with someone friendly is just a simple invitation away.

2

GEORGE—A WALK ON THE WILD SIDE

THE NEXT DAY, I MOVED into my first hostel, the Paw Paw Lodge. Situated inside a rusty iron fence on the suburban side of the park, dthe lodge was surrounded by a dirt yard with sparse blades of dusty grass hanging on like retired men with no more mountains to climb. The only thing painted in modern times was a concrete sidewall that was graced with psychedelic ocean waves. Inside the hostel, metal bars on windows cast shadows into grimy once canary-yellow rooms with cement floors worn smooth by years of traffic. Budget travelers who couldn't afford two dollars for a double room slept in the dormitory. I settled for a double room with only one occupant—me.

On the bright side, my African hosts were cheerful and warm, and the guests intelligent and interesting. I met a personable young Canadian couple sitting on a tattered sofa in the lounge. They had recently graduated from college and were traveling because they couldn't find a job. A rough Australian woman said she had been on the road for three years, after working nine years in a mining town. And a contingent of Ethiopians taught me how to stand a coke bottle on its edge without it falling.

The company was enjoyable, but the facilities took getting used to. Sleeping in a dorm was just too far back in my life to tackle just yet, and I definitely distrusted the beds in my room. I spread my sleeping bag on top of the best-looking one to avoid lying directly on whatever might be inside.

Outside, in Harare, was more unnerving—especially alone at night. Mostly unlit, the city's streets undulated with waves of humans blending into the darkness. Feeling isolated and vulnerable, I was wondering if a black person walking in a white American neighborhood felt like me when an African approached me at a quaint cobblestone plaza encircled by lamps. I was in the mindset of labeling blacks as "Africans" and white people of any origin as "whites."

"Excuse me," he said politely, "my name is George. Would you mind talking with me for a while?"

The first impression was favorable. Barely shorter than me, maybe five feet eight, and thin, George had a pleasant face. I wanted to think positive; that he was just being friendly. Although I was anxious, I told myself I was safe under the sparse lighting. I put aside the cynicism born of my early street schooling in New York, and let the positive win out.

He led me to the single wooden bench in the plaza, under an oak tree, and began a barrage of personal questions: my age, marriage status, children, why I was in Zimbabwe. After a while, curious about him, I turned the tables. "Are you married?" I asked.

"No," he replied. A suggestive hint on his face carried the remainder of his response. "I do not like women."

"Well," I said perfunctorily, "I need to be getting back."

"You like women?" He smiled, fingering a silver cross and chain dangling from his neck. "I can get you a woman!"

My curious nature took over. "What else can you get?"

"Anything you want—" He flashed a smile. "Hash, hard drugs. I can change money. Anything you want. Come, we get a beer!"

"I gotta go, George. You seem like a nice guy, but someone is waiting for me at the hotel." But as I was lying my way out of the situation, a thought occurred to me. George could be a golden opportunity to understand the underbelly of African cities.

"Listen, George," I said, "I don't want to buy anything except information. I want to know about your business, what you do, how the black market works, dangers to avoid—things like that. Come over to the Brontë Hotel tomorrow afternoon at two. I'll buy the beers and we'll talk." A deal was struck. At the Brontë, I couldn't be traced.

George arrived promptly. We sat in the back patio, at a table surrounded by manicured grass. The garden of red bougainvillea added glorious color to the balmy day. Birds scampered and sang. Before we began, George increased the discussion "fee" from just beer to include a pack of cigarettes and beer money for a starving friend.

"Do not walk alone on back streets in Harare," he instructed. His African-inflected Queen's English reminded me of a Caribbean accent. He leaned back and casually waved to a waiter he apparently knew. "There are no lights, you understand? Unemployment is high, and people need money. Sometimes a man has more than one family. It costs money to support them, you understand?"

I nodded.

"Can a guy have more than one wife?" I asked, raising an eyebrow.

"Yes, of course! Is it not like that in the Unites States of America?"

"Are you kidding?"

"I do not need to worry about it." He grinned, leaning back in his chair.

We chatted while George polished off his second beer and dragged deeply on a hand-rolled cigarette. The cigarettes I paid for had been tucked away in his shirt. I shifted in my seat, flagged the waiter for another round of beers, and watched a chipmunk skitter across the grass. George brazenly requested a second pack of cigarettes—for his friend. The whole exchange felt like putting coins in a meter. But now the topic was the black market.

"How does the black market work? Who hires you?" I inquired.

"Shop owners hire me. They are buyers, or they buy for someone else. I look for tourists like you who want to change US dollars into our currency at a favorable rate. Sometimes I find a large seller of US dollars who has a particular need for Zimbabwe dollars."

"Would large sellers of American dollars get a better price than me?"

He held his palms out like a garment district merchant. "Is that not the way of business?"

We laughed, and then I went back to the interrogation. He told me that buyers were mainly interested in US currency, adding: "The government limits the amount of foreign exchange citizens can legally spend to buy foreign products, you understand. Also buyers want US dollars to deposit into foreign banks. I do not know what they do with the currency. I think they have an expensive vacation or hold the currency for—what do you call it?—a contingency?"

Our discussion lasted about three hours, during which time I bought George five beers, the cigarettes, and a bottle of wine for a female friend. All the time, I'd been dying to ask one question.

"The woman you offered me last night, who is she?"

In the limited time that I had been in Harare, I hadn't seen any prostitutes in the street, and the women in the club we visited seemed too meek to be hookers. I got the impression that this was the type of place where prostitution would be hidden from view—possibly by tribal law. I was curious about how the process worked and, to be candid, my interest in a fling with a black African woman was definitely piqued. After all, I was on an adventure.

"She is a friend of mine," George explained.

"Is she a prostitute?"

George sidestepped the question by saying that she would like to meet a white man. "If you would like to meet her," he said, "buy her a present like a bottle of wine. I am sure that she would like to meet you. I could bring her to the park tomorrow and introduce her to you."

The thought of this woman was enticing and the percolation in my loins made her severely tempting. What would she be like? Was she a professional or a woman attracted by the novelty of a white man? Then there was the danger of AIDS in Africa. I decided to pass up the offer after a struggle between the forces of lust, curiosity, health, and the hesitancy of beginnings.

Before George and I parted he told me of his dream. He wanted to earn enough money to visit his uncle, a mechanic in South Africa. The dream was to buy a car and set up business as a taxi driver in Harare. His eyes had that far-away look. Then he snapped out of his daze and drained the fifth beer.

3

THE DREAM

E LLIE HALSEY PICKED ME UP in a white Volvo station wagon, the first of many errands before meeting her husband, Brent, for lunch. I judged Ellie to be a few years older than me, in her early fifties. She wore a gray skirt and a floral, sleeveless blouse, and trussed up her chestnut hair so that pearl earrings dangled aside her bare neck. The style gave her a sporty look. Long eyelashes and full eyebrows enhanced her amber eyes that, along with a pug nose, betrayed a touch of elegant mischievousness.

"I'm so excited to meet a friend of Gordon's," she said in the refined English of the white southern African. "He's my only brother, you know. I absolutely adore him. Do hope you don't mind the errands."

I told Ellie I'd met her brother only briefly. But it didn't matter, she acted as if I was his buddy. We drove to a section of town where clean streets and shops catered to whites, then into a parking lot servicing a small chain of specialty stores to pick up a few cases of beer and soda pop. After turning off the ignition, Ellie reached under the seat and hauled out a serious looking iron-link chain covered by a plastic sheath. It must have weighed twenty pounds. She slung the chain on to and through the steering wheel. An action out of character with her appearance, but that definitely fit the pioneering element in her manner.

"Let's move the seat closer to the steering wheel, so I can hook this chain." She nodded towards two black men chit-chatting under the shade of a tree. "You simply cannot leave a car without security, or these buggers will pinch it for sure. They will strip it and sell it as a taxi in Bulawayo."

"Do you always use chains?" I asked, gripping the seat with my legs.

"No," she grunted as we shimmied forward. "Our other car has an electronic plug attached to the steering column. It unhooks the electrical system. Otherwise, there are armies of security guards everywhere one goes here in Harare to watch one's belongings. I'm sure you have seen them." She snapped the lock. "But I wouldn't rely on them to protect my car unless I knew them personally."

In the Seventies, Rhodesia often made the international headlines as Ian Smith's racist government engaged in a brutal white versus black power struggle. But the country dropped out the newspapers back home after the revolution and name change, so between stops at grocery stores, Ellie filled me in on politics.

"After the war, the main rebel leader, Robert Mugabe, seized the presidency and immediately tried to set up a single-party Marxist government. He never got his wish, but he's had a stranglehold on the government ever since. Foreigners thought the downfall of Ian's administration was the worldwide embargo against us. But it wasn't the embargo that got us to throw in the towel. We handled that quite nicely." She rounded a corner with the expertise of a truck driver, pumping the accelerator with one-inch heels. "It was the sanctions against South Africa, because they buggered our distribution to international markets." She lifted her sunglasses to look at me. "By the way, your Henry Kissinger negotiated the settlement between the whites and blacks."

"Why?"

"I haven't the foggiest idea. Maybe it was because the Chinese backed the rebels, and the US felt compelled to wave the banner of democracy."

She began to reminisce about a trip she and Brent had taken to California. Their car had broken down in a small town nestled among the foothills of the Sierras. While waiting for it to be fixed, she and Brent spent the afternoon getting soused in a cowpoke bar.

"Brent made friends with the owner, a rather stout, boisterous woman who had a hard time understanding where we came from," said Ellie. "'Where ya from?' Brent told her Zimbabwe.

"'Zimbabwe! Never heard of it! Where is it?'

"'Africa.'

"She was visibly impressed, no doubt about that. 'Africa!' she hollered, 'No kidding. What's the president's name over there?'

"'Mugabe.'

"'Never heard of him. What's the vice-president's name?'

"'Banana,' Brent said with a chuckle.

"That is his name," Ellie concluded, "but, of course, all of our credibility went down the drain when he told her."

After errands, we took a bumpy road from Harare to the Halseys' tobacco farm about twenty kilometers away. En route, Ellie talked about growing up as a young mother and employer, mentioning how she acted as matriarch and sometimes midwife for the black workers.

"Zimbabwe is mostly agricultural," she said. "We grow maize to feed the black population, export tobacco, tea, and our world famous beef. We were self-sufficient under Ian's government. The blacks were a lot better off, I can tell you! Now the bloody government is corrupt beyond belief. We have to import food, hunt for foreign exchange, inflation is over forty percent a year, and the roads and buildings are falling apart from lack of maintenance. Blacks do not plan! I'm quite serious when I say that a building isn't replaced until it falls down."

She turned right on to a perfectly maintained red dirt road lined with leafy trees. Tall green tobacco plants blanketed the fields as far as the eye could see. It was as if we'd driven into Gone with the Wind—all neatly groomed, rustic, smelling of lilac. But these peaceful roads must have been very different during the war.

"They were bloody dangerous!" Ellie agreed. "There are loads of these lonely roads. We drove in convoys to town or to Lake Kariba for our holidays. Life was gruesome for both sides, but this is our home and whatever happened we planned on staying here. I never went anywhere without a decent rifle—like most farmers during the war. I liked my body just the way it was, and I wasn't about to lose any pieces." She knew life for whites was now tenuous in Zimbabwe—they were needed to make the economy work, but were political pawns that Mugabe could blame for poor economic conditions.

Our discussion was interrupted by the appearance of a weathered shingle house surrounded by shady trees and a generous emerald lawn, where three peacocks meandered and poked for food under mustard-colored leaves.

"Look, that's our house! And that's Joshua!" She pointed to a black man who looked to be in his late sixties. "He runs the farm. Been with the family since he was a boy. Can you believe he is eighty-two?" Joshua's dignified demeanor and snow-white hair completed the picture of the Old South.

He walked slow and easy to the driver's side and opened the door for Ellie. He took my hand softly as Ellie introduced us, and then, with a look of concern in his brown eyes, said: "We lost a hen last night—looks to be a wild animal."

Accompanied by the cat-like wailing of peacocks, Ellie and Joshua chatted briefly about business, before showing me around the farm. "The peacocks sleep in trees to avoid being eaten by wild animals," Ellie said. She strode with grace and purpose, pointing out the various crops and fields. "This week, we harvest the tobacco," she told me. Meanwhile, I was still looking around wondering what exactly wild animals meant.

We toured the house with its quietly elegant views, before entering a lounge with a full-size billiards table. It reminded me of my pool table at home that was modified to double as a large dinner table when we had guests. Before excusing herself to check on lunch, Ellie introduced me to her husband, Brent, who stood behind a heavily stocked mahogany bar. A white shirt stretched over his bulky frame, and he wore a red tie with giraffes. Perspiration seeped through the armpits.

Brent told me he was negotiating a buyout of the company he managed from its multi-national parent. "Africa apparently is not a good investment for the big boys these days," he said, while fixing pre-lunch drinks—a frosty beer for me and a scotch and soda for himself.

Brent rushed through lunch, a smorgasbord of yams, sizzling corn, Zimbabwe's famous beef, one-bite barbequed lamb cutlets, and fresh vegetables. He leaned over his plate, and, between forkfuls, queried me about my itinerary and family. Like many busy people, he barely chewed his food before quickly swallowing so that he could return to the office. I recognized the habit—gulping life with no time to digest.

I recalled the routine of waking in the morning with tension-induced neck pain, showering, shaving just slowly enough to avoid cuts, putting on the suit and tie, and grabbing a bulging attaché case. Then it was listening to self-improvement CDs in the car to work, and a long, stressful day before returning home to crowd extra work in with some family discussion. At times, life was one long run-on sentence.

"So," he said, after I explained why I left the business world, "why travel? You could be at home relaxing, watching sports, and enjoying the good life."

"Yeah, but everyone is so busy I wouldn't have anyone to watch the games with." We laughed. "I'm playing out a dream I've had since I was a kid."

"Mmm, dreams take on a life of their own," he snorted agreeably.

"In Silicon Valley, where I worked, we referred to them as visions."

"Zimbabwe could use a vision right now. We are seen as a business risk, not a money-maker."

"Unfortunate for Zimbabwe... Anyway, I had a strong vision as a kid," I said, finishing the thought because it needed to come out of my mouth.

"Ah, yes, the dream," he said with a chuckle. "So what is the dream exactly?"

"I guess it's the American dream," I said, wincing at the cliché. A great family and enough money so that no one could pull my strings. Fourteen words, perfect length for a vision.

"And now you're on the no-strings part?"

I let the no strings sink in for a few seconds, making a mental note to think about what exactly qualified as strings. "Something like that. Actually, I never imagined how consuming the pursuit of family and wealth could be."

"It's a heap of responsibility," Brent inserted with an air of certainty, uplifting his eyebrows as a signal for me to continue.

"I was burnt out. Then a few years ago a comment stuck to me like tar to a shoe. It was during a conversation with my physical therapist, who was working on chronic tension in my neck. She said her former husband used to beat her, and that she went to a friend for advice. The friend told her: 'You're traveling down this highway of life. If you come to an exit and want to get off, but miss it, that's okay. Those things happen. But if you miss the next exit, you may be on that highway for a long time.' I took the exit."

Ellie, who had been quietly sitting and listening, nodded her head in thoughtful agreement, then rose and walked into the kitchen to summon the maid.

"Wise advice," Brent said, his eyes fixed on the china plate he scraped with his fork. "So now what?"

"I've given myself a whole year to screw off."

"You want it all! Good luck, matey. A year with a backpack, that's a lifetime!"

"It's 1.3 percent of the average person's life. I already made the calculation." I remembered the early years when I was away from the family on business trips calculating the percentage of time away. The tiniest percentage away seemed so large.

He looked up from his plate to stare at me. "You already made the calculation," he observed wryly. "You must have come up through finance."

4

Intimacy Among
Long-Term Travelers

A FTER A SOUND NIGHT'S SLEEP and an English breakfast of beans, eggs, and sausage, I boarded an overnight train to Bulawayo in the southwest of the country.

The train traveled sluggishly on its 490-kilometer, thirteen-hour mission. We clickety-clacked across vast stretches of savanna sprinkled with villages. Instead of marveling at elephants and rhinos, I looked out with the same fascination at huts, children playing, and groups of thin men talking. The sienna plains provided an ideal backdrop for the brilliant orange, canary-yellow, and flamingo-pink cloth wraps worn by the women, who ambled along the dirt roads or stood and socialized—all the while balancing heavy loads on their heads. The train stopped frequently at hamlets where people milled around the railroad platform, helping family members load everything from cloth bags to chickens.

The discussion with Brent made me reflect on my Silicon Valley days when I worked for an early-stage video game company. Hundreds of companies in the industry had just collapsed like so many palm-leaf shacks in a hurricane. Product glutted warehouses. Our venture capitalists handed me control of our battered shack until we could find money or a buyer. My life was forecasts, operations, laying people off, and trying to motivate the ones remaining. At home, Kathi was starting a business that required cash. I needed counseling, so I arranged to meet a friend and trusted advisor from my consulting days in New York, Frank Zolfo.

Frank looked like Al Pacino at his desk in the ending scene of *The Godfather Part I*. Slightly paunchy, dark hair cut around the ears and meticulously parted, open collar, and black, polished shoes. I remember him sitting in the Los Angeles hotel suite where we met up, a pack of non-filter Camels in easy reach on the mahogany coffee table, pouring whiskey into glasses filled with ice. He stretched across the table to hand me one of the glasses. I was sprawled on the bed as if I'd been crucified.

"Take a deep swallow," Frank said with a mild dose of the Bronx. "You look like shit!"

I confessed I was worn out, defeated, a millionaire one day and a thirty-eight-year-old pauper the next. There was more. I recalled a dinner that Kathi and I shared with him and his wife before their divorce. Frank was a forceful businessman adept at being right, and twenty-two years of marriage had created unlimited triggers for rebellion in his wife. If Frank said "A," his wife said "Z." He was saddled with a history of control and his wife didn't want to be wrong anymore.

Frank snapped the pack of Camels against his fist and a cigarette shot out. "You know, Denny," he said, cigarette in mouth, "when we were young we assumed the job of advising our wives. We did it to help the people we love. And they wanted us to take charge. Ten years go by, now they've had it with our advice. But our habits are set."

"I don't like some of my habits. I don't like coming across like I'm always right." I thought for a minute and Frank let the silence be.

"I'm walking down the same road that you did, Frank." I swallowed a large gulp of whiskey and let myself comfortably wallow in self-pity. "You know, I always believed in equality. We painted the girls' rooms anything but pink, gave them basketballs as well as dolls, required that they work for their allowance. I lived by my grandmother's message that women need to have their own money or someone will always be pulling their strings.

"And here I am, on the other side of that advice, bankrolling everyone and feeling like a workhorse. I yelled 'Taxation without representation!' until it lost all meaning. Kathi and I used to rely on each other. Somehow things changed. Now I'm alone at the top, and *she* doesn't want to be wrong anymore. So basically, between my business prospects and marital habits, I'm fucked!"

"What else?"

"Well, being the strong one is ingrained in me, like you. I don't know how to be vulnerable. I'm shackled by chains of never-ending responsibility. I dream of traveling to faraway places, or living without possessions, like Christ and Buddha. I envy the lone man hitching in wide-open spaces carrying only his guitar."

Frank lit another cigarette, and refilled our glasses. He looked deep into my eyes and leaned forward with his hands folded as if in prayer. "Let me tell you something, Denny. The success I've had in business, you have had as a husband and father. Now I'd like you to do something for me. Close your eyes and think of yourself as eighty years old. Tell me what you have achieved from here on out."

I followed his directions. "You know, my grandmother began her business career at fifty. At fifty, I see myself free from business."

"That's it?"

"That's it! Fifty is twelve years away. I can do that. It's not that long a grind."

"Then that's it!" He leaned back proud of himself and sipped his whiskey.

The first night in Bulawayo, I sat alone at one of the two Formica tables in the kitchen of an eight-dollar-a-day hostel, slicing cheese with my Swiss army knife and loving the simplicity of it all. The place was clean and neat, with communal bathrooms and a lounge filled with vintage Salvation Army furniture. At the other table, an African, Englishman, and an American in their mid-twenties engaged in a lively conversation about the effects of colonialism. Plastering the cheese on bread, I leaned into the flow of the discussion, proud to be a low-budget traveler. Up until that moment, I had eaten only at restaurants.

"The imperialists *savaged* Africa!" the thin, freckle-faced Englishman bellowed. "Let's face it, Europe avoided economic strife by sending its excess manpower to Africa. But they kept their bloody factories going at full tilt exporting crap to Africans and building a demand for Western products. Then they pinched Africa's natural resources in payment."

"Maybe you are being harsh," the African said. He spoke quietly in precise English. His dark eyes and articulate manner exuded a sense of quiet intelligence. "Your ancestors also built our roads and railways. The English built infrastructure and they taught us a way of government that can handle larger populations. We now have eleven million people. At that level, the tribal structure no longer works as an effective governing institution."

The American jumped in, passion in his eyes. "But don't you hate whites, Rayford? For treating your people like serfs, while you worked in their kitchens and farms for peanuts?"

Rayford carefully chewed and swallowed a spoonful of beans, then politely responded. "You must understand that the African in Zimbabwe did not hate whites. We are easy to forgive and forget. Our nature is to be hospitable to visitors. That is how Rhodes and the English conquered our Matabele king Lobengula and settled this country. In my tribe, for instance, it is my responsibility to treat visitors better than I would my family. We welcomed the English and they took advantage of the situation."

"To your regret, I reckon!" the Englishman interjected.

"We are patient. When you consider the history of invasions into other cultures, we did well to oust the whites from power in less than a hundred years. The African understands patience. We were willing to take time to get our country back. Speed is not characteristic of Africans, but tenacity is."

By this time, I was all ears.

The American stroked his beard casually. He slouched and stretched his legs, plopping his feet on to a chair while he spoke. "Rayford, do you think this willingness to forgive was key to Zimbabwe's ability to achieve peace so quickly after the revolution?"

Good question, I thought.

"Perhaps," Rayford replied and smiled easily. "We need business expertise and links to the Western world because our adaptation to Western culture is inevitable." He turned toward the Englishman, who was absorbed in the spiraling smoke from the cigarette between his fingers. "We needed independence— this is our land. However, as I have previously stated, it is also true that my people benefited from colonialism. I fear the benefits will be forgotten in the future."

"What benefits?" the Englishman shouted with indignation, his face almost redder than the cigarette's glowing end. "To trade a way of life where a bloke's got time for family and friends for a culture where people watch TV instead of nature? Get sucked up—a number in a computerized vacuum cleaner? Pollute the land with concrete, cars, and Big Mac wrappers?"

"Societies change. That is inevitable, is it not?"

"Rayford's right, Victor," the American said. "Change is already here. How can Africa go back to the old days when the world is moving forward? The African way of life is a goner—it's just a matter of time."

Rayford shuffled his legs. "Perhaps it's a 'goner' as you say. But whites will never teach us how to hurry. *Slow* is what we can teach them."

Eager to join a good conversation, I pulled up a chair and introduced myself. The American's name was Jeff. Starting in Egypt, he had traveled the length of East Africa. Victor, the son of a rich British barrister, worked for a charitable organization and lived at the hostel along with Rayford. It was news to me that people could rent rooms in hostels long-term. Victor didn't care much for his family's lifestyle, and charity work helped him give back part of what he believed his ancestors absconded with. Nevertheless, when he returned home he wanted to be an entrepreneur. Rayford, a twenty-six-year-old of Matabele descent, worked as an administrator for a local company. He was the only child of parents high in the political chain.

Although English was Rayford's second language, I was impressed by his fluency and grasp of nuance and idiom—American and British. Nevertheless, I constantly found myself interrupting or finishing his sentences. He would calmly wait until I finished before continuing, apparently accepting my words as enhancements to his own. My intrusions would have been subtle in the United States, where interruption is a national priority, but in this conversation they stuck out like zebra stripes. Each interjection embarrassed me, but the habit proved difficult to break.

Later in the dorms, Jeff and I got absorbed in discussion until the crickets slept. He had recently received his master's degree in African Studies from Yale. He loved the program but abhorred the predilection for political correctness. He believed it absolutely killed the ability to see and deal with reality because it sanitized the facts and made people paranoid about voicing ticklish thoughts.

"For instance," he complained, "we are dropping the word 'tribal' in favor of 'ethnic group.' Why? 'Tribal' denotes inferior culture. But Africa is built on tribal culture! It dominates the politics and daily life. It's social security, welfare, police protection, and identity all rolled into one. Tribal chiefs are top dog. Look at Mugabe! His face stares out from every dollar bill in this country. 'I'm the boss,' it says, 'and don't you ever fucking forget it.'"

The next day, wearing shorts and bandannas, Jeff and I hitched into town. It was eighty-five degrees with a slight breeze, which reduced the impact of the humidity. Miniscule bubbles still popped on the skin and our T-shirts got wet under the armpits, but at least we weren't actually dripping. I hadn't hitched since college. Walking slowly along the narrow two-lane modestly paved road, Jeff showed me how to make a cap out of a bandanna. Youth and a bushy beard gave his cap a more natural flavor, yet still I felt like a hippie blowing with the wind.

Cars were scarce on this major road. Blacks who didn't stop used their hands and eyes to pantomime the reason why, while whites drove by looking straight ahead. Finally, a black man gave us a lift to the City Park.

As we sat comfortably on warm, dry grass under a leafy oak, locals would stop to look at us or ask for money. This is when I began to think about rules for treating beggars, since they were part of the landscape. One man, his fingernails cracked by common labor and eyes slowed by the sun, sat next to us for a while.

"How is President Clinton?" he inquired with concern.

"He is doing well, I said. It is a tough job."

This was enough to satisfy the man. Then, he asked if I had a big family in America. I unzipped my daypack and pulled out pictures of Kathi and the girls. I'm a Leo, so my pride was glaring. The man was interested in details, such as why my girls were laughing or what the print on Chimene's shirt meant. After we looked at seven or eight photos, he pointed to my hiking boots: "How much you paid for those shoes? They are very good!"

I considered a comment Rayford dropped the night before: "White tourists are targets. When a black sees a white, he thinks of three things: white, rich, and superior." I would have added that the locals were also very curious people.

After the man left, Jeff began to open up about his reasons for coming to Africa. In addition to exploring the world, he wanted to get out of his parents' way for a while and establish his personal space. He described his mom and dad as solid.

"But they struggle to stay connected to each other," he said. "Mom always has things to do and places to go, and my dad seems to have lost interest in everything but work. I mean, we go fishing together on the odd occasion, but he's listless. I think his sense of excitement is gone."

As much as I was interested in Jeff's family, he was taken by mine. He grabbed the pictures lying on my lap and pointed to my daughters. "Wow! Maybe I should plan a special trip to California—a redhead and a brunette. They're babes. And I like their smiles."

"The strawberry blond is Shannon. Chimene's the younger one. Doesn't she have the most beautiful eyes?"

"That's your wife, Kathi, right? You mentioned her earlier. She has a very feminine look about her. Looks like Shannon got your coloring and Chimene her mother's. You're a lucky man."

"My trial in life! I've always been surrounded by strong, beautiful women. You should meet my cousin Sharon. When it comes to zest for life, Zorba had nothing on her! If there's something interesting or fun going on in town, Sharon's there."

"Tell me about the personalities behind the pictures," he asked.

Stretching my legs on the grass, head pillowed in my hands and looking up at twittering leaves, I conjured up a vignette that would do them all justice. "One Saturday, when the girls were in their mid-teens, I rose from my desk in the den, walked into the living room and saw Kathi engrossed in a book, studying psychology. After a while, I asked in all seriousness, 'Kath, what are you going to do when you get the impossible patient?' She looked up, briefly acknowledged my presence, and then continued to read. 'There's nothing you can do with this patient!' I persisted. 'You treat him and treat him, but there's no visible improvement. You could tell him what a schmuck he is, you know, destroy his self-esteem, ravage his male dignity. It doesn't matter! It doesn't matter what you say.' I paused. 'He's driving you crazy! You come home and make my life miserable because you can't get him out of your mind! Our marriage is becoming mush. Tell me, what are you going to do with this patient?'"

"What did she say?"

"She looked at me like she was brushing a pesky fly off her shoulder, and said: 'Are you bored? Why don't you watch a game on TV?' Then she went back to the book.

"A little while later, I was sitting on the pillow-couch in the TV room, when Shannon walked by on her way to the kitchen. I grabbed her leg. 'You're a psychologist,' I said. 'You have this impossible patient.' I went through the whole routine. 'There are three things you can do. You can continue to treat him. You can tell him to get out of your office, that you want nothing to do with him. Or you can raise the price. What would you do?' She frowned and in an exasperated, humanistic tone said: 'Dad, everyone can be helped. Of course I'd treat him.' Then she continued into the kitchen.

"Later, Chimene comes home from playing basketball, a little sweaty. 'Hi Dad' she said, and gave me a peck on the cheek. I followed her into the living room. She gave her mom a kiss. I recited the spiel to her: she's a psychologist, has this impossible patient, blah, blah, blah, and then the three choices. She said: 'And there's nothing I can do with this patient, right? He's ruining my married life.'

"'Yes!' I say.

"'And no matter what I do, he's never, *ever*, going to get healed?'

"'Right!'

"She shrugged. 'The answer is simple, you raise the price!'"

Jeff gave a hearty laugh and said Chimene and his sister would get along great. He nonchalantly went on to ask, "What does your wife think about a year-long absence?"

I should have been good at answering this question, but people's perceived judgments made me uncomfortable. "She supports this trip," I said. "If she didn't, I probably wouldn't have gone. As a matter of fact, she told everyone about it. Then, of course, I had to go." We laughed. "She said she could use the time alone to juggle an internship and write her dissertation."

"What does she really think?"

"She's nervous about being alone, although the house is rarely without visitors. Also, I think she's quietly excited that the removal of my shadow will allow her finally to be the center of her universe. I like that idea, too. At the same time, I think she's melancholic."

"Yeah, a year's a long time. My mom would never let my dad go. Dad was excited at the thought of my trip—you could feel his vicarious pleasure. But he'd never attempt it himself. So, what caused you to jump ship?"

What caused me to leave? I found myself opening up to this relative stranger—even if I still side-stepped the incident that triggered my flight. The wanting to share with him came easily. He was eager to hear. I told him about my meeting with Zolfo, about the grind of achieving, my fatigue, and about feeling unappreciated.

"After the meeting, I started my own company, figuring I had twelve years to be successful in business. I also began to save for a round-the-world trip with a friend to purge the rebellion and exhaustion I felt. This is not to say that my family didn't make me feel special, they did, but it wasn't enough. Anyway, as I began to close in on fifty the notion of escape to live the simple life of Buddha became my mantra. I guess, I needed to rewire who I was—change a few habits."

"What habits?"

"Well, how I spend my time, for instance, or being a better listener with Kathi. I asked myself the age-old question: what's the purpose of life? Should I endure, or change?" Given the direction of the conversation, I felt compelled to add an afterthought. "I'm sure your parents have had their tough times, too."

"They were going through them, but I'm not convinced they were facing them. My mom makes the major decisions, but my dad makes the money in my family. Funny, I never really considered how he thought about his role, or his pressures. Dad doesn't talk about those kinds of things. He talks about fishing." Jeff was pensive for a few seconds. "I think underneath it all, Dad's bored with life."

He paused again, and then smoothly changed the subject. "Did you feel guilt at the thought of leaving your family?"

"I felt relief. Relief that I could finally purge a growing rebellion against aspects of life that had been so vital to me, without anger and bitterness. My kids didn't really need me anymore, and I was disillusioned about features of my marriage. But the trip wasn't a surprise to anyone. A friend and I had been squirreling away money for it for years.

"How about you, Jeff, how did you feel about leaving home?"

"Sure I suffered bouts of nostalgia being away from the family and everything dear to me. But the homesickness was accompanied by seductive thoughts of having *time* to meet fascinating people and visit exotic places. You must know what I mean?"

"I know exactly what you mean."

"How about your daughters? What did they think?"

"They were enthusiastic about my journey. They had traveled a lot, like you. Both had studied abroad and traveled extensively around Eastern and Western Europe as part of the family's plan for their enlightenment.

"We shared the excitement of comrades. They knew I was frustrated. They helped me prepare and pack, and inspired me. At my going-away party, Chimene said, 'Dad, consider this trip your mid-life quest. And don't worry, we can take care of ourselves.'"

"Okay," Jeff said, going for the bull's-eye, "What about sex?"

"What about it?"

"Do you plan on … You know …"

I laughed. "My friends all wondered the same thing. Sex is the spice of life, and people want to know how spicy you like your food. 'What did Kathi think?' was often their way of priming the pump. My response was that a year is a long time to be away, and whatever happens, happens. What's the sense of lying?"

"A good way of stepping around the question. I hope I'm not prying," he said, with a mischievous twinkle in his eye. "That question is going to travel with you."

"Looks that way."

How do you say what you feel when you are used to being an authority figure and the answer is ambiguous and changing? Secretly I dreamt of an intimate love affair on some warm secluded island. I sighed, unsure about how to arrange the words. "Fidelity is such a touchy aspect of marriage. I don't endorse screwing around indiscriminately or falling in love with a third party if you want to be in a long-term relationship. Neither do I think fidelity is the cornerstone of good marriages."

"That's not a popular philosophy. I'm sure most people count on fidelity."

"It's the best I've got on the subject. Right now I don't want restrictions."

"Fair enough."

"How about you?" I said, "How has traveling affected your sex life?"

"I had a couple of experiences that were unique looking back. Sex is harder to come by than you think when you're on the move." Then a grin surfaced, slowly spreading from his mouth to the outer reaches of his face, like the ripple a pebble makes when dropped into a glassy lake. "There was this place in Nairobi ... You should go there. It's called the Modern Green Day and Night Bar. Been open twenty-four hours a day since 1967. The Modern Green is a trip, man! A grab fest, African women over you like locusts. I don't think most of the babes are prostitutes. Just want a white body to hold because we're different, superior maybe in their view. Or maybe they want a nice place to stay for the night."

From the park, we walked to the city center. With a quarter of a million residents, Bulawayo was the second largest city in Zimbabwe. But it looked like a farming town—no building taller than two stories and dusty streets used mostly by pedestrians. Not enough cars to pollute. No one hurried. People threw everything on the ground or in the street, but it was all biodegradable— mango skins, cornhusks, and so on. No plastic yet. Bottles were recycled because the glass was worth more than the contents.

As in Harare, I had noticed that males held hands with males. Rayford said that this was normal in Africa, and Africans like him would be shocked at the suggestion of homosexuality. "Our handshake, for instance, is totally different from Western handshakes," he said. "It is soft, and denotes intimacy and friendship as opposed to power or weakness. Like many Africans, I received lessons in the art of the Western-style handshake. We were taught to hold the hand firmly, and then to jerk it away quickly."

We found a small African restaurant with eight empty tables and dangling beads for a door, like in an old Bogart movie. We ordered crocodile tails, beans, and a couple of bottles of beer. While we pecked away at the crocodile, which tasted like the offspring of a chicken and a fish, Jeff gave me a few pointers on traveling. "You can drink the water in most of Africa, Denis.

People will advise you against it, but I didn't have a problem. Be careful of mosquitoes, you don't want to get malaria. Pills are good, but not getting bitten is better. And don't forget to wear long pants after four, that's when mosquitoes hunt.

"And another thing: If you catch someone stealing, make sure your loss is important before you yell, 'Stop thief!' Africa is instant justice. Once in Zaire, I shouted at three dudes who ripped off my daypack. They clipped it right outside the bus. The locals chased them down and beat the guys to death, then casually threw a piece of canvas over the bodies. As long as I live, I'll never forget watching one of the legs sticking out still quivering. Man, I was in shock for days. It's like everything in Africa moves slow, except for the kill."

I observed how the conversation flowed easily between us. "Traveling does that to you," Jeff agreed. "People travel to explore the environment and the mind. We want to see the world for ourselves, not read about it in papers, *and* we want intimacy."

"In your exploration, Jeff, what struck you the most about Africa?"

"The pace. Like I said, everything moves slowly—from eons of exposure to the sun. There's a feel to this place, like nothing I've ever experienced before. The sheer space, the smell, the people, the animals. You're constantly in nature and your genes recognize it."

5

Encounter with a Lion

E ARLY THE NEXT DAY, JEFF and I parted ways without fanfare. He headed south, and I boarded a bus to the Hwange
National Park—as recommended by Ellie. "If you've come
all the way to Africa," she advised, "you might as well see the
animals properly, that means with a guide qualified to take you
walking into the bush. Nothing beats the first impression!"

The bus driver stowed my gear on the roof rack of a dusty
local bound for northwestern Zimbabwe. Losing sight of the
backpack made me nervous, but it was time to trust. A family
tradition was to pick an inspirational card for New Year's from a
collection Kathi kept in an abalone shell. Mine had been *Trust*. I
took that card out of my pocket now.

After just a few days of lugging around my backpack, I could
feel my body getting stronger and lighter, feel the fat melting off
my bones. While my spirit soaked up the sleep that twenty-five
years of hard work had denied it. Old hurts vanished. The pain in
my neck, back spasms, cracking knees—all gone.

Since I had been in Africa, I noticed that babies didn't cry. I
chalked this up to the mother's method of carrying them bundled
up on her back—the kid was secure and could look around but
had no choice except to stay put. Since the mother worked hard,
and had on average six other kids to contend with, the kid probably figured it wouldn't do any good to cry and therefore learned
patience.

I was dwelling on this thought when, to my surprise, a
mother handed me her one-year-old, bare-bottomed, little boy.
I had been making him laugh, so she must have figured I also

had a hankering to hold him. It was a shock, though. The tight texture of the baby's skin was unfamiliar, but my main thought was the worry that the little tyke was going to piss on me—at the very least.

The bus stopped at an old hotel near the entrance to Hwange National Park, where my guide, Mike, was waiting in a Land Rover with a retractable canvas roof. Stocky with crew-cut, blond hair and hunter-green Bermuda shorts and shirt, he looked like an outsize Eagle Scout. He stowed my gear beside a pair of rifles in the back and we set off into the bush. Under the grandeur of the African sky, grassy plains extended to the horizon. The air smelled arid. Starlings flittered in the green canopy of umbrella-shaped acacias.

We bounced for an hour along a dirt road in near silence. Mike's conversation was largely confined to his guns. They were powerful enough to propel a long bullet through an acacia, he explained. "I never aim a rifle at animals unless human lives are threatened," he added, avoiding my eyes.

The Hide was a luxury camp consisting of six army-green sleeping tents for guests, each the size of a large bedroom, and a permanent two-story dining tent. In my tent, the bed was neatly made with a corner rolled down, like at the Hilton, and a fancy hard candy lay on the pillow. A clay water pitcher rested on a lace doily on the night table. The tent had lights to read by, full bathrooms and showers with hot water, and smoke burners to ward off mosquitoes. The bottom floor of the dining tent was big enough to house a long, shiny teakwood table that Hewlett-Packard would have been proud to use in its boardroom. The upper level allowed guests a full view of a waterhole fifty yards away—animals quenched their thirst while we human spectators could sip wine and watch. And, at night, if moonlight wasn't sufficient, a soft, yellow electric light gently illuminated the pond.

During orientation, Mike explained that the park occupied thirteen percent of Zimbabwe's landmass, and that camps provided hope for wildlife. "Tourism brings in more money than subsistence farmers can earn," he told us. "So the land goes to animals because the government needs foreign exchange." He paused, then gave a warning that made my skin crawl. "Oh, before I forget, please do not venture outside your tents at night if you can help it. We can't vouch for your safety. Last week, at another camp, a chap lost his arm to a hyena. He forgot to secure the tent, and slept with his hand outside the opening."

It was only at lunch that Mike formally introduced his seven clients to each other: an older Irish couple and their accountant son from South Africa; another South African couple of Greek lineage, Panos and Jane; Nancy, a red-haired, middle-aged Floridian who sold pharmaceuticals; and a businessman turned backpacker from California—me.

Conversation was polite, with a sprinkling of humor from the Irish gentleman. Despite the laughter and Panos's youthful exuberance, an air of formality presided, as if looseness and genuine feeling were luxury items we couldn't afford to buy. I reflected that formality is a pride and fear we carry around inside. I was reminded of my surprise fortieth birthday party, seven years before, in a Yosemite cabin. When I watched the video of it afterwards, I saw a fat cat whose only moving parts were his lips. Each word was carefully orchestrated, but he was speaking through hardened skin that looked plastered in place. The smugness of the image had shocked me. How long would I take to loosen that face?

After lunch, we set off in the Land Rover. Peeping through the open canvas roof, we saw our first wildlife: paranoid jackals, long-tailed secretary birds with crimson bibs, and a sleazy-looking red-beaked vulture on a tree branch that barely supported its weight. Periscope-necked ostriches flapped their useless wings as they ran. Legions of zebra foraged with wildebeest and baboons, while from the highest trees, eagles regally surveyed the angry-looking Cape buffalo and elephants. Mike hollered animal facts above the bouncing clatter of the car, such as the discovery that elephants can communicate from miles apart, arranging the time and place of clan meetings months in advance.

We stopped by a long lake to watch giraffes. Four sentries roamed in a diamond formation around the herd, about a hundred yards from its center. The aloof herd grazed peacefully, plucking leaves from tall trees and swishing their tails while oxpecker birds pranced on their manes searching for parasites.

"Look to the left of the trailing giraffe, about three hundred yards!" Mike whispered, as the rear giraffe sentry suddenly extended his ears upward in alarm. "Do you see them?"

I scanned the landscape unsuccessfully. Finally, I spotted four lionesses in the deep grass, spread out and moving stealthily towards their prey. The lead lioness crept to within fifty yards of the rear sentry before breaking into a sprint. To my astonishment, the sentry was off and running at the lioness's first step. A second later, the rest of the herd bolted and the chase was on!

We sat spellbound, biting our knuckles. The lionesses closed tight on the sentry, but just ran out of steam before they could attack. Meanwhile, the herd galloped the exact distance again that they had before the charge, then nonchalantly began to nibble grass as if nothing had happened. Even the oxpeckers resettled into their positions.

The lionesses attacked again and again, repeating the scene as if caught in a time warp. The charge, the escape, the measuring of distance, the casual grazing, it went on for an hour down the entire length of the lake. Spent, the big cats eventually accepted their loss. Though glad for the giraffes, I also noticed my disappointment—as if some ancient lust for blood was unsatisfied.

That night, finally unwrapping the candy left on my pillow, I felt strangely at home in this hot place, alive with smells of grass and dung and dryness. Outside, the animals howled, bayed, and shrieked, while insects clicked and buzzed. Inside, I wondered if I could ever go back to the fast-paced life and the bulging briefcase.

The next day, Nancy, Panos, and I returned to the bush with Mike. It was late afternoon when the glare of the sun lessens— prime hunting time. We walked at a leisurely pace in the soft, pepper-colored sand and dried grass to the right of the waterhole. I sniffed the air for fresh animal droppings—amazed at the acuteness of my sense of smell—and searched the grass and prickly acacia trees for hungry eyes and mouths. My ears leaned into every sound, jumping at the dog-like bark of impala.

I barked a few questions myself. "Hey, Mike, how long have you been a guide?" and "How good are you with that rifle anyway?" and "Have you ever used it out here?" He said that he'd only had one occasion to use it out here, and repeated that a slug from the rifle could go through an acacia.

Not more than half a mile from camp, we stumbled on moist elephant spoor infested with dung beetles. The size of my thumb, the beetles busily bulldozed elephant feces into neat little piles with their snow-shovel heads and lobster-like pincer-claws. Then they turned around and used their behinds to push the dung into nickel-sized holes in the ground, where it would later be consumed as food.

Trekking further into the short grass, we ran into an eight-foot tall cone. "Termite cones always face north," Mike said authoritatively, pointing to the phallic-looking stack of hardened mud. "The temperature in every inch of the cone is regulated at eighty-six degrees Fahrenheit, in order to grow fungus to feed the queen. These blokes are the best engineers in the world.

"Their queen is about six inches long. She is chemically fed information to determine the mix of soldiers, workers, and other females needed to achieve balance in the community."

"How many can she produce?" I asked.

"Oh, I reckon the queen can lay as many as thirty thousand eggs a day."

"A day! She must really like kids."

Mike scratched a leg itch with the butt of his rifle and set off again, still imparting information. "Nature keeps everything in balance in the bush. Aardvarks keep termites from overpopulating, just as the food supply keeps animals under control. When food is plentiful, the more passive herds grow and predators flourish. When it's scarce, herds die off and predators starve. Trees, bushes, grass, insects, and animals all work together. Sort of like pistons firing to make a motor hum, they give and take from each other."

As we followed Mike single file into the high grass, my mind was still with the dung beetles. I contemplated how they organized communal living and whether humans would evolve a similar groupthink in a billion years. Only remembering a travel book warning broke these slack-minded speculations: "Avoid high grass. Large cats use it for cover to stalk prey!"

I began to carefully scour the straw-like blades of grass, nervously thinking that anything could happen at any time. The previous night, Mike had recounted another incident. A family of five was traveling through the bush in a Land Rover and stopped to watch a pride of lions feeding on a zebra. The father got out to take pictures with his video camera, ignoring the unarmed guide's order to get back into the vehicle. Instead, the dad moved closer for a better shot of the munching adults and sweet little cubs. Then, out of nowhere, a powerful male lion swept around a knoll and was on him. The swipe of a huge paw probably killed the guy before the cat bit into his neck. In front of the family, the lion dragged dad back to the pride where they ate him, too.

The stories served their purpose. I quietly moved past Panos into second place, looking around slowly and sniffing like a bloodhound for the scent of anything peculiar. Mike pointed out the distinctive bottle-shaped baobab tree. He identified larks gliding over the grand savannah, and crimson-breasted bush shrikes as they flittered in and out of acacias. When Mike stopped talking so did the rest of us, our single-file line closing ranks enough to smell each other's sweat. There was no "protect the lady" colonial gallantry. Rather Nancy appeared perfectly capable of protecting herself or—probably closer to the truth—as equally incapable as Panos and I. She was now in third position and Panos last. The animals kept their distance as we walked—further away than if we were in the Land Rover.

"Animals," Mike explained, "get a heightened sense of danger when humans are in the open bush. Blokes inside vehicles are of less concern to them. All they see is an inanimate object."

After a few hours, we had carved a wide arc that placed us several miles in back of the waterhole. At ground level and eyeing the animals in the distance, I got a sense of their world. The lack of concern for time, the freedom of the moment, and an awareness of unlimited space resonated within me.

Though the high grass obscured the lie of the land, I soon realized we were heading back toward camp. We were finally exiting the grass to reach home when we halted in our tracks. Two hundred yards ahead and downwind were four monstrous bull elephants. They were whacking tall trees with their trunks to shake off the nuts. Their flapping ears and waving tusks looked huge, prehistoric. The onset of dusk over the savanna added to their awesome power. I was nervous.

Mike raised his right hand. "I reckon we ought to stop here a while," he said. "See what they have in mind. Bull elephants are cantankerous and dangerous. We have to be careful." Then he rested the butt of his rifle on the ground and chewed on a piece of straw.

Suddenly, we heard a rolling, engulfing roar. The roar sucked in miles of open space and rumbled through my bones into my head.

"It's a male lion," Mike whispered calmly, bringing his fingers to his lips to keep us quiet. I could see Panos frozen in place, nervously biting his lower lip. The elephants immediately took a lower priority.

"How far?" I asked, while looking around for an escape route. Nancy and Panos locked eyes with me while we instinctively moved closer to the guy with the gun, until we were almost in a huddle.

"Not far and getting closer. Don't go any further."

No one saw a problem with that suggestion.

Mike advanced a few steps, and then pointed to the right. "There he is under that bush, to the right of the acacia, about sixty yards."

I looked through my binoculars. A regal mane framed the fierce face and indifferent eyes of a male African lion. He stared directly at us—as if sizing us up.

Great! Dead ahead (poor choice of words) were gigantic elephants. To our right was a lion, probably famished. To our back, high grass. Again, travel book instructions flooded my mind: "If you chance upon a lion or other predators in the cat family, do not panic and run. They will think of you as food and chase. Back away slowly. Show no fear." Then another flash: "Evening is prime hunting time." Letting the binoculars drop to my chest, I could see the lion clearly now. He looked cool and to be enjoying his rest. What was he thinking? Did he notice the rifle? My blue bandanna was soaking up a lot of perspiration. As time slowed, I wondered if blue was to lions what red was to bulls.

Mike gestured against the wind—we should backpedal. The *Homo sapiens* slowly retreated to the edge of the high grass in the soft evening air and settling darkness. Crunching clay underfoot, we crept gingerly back towards the waterhole through the bristling grass. The lion watched every step of the retreat, his massive head and impassive eyes never moving. The elephants remained engrossed in their work, flapping their ears, bellowing, and pounding trees.

We rounded a clump of acacias and saw the waterhole half a mile away. Next to the water lay the beautiful sight of tents and a plume of smoke spiraling into the darkening night. The final confident strides to camp instilled in me an exalted sense of the majesty of savanna landscape: even elephants shrank in its vastness. When we had reached camp the lion roared in the distance—as if to remind us who ruled out there.

6

KILLER!

ELLIE MET ME AT THE bus station on my return from the game reserve and we drove to her city home in the suburbs of Harare. From the outside, it could have been a modestly well-to-do home in Los Angeles. I was to spend a couple of days there with the Halseys before we headed five hours east to Lake Kariba for a week on their houseboat, *Calle II*. My room was in a quaint guesthouse outside the main building, accessed through a Dutch door.

"We usually keep the bottom door shut," Ellie told me, "to stop the dog from coming in."

"Dog?"

Just then this Rottweiler showed up weighing in at roughly the same as me—158 pounds. His head came to my nipples. And it was no ordinary head. It was dense, solid muscle, like the rest of the body, with wide, tight jowls and teeth so big I doubted the dog could close his mouth. The mouth dripped saliva, while the inscrutable eyes looked directly into mine.

I stared at the canine King Kong for a while, trying to size him up before even thinking of making an attempt to cross to my room with my backpack. He looked like he had the potential to be playful—after all, Ellie informed me, he was only two years old—but I had the feeling that "playing" to this dog would be like a cat with a mouse. I don't recall the dog's name—since there was a compelling reason to forget—so I'll refer to him as *Killer*.

I tried to communicate from behind the half-door, being very careful not to endanger any part of my body. "Nice dog. Have you had a good day?" His eyes, like those of a shark, showed no sign of emotion either way.

"Oh, don't worry about Killer," Ellie said. "He's a good boy. But once in a while, he gets boisterous. Wouldn't hurt anyone, unless of course they were trying to harm one of us, or break into the house.

"Then again," she reconsidered, "a couple of weeks ago, he did rip a hole in the trousers of a guest staying in that room. Nipped him a little. Killer must have sensed some ill feeling.

"Here!" She passed me a handful of beef chunks left over from the previous night's dinner. "This might help establish a relationship."

Ellie didn't seem worried, why should I? But what did she mean "nipped him a little"? This dog wasn't capable of a "nip." I opened the lower door, subjected myself to Killer's sniff inspection, and followed the travel book's instructions for lions: "Back away slowly. Show no fear."

Killer nudged me in between my armpits, like a horse would. "Here, boy, I brought you a gift. Maybe we can be friends!" I dropped the beef. The diversion worked long enough for me to open the guesthouse door and slide in fast. Jesus! I felt like this was a guest test—and I wasn't sure I passed.

I love dogs, but needless to say, I planned excursions from the guesthouse to the kitchen very carefully. I know exactly how many times I walked that distance—eight. Each time was a test of courage. Despite my efforts, Killer did once manage to get into my room before I had a chance to shut the door. I got pissed! I had had enough of his intimidation. This cheeky dog had pushed me too far. "No fucking way, Killer!" I said in a careful monotone, my knees shaking. "This is *my* room. Out!"

Killer sized me up, a few drops of frothy saliva hanging halfway to the floor. Then grudgingly he turned, and, like the stud he was, slowly strolled out.

7

DANGER ON
CROCK-INFESTED LAKE KARIBA

IN THE LATE 1950s, THE Federation of Rhodesia and Nyasaland (a colonial grouping of what is now Zimbabwe, Zambia, and Malawi) created Lake Kariba by damming the eastern portion of the powerful Zambezi River. The resulting lake is about 280 kilometers long and 48 kilometers broad at its widest. It is one of the largest man-made lakes in the world, and probably the only one in which, if you fell in the water, you would risk being eaten alive by a crocodile or crunched in half by an angry hippo. The non-amphibious species from the area had to be rescued during the creation of the new reservoir, as thousands of wild animals were left stranded on the tips of "landbergs." Their offspring now live on the banks of Lake Kariba, where the cleansing aroma of water mixes with a penetrating smell of honey-colored grassy savanna. The government couldn't do the same for the trees, though. They drowned the forest and the trees' ghostly limbs still pierce the surface of the water that killed and entombed them nearly half a century previously.

On the way to the lake, Ellie gabbed and entertained us with jokes in different brogues, a talent no doubt inherited from her well-known British actress mother. The back of the Halseys' pickup was packed with beer, soft drinks, hard liquor, and a variety of foods, including a couple of pounds of an African culinary fetish, biltong (cured beef cut into thick strips). I was about to spend a week with white farmers and get their side of the story.

The fifty-five-foot *Calle II* had three levels. The lowest contained sleeping bunks and two bathrooms, both with a full-pressure shower. A walkway railing surrounded the second-level bridge, as well as the kitchen, two dining rooms, and an area for fishing at the stern. The larger outdoor dining area had the upper deck for a ceiling and was shielded in foul weather by bamboo curtains. The third level was the upper deck. It covered the entire boat, and was used for sunning during the day, cocktails and hors d'oeuvres in the evening, and sleeping under the Southern Cross at night. A forest-green canopy, matching the green and white decor of the boat, covered the stern.

Standing on the upper deck, beer in hand, Ellie introduced me to the crew and long-time family friends: Captain Robert and first mate Paul, both black Africans, who had worked for the Halseys for fifteen years; Harry, a thin, sixty-year-old South African accountant with a friendly mousy-quiet demeanor; Jan (pronounced Yan), a retired white hunter with a devilish smile; Rachael, a tall American in her mid-forties who had beautiful long blond hair, a sun-hardened face, and near anorexic body; Brent's cousin Audrey, a hard-to-read matronly woman in her late fifties, with more salt than pepper in her hair; and Daryl, whose distantly courteous demeanor epitomized the English colonialist. Jan and Rachael had lived together for eighteen years, but never married. Audrey and Daryl owned a tobacco farm north of Harare.

"Here's to our six-day exploration of Kariba," Brent proposed a toast. "May it be exciting and welcoming to our friend from America." As we raised our glasses, Paul unhitched the mooring ropes. The *Calle II* plowed through the water pulling two dinghies and a skiff like a mother goose with her young. Before long, all remnants of civilization disappeared, replaced by the golden sheen of the African bush that appeared to grow out of the sparkling blue of the lake.

As the *Calle II* glided east, Paul placed a lunch of fried meats and fruit on a glass table covered with a thick, fitted tablecloth. As we watched elephants play in the water, Ellie filled the group in on my itinerary. "Denis is planning to backpack around the world. Can you imagine? And he's staying in *hostels*." Her intonation of "hostels" implied lice-ridden flophouses, but also there was a note of pride in her daring new friend: "He sold his business to his partner, and left his two daughters and wife to explore the unknown."

"That's bloody brilliant," Jan said with a thick Dutch accent. "We live too soft a life these days." He was a debonair figure even in his mid-sixties. His silky-white hair sat comfortably on a sun-weathered brow. His body rippled with deep muscles only recently layered with age-loosened skin. And under his penetrating blue eyes, a scar that slashed the length of the left side of his face spoke of a dramatic life.

As a sixteen-year-old, Jan had joined the Dutch resistance to oust the Nazis from Holland. When the war ended he worked on construction projects in South America, before traveling to Nigeria in 1950 at the adventurous age of twenty-two. From there, with an assortment of rifles, he and a buddy headed across Africa in a jeep. It took them two years to cross the Belgian Congo and travel southeast to Rhodesia. Along the way he acquired the skills of a big game hunter, and later set up a business leading safaris.

"I wouldn't do it now," Jan offered. "I just don't have the heart to kill these beautiful animals. Times have changed. Me with them.

"Rachael used to be a hippie traveler before she hit these shores twenty years ago and ran into the man of her dreams," he said jovially. "Right, Rach?"

"Don't flatter yourself," Rachael sneered, "I just needed a place to stay and you were available."

Ellie piped up: "He's going to Vic Falls next."

"And what does your wife think of being separated for so long?" Rachael shot in.

Audrey, who had been silent, followed up with: "Yes, why did she let you go?"

The ladies put me on the hot seat. "She's been very supportive," I said, slicing a piece of sausage uncomfortably. Women, I'd noticed, have a way of fitting men into categories. "But I still haven't been able to figure out a woman's mind, so I'm not sure that I can really answer that question."

"Bloody right!" Jan said. "Women can't even figure out what is in their own minds, how could we be expected to have a go at it?"

"We're not confused," Rachael snapped, "We're too advanced for small minds."

Rachael herself had a sharp mind and her speech was laced with sarcasm, but I was to find her exterior masked a warm heart. Already it hadn't escaped my notice that she quietly, almost shyly, made sure I enjoyed myself.

Later that afternoon, as we lounged on the top deck in the sun, she described how she had dug in shortly after arriving in Africa. Now she gathered and summarized intelligence information for the Zimbabwe government—as the only white in her department. I was surprised to learn she was also a keen bird-watcher and was hoping to catch sight of some new species. She confided that she was down on Americans because they were like her parents. "They're preoccupied with filling every minute of each day, forgetting that people are important," she believed. "Friendships and family need to be watered with time in order to blossom."

We traveled deep into the savanna that first day, before Captain Robert picked out one of the many inlets off the main body of water to moor for the night. Darkness settled and the sky dominated. Although the moon was bright, clusters of stars packed the heavens. After Paul outfitted the top deck with full-length bed cushions, pillows, and neatly tucked sheets and blankets, we vacationers climbed up a narrow ladder and bedded down under the canopy like campers.

I woke to a dark sky, crimson invading its eastern edge. Everyone was asleep except for Harry. We smiled "Good morning," then silently watched darkness clinging to the clouds. Eventually an angel's breath blew away night's outer layer, leaving a velvet glow. The rising sun slowly turned the African sky baby blue, and olive-green and golden grasses revealed themselves across the landscape. Drowned trees rose from the lake around us. In the grass just above the clay riverbanks, two mountainous Cape buffalo snored and dreamed. Suddenly, we were all wide awake, speechlessly watching snowy-white egrets float past the skeletal trees.

Rachael, Harry, and I decided to go for a pre-breakfast hike, while the rest of the gang loafed on deck or equipped the dinghies for fishing. Before leaving, Ellie informed me that the government prohibited walking in the Kariba reserve because of the risk. There were buffaloes around, also hyenas, lions, and elephants. "But bugger it," she concluded, "We do it anyway."

Onshore, we began to follow a narrow trail through the grass, stepping carefully to avoid snakes. Jan called out to Rachael from the boat, joviality barely masking his concern: "Now, don't be so absorbed with birds that you don't see where you are going." Of course, the warning only inflamed my paranoia of creeping predators in tall grass. And I was teamed with a bird-watcher and a retired accountant—while the former white hunter stayed behind to fish. It was an unsettling thought.

Muddling through the bush, Rachael lifted her binoculars and nonchalantly scanned the horizon. She pointed out African fish eagles and a hornbill with a yellow beak like a toucan. While she got excited by a spotted something or other, I carefully looked around for escape routes.

Finally, we climbed uphill into a clump of trees and watched grazing eland and the delicate-legged impala leap and scamper at our scent. High ground had the feel of safety. It provided visibility and tall yellow acacias to climb when the attack came. Rachael led the way through the trees to a cliff overlooking muddy flatland. Harry protected the flank. Down below a herd of at least three hundred mean-looking Cape buffalo splashed in waterholes, rolled in mud, or grazed suspiciously. A few stared up. I immediately doubted the security of the knoll.

Suddenly, I felt a tap on the back. I turned to see Harry's finger planted on his lips—shh! He slowly moved his finger away from his mouth to point. Rhinos! Behind a thicket of bushes beyond the trees. We tiptoed and then crawled to within forty yards. From there we could see more of the group, including a calf the size of a Volkswagen Beetle nuzzling its mother. The mature ones nibbled grass, moving so close to one another that they could have been whispering between bites. Each breath sounded like a large bellows. The only non-gigantic aspect of these huge beasts was their tiny eyes. To try to take the profit out of poaching, rangers had sheared their horns off. But sadly the poachers machine-gunned these magnificent animals anyway, so as not to lose time tracking hornless individuals in the future.

Moving with confidence, the rhinos failed to notice us lying prone behind the bushes spying on them. I was caught between the instinct to flee and the exhilaration that accompanies exposure to nature's risks. They snorted, sniffed, and casually looked around. And with each inhale and exhale of their breath, I felt my fear. However, these animals, which could have crushed me like an ant, exerted a primeval pull. In the end, we did not wish to tempt fate too far and slowly retraced our steps. Back on the path, we made a triumphant return to the boat.

The third morning, I opted to fish with Brent. We took one of the two dinghies to a calm spot on the lake. Brent began to bait the lines. His chunky, red face looked vexed. I guessed the pressures of owning a sizable business in an unfavorable economic climate were getting to him. He often wiped his brow and would squint behind his glasses when the perspiration flowed into his eyes. Finally, he sat down, popped a cold one for each of us, and inquired further about my profession before I set out to conquer the world.

"They call it crisis management," I responded as I flicked my line out into the clear blue. "My firm was engaged by large interests to consult with companies in considerable financial trouble. Occasionally, we were called on to run one of them."

The boat could have been on dry land, the water was so still. The only movement was the rings that formed after our lines plopped in. Brent paused, pursed his lips, and then conversed as if very carefully peeling a banana. "How does that work?"

"Well, first we figure out how critical the situation is and what to do about it. Then we build a salvation strategy and operating plan, and organize the various constituencies, like management, banks, lawyers, stockholders, suppliers, and bondholders, to approve the plan and work together. Meanwhile, we'd guide management to break down the organization into building blocks. Keep the winners. Get rid of losers. Rebuild credibility. That's it in a nutshell."

I recalled how, by the time we arrived, management had fucked up communication by reporting confused information, or worse, by giving no information at all. How constituents got nervous and often began to act independently, each party employing its own lawyer like an unfriendly divorce. How credibility eroded faster than mud under the Victoria Falls. And how our first task was always to analyze each constituent and understand where they were coming from. Bankers were first in the pecking order, and generally wanted their money back, whereas stockholders were last, and needed to keep the banks' money in play so they could hit a home run. With everyone's point of view understood, it was possible to predict reactions and strategize to keep the groups working in concert. For me, the practice also honed a wider ability to understand people's motives.

"Did you help the companies obtain financing?"

"Occasionally."

We tipped our heads towards the other and chugged beer. "You know I've been looking for financing to buy my company from my former bosses," he said. "It's not easy to raise money in Zimbabwe under the present government."

We sipped and talked, while we reeled in and flicked out, our lines sailing through the air and plopping into the water. I asked him a few questions about potential lenders, and what he thought about going out on his own, but nothing was settled. In fact, while I was interested in hearing, I was not interested in addressing his problem, which is unlike me. I had been built to solve problems. But in this setting, you didn't need to catch fish or solve the world's business issues.

Our daily routine was to wake before sunrise and, as light chased away dark, the ladies would silently take turns to serve tea and biscuits to the stretching and yawning males. Then we politely broke into pairs or threesomes to fish for bream and tiger fish while chugging beer, go for nature walks, or loll around the boat. When the fishing boats returned, we breakfasted on fried eggs, bacon, thick sausages, potatoes, and cereal moistened with fresh fruit juice. Conversation ran the gamut from the morning's catch and sightseeing experiences to good-natured kidding, jokes, and politics. After breakfast, Ellie, Harry, Audrey, and I played bridge, while the others lay in the sun or played a dice game called Minefield. Beer and hard drinks started just before a fish lunch, followed by more fishing and nature walks until the infallibly spectacular setting of the sun. There followed pre-dinner drinks, appetizers, and, eventually, dinner.

Everyone agreed my American way of eating, switching the fork to the right hand after cutting, was amusing and inefficient. When in Rome ... I adopted their method: the knife used as a steam shovel to pile food on the back of the fork held in the left hand.

One evening, everyone dressed up and relaxed on the top deck. I donned my fanciest wrinkled clothes. The bar was opened as the first stars appeared in fading light. Nibbling fare included biltong and miniature quiches filled with cheese, potatoes, minced beef, and herbs. Fireflies blinked on and off in the distance and an occasional mosquito hummed in the lingering heat. The talk centered on the dismantling of Zimbabwe by President Mugabe.

"The infrastructure that the whites built is deteriorating year by year," Brent groused, to general agreement. "The buggers just don't have the capacity to plan anything. And we watch our tax money go into someone's bank account in Switzerland."

"It starts right at the top," Ellie cried. "Mugabe and his gang are looting the treasury. Did you know, Denis, that his recently deceased wife was one of the richest women in the world?" She sighed and crossed her freckled legs. "It's the same all over Africa, black leaders ripping off the very people they fought for. Now, for his own safety, Mugabe's constructed miles of buildings to house ten thousand guards."

Jan poured himself a scotch and water. "Don't forget Mugabe's new football stadium," he added with a mischievous grin.

Daryl lowered his pipe solemnly from his mouth to follow up. "You see, Denis, the Chinese supported the rebels during the war, so we compensated them with construction projects. They designed and built our football stadium without snack bars or ticket booths. Evidently in China people bring their own food to free sporting events. It cost a bloody fortune to rebuild."

"Shouldn't we allow a learning curve for blacks to govern effectively?" I asked. "After all, it took Europeans a couple of thousand years to figure out how to manage large societies."

"You probably think we're racists!" Jan said. "But we have to put up with this unorganized lot. The only thing that we have too much of is government workers and security guards to protect us from theft!"

Back home, I didn't hear directly derogatory racists anymore, but the number of blacks in my town in California could be counted on one hand, and in all my years in senior management and consulting, I couldn't recall more than ten upper-level black managers. Although I philosophically abhorred racism, it hadn't played a major role in my life. Yes, I guess I did consider my hosts racists, but I wanted to hear them out without making a judgment call. I was beginning to think that was the way of the traveler: to see, listen, and piece together the puzzle that is society.

"You have to do something to keep them employed; they multiply like rabbits," Rachael added. "And if you think we're hard on the blacks, you should see the way they treat their women. The poor things grovel in the kitchen while the husbands dine. And who do you think does all the child raising, farming, and fetching water while the men—who probably have two or three women—hang around bars with their buddies?

"When women marry, their property rights go to their husbands, making the wives legally invisible. People romanticize Africa, but I don't think women in the United States would put up with these bastards." Then she leaned over and whispered to me out of earshot of the group, "Course, in some respects when it comes to treatment of women, most white men in these parts aren't much different. They treat their women like furniture."

I listened, occasionally asking questions to understand where my companions were coming from. They all believed blacks discriminated against whites for government jobs, but needed the whites for economic stability and tax dollars. It was also clear to me that though the whites acted appalled by the inefficiency and injustice, they economically dominated the majority of the blacks. White men dominated white women. White women dominated black servants. Black men dominated black women. I felt like a witness to a multi-car accident.

Two days later, Daryl, Rachael, Harry, and I took an evening sightseeing tour. In our twelve-foot boat with a five-horsepower outboard, we putt-putted out into the lake under soothing pre-sunset skies, our hair barely moving in the perfect warm breeze. Daryl piloted the boat, pipe in mouth with a hint of a smile on his face. Cameras and binoculars dangling, Harry and Rachael occupied the middle plank, while I commandeered the narrow front seat. Daryl maneuvered into a wide channel between a maze of dead tree limbs bordering the shoreline. Suddenly, the boat rolled over an object below the surface and leapt into the air.

"Hippo," Rachael figured.

An omen, I decided.

Hanging perpetually from his tight lips, Daryl's aged, brown pipe disengaged almost imperceptibly when he smiled. If he removed the pipe from his lips, it became part of his left hand, and his face changed to a kind of smugness. His skin looked like sun-cured leather. V-shaped ridges in his forehead ran deep and his bloodshot eyes, like red rivers meandering through grimy snow, became moist when he smiled. The smile stretched the skin of his face and revealed tobacco-stained teeth. It dug deep dimples in his cheeks and accented a nose that rippled at the top and almost touched his teeth at the bottom. Overall, Daryl's grin, with the exception of an inscrutable glint in his eye, looked more like a cat's reaction to the unexpected arrival of a dog.

Our destination was a secluded lodge in the hinterlands of Lake Kariba. We were meant to be going for tea and a walk in the bush, but the exact order was not quite clear in my mind. I listened to the chug of the small outboard, while Rachael focused her binoculars on an eagle perched on a cadaverous tree. Harry sat quietly and Daryl hummed a tune. Two little kids played tag on the shoreline near their houseboat. The wind began to pick up.

The further the dinghy headed into open water, the more it was clear that a storm was brewing ahead. The clouds went from white to gray. The patches of blue dwindled. Waves rolled with increasing intensity. In the distance, ugly black clouds spewed rain and ferocious lightning. This was not a passing squall, and we were heading straight into it. Rachael and Harry were anxious. But Daryl was happily singing to himself. "We all live in a yellow submarine, a yellow submarine, a yellow submarine...." Occasionally one of us offered a comment about the approaching gloom, but he kept going forward. Did Daryl know something we didn't? Was there a teahouse around the next bend?

The wind continued to notch up, and the first droplets of rain struck my bare arms. Waves now slapped menacingly against the boat. The warm, thin aroma of the friendly lake changed to the chilling, heavy scent of wind-whipped waters. Blue sky was a memory as we entered the tempest's fringe. Still we went forward. I turned around to see Harry and Rachael rubbing their arms and cowering against the pelting rain that also whipped Daryl's face and dripped steadily from his nose into the bowl of his pipe. Still there was no change in Daryl's expression. In his rough smoker's voice, he had progressed to Irish folk songs. "The pale moon was rising above the green mountains, the sun was declining beneath the blue sea ... She was lovely and fair as the rose of the summer, yet 'twas not her beauty alone that won me, Oh no, 'twas the truth in her eyes ever dawning, that made me love Mary, the Rose of Tralee."

His unconcerned look conjured up an image of the English commander sternly ordering his troops forward at the Charge of the Light Brigade. Like the ill-fated cavalrymen, none of us said a word about turning back. Suddenly we were in the thick of the storm. Four-foot waves pounded the little boat and rain punished our faces. Daryl shouted above the wind in a tone bordering on the blasé: "Shall we turn back?"

"Yes!" we bewildered soldiers cried in unison. At last, we turned for home—but where was home? I squinted into the swirling mists, barely able to make out the shoreline. How far had we gone? Normally, I wouldn't have been concerned. We were only a half-mile from shore. Not a bad swim—but for the hippos and hungry crocodiles licking their chops in smiling anticipation. Rachael, Harry, and I bailed furiously using our hands as pails. We tried to ignore the increasing chill and concern seeping into our bones. Daryl was cool though. His pipe continued to bob to the rhythm of his latest tune.

"Shall we stop at the houseboat we passed earlier? I don't think we're going to make it back!" His voice punctured the veil of howling wind.

"Good idea!" Harry screamed to unanimous head bobbing from the crew, before yelling a suggestion of his own. "Why not change the angle to cut down the water we're taking in?"

We made it to the houseboat, drenched and chilled and longing for its warm shelter. Shivering, I tossed a rope to the first mate and he hauled us in like spent fish. Daryl climbed on to the stern, like General MacArthur inspecting a cruiser. "Do you mind if we visit for a while?" he said, smiling through the pipe. "We've had a bit of bad luck, you know. What with the storm ... Tea? Why, yes, we'd be delighted."

We sipped hot tea in the comfort of the cabin with our new hosts, a family of seven white South Africans, including grandma and grandpa, who chatted amicably about the dramatic changes occurring in South Africa as if we were expected guests.

Meanwhile, as the winds raged, the boat's black captain radioed the *Calle II*.

We returned home aboard a skiff not much larger than our own but much sturdier and with a more powerful engine. *Calle II's* captain, Robert, met us at the halfway point and we attempted to transfer amid the rough waters, wailing winds, and cracks of lightning. However, the waves were too high to make it safely, so Robert's skiff became our escort.

Though not much was said, the relief among the folks on the *Calle II* was clear as they helped us aboard the mother ship. We all felt sorry for the other captain having to brave the waves back again. Daryl gave him a good tip, and we were relieved to hear later he made it back safely.

That night, we buttoned down the side curtains, drank a lot of booze over dinner, and ended up enjoying an old-fashioned songfest. It turned out to be the worst storm in Lake Kariba's recent history, and by morning, dead bugs were plastered over every inch of the houseboat.

Two days later, I was off to Vic Falls. My hosts had booked a room for me at the famous Victoria Falls Hotel. "Denis, I know that you like to rough it," Ellie said, "but even if you spend only one night at that hotel, you must do it. You won't have seen Africa if you miss its colonial elegance."

"I remember the first time I saw the falls," Brent said wistfully. "It was one of those once-in-a-lifetime experiences. Just wish I could live it again."

I felt like a jack-in-the-box before its lid is opened. The falls were the reason I came to Zimbabwe—another childhood dream.

8

VICTORIA FALLS:
FIERCE FORCE OF NATURE

T HE VICTORIA FALLS HOTEL WAS indeed elegant. Its spacious
carpet of lawns and European-style gables were a glorious
relic of English gentility. After spreading the contents of my
backpack throughout the surprisingly small room and washing
clothes in the sink, I found my way to the expansive teakwood
dining room and sprawling buffet-lunch. Plate heaped with food,
I stepped out on to an open-air porch and took the glistening,
white stone steps down to a graceful garden. There, surrounded
by pink bougainvillea, proper patrons sipped proper fruit-laced
drinks—all served by black waiters in white jackets and bowties,
who said, "Yes, boss," and "Can I get you anything else, boss?"
I looked out over rainforest stretching as far as the eye could
see. Beyond the green blanket, rich blue sky collided with mountainous clouds of vapor to form a rumpled white mass. THAT! I
thought, has got to be the Victoria Falls.

After lunch, I headed out. At a wire fence marking the rear
edge of hotel property, I followed a dirt path into the forest. The
path was devoid of humans, but was peppered with funnel-faced
mongoose, playful monkeys, and families of menacing baboons
with red, bulging rear ends and huge teeth that scared the living
shit out of me. The air hung heavy from the steamy cauldron
rising from the Zambezi River. After a while, the foliage became
dense and damp and the ground shook as if I was in an earth-
quake. The falls had to be a mile away, yet they roared like the

Pacific on a stormy day. Logically, the native name for the falls is Mosi-oa-Tunya, *the Smoke that Thunders.*

I walked, carefully avoiding any baboons, until the path bisected another near the river's bank. Back home there would have been a warning sign: *Proceed at Your Own Risk.* Transfixed, I peered through drenched ferns at the rolling, rust-colored water that sparkled peacefully in the sun. The sound was overpowering. I parted the ferns and crept cautiously to the river's edge. Only yards ahead, the sparkling water suddenly hurtled over sheer cliffs to brutally drop four hundred feet into a smoky abyss, where it disappeared into a canyon—the spray rising high enough up to look like rain clouds. Through it I saw the Devil's Cataract, the first of the nine contiguous falls. I had to resist the hypnotic urge to leap into the smooth power of billions of gallons of free-falling water.

The next day, I ventured across the river from Zimbabwe to view the falls head-on in neighboring Zambia. The sun shone brightly, yet I walked over a mile in heavy drizzle. Along the way, I passed a curio market, which offered "ebony" woodcarvings from the densely grained mopane tree. Hawkers greeted me with hard sells: "You make sure to see me when you come back … My name is … I remember you … Make special deal." I bought a walking stick with a serpent's head handle baring bone fangs and shining demon-red eyes.

At the edge of the jungle, a young man, who said his name was Paul, offered "special" guided tours under his large rainbow colored umbrella. "Thanks," I said, "but no thanks. I can take care of myself." Right! Two minutes after walking down into dense jungle in shorts and T-shirt, I was back. My panama and body had been pummeled every step of the way by waves of heavy rain. "Okay," I said, "lead on!"

Paul wore a charcoal-gray shirt, long, blue pants, and black lace-up shoes ripped open at the soles. He said his father was a doctor in Victoria Falls, and that he, Paul, needed money for books in medical school. We walked toward Zimbabwe along a grassy path below the rim of the falls, so that we stared into the downward flow at close range.

That was the magic of the Zambian side. The churning waters accumulated in a chasm, then at the far end blasted into a perpendicular gorge with huge, algae-covered granite walls that propelled and funneled the Zambesi from Africa's interior. Directly in front, the falls spanned at least a mile. Devil's Cataract abutted the banks on the Zimbabwe side in the distance. To its right Cataract Island, a desperately deserted hunk of land teetering on the very edge, then Main Falls, Livingstone Island, Horseshoe Falls, Rainbow Falls, Danger Point, and Eastern Cataract. Finally, Knife-Edge Point finished the spectacle.

Not far from Rainbow Falls, where there *was* a rainbow, we crossed a one-person wood-slat bridge suspended across the narrow gorge. The shaky and slippery bridge, weathered by age, seemed to cringe under the constant battering of wind and rain. Paul distracted me by chattering about Christianity as I inched across the bridge. My hands gripped the slimy rope railing. I tried desperately not to look down.

"What religion are you?" he inquired.

"WHAT?" I shouted above the roar.

"WHAT RELIGION ARE YOU?"

Back on solid earth, he held the umbrella above our heads while we watched the rainbow. "I'm not," I shot back. The colors were so vivid the pot of gold had to be within a half mile.

"Do you not believe in Christ?"

"I believe he was probably a great man," I said. Was this the start of a conversion effort?

He looked at me wide-eyed. "Do you *not* believe he is God?" This guy was persistent. He could probably work a couple of conversions a day using the falls as a demonstration of God's power.

"I don't really care. It's not something I think about."

Paul looked puzzled, but charged on. "What do you call what you are?"

"What?"

"What do you call what you are?"

"An agnostic."

We crossed back over the bridge—another hurdle on this crusade completed. I took a picture of Paul standing on the edge of a bluff, with the full intensity of the snowy-white falls and crinkled clouds in the background. He crouched down like a boxer—back foot pointing towards the falls and front towards me. One hand holds the rainbow umbrella, the other sweeps the panorama of the falls as if to say: "All this is God's!"

Paul motioned the umbrella towards an alternate path, one less rained on. Even with the umbrella, water ran off my nose from the constant downpour, and I regretted wearing walking shoes instead of sandals. Paul's shoes at least expelled water through the hole in his sole. We stopped about two hundred yards away from the roaring falls for more questions from Paul.

"Never heard of those 'agnostics.' Do you not believe in the Bible?"

"It's hard for me to believe anyone's written account could survive thousands of years of translations," I said, then tried to turn the tables on him. "What color do you think Jesus was?"

"He was white, of course!"

"Why do you believe in a white man's god?"

"That is what the missionaries taught us."

Paul spoke clearly and articulately, with a hint of playfulness in his voice and eyes. He looked about nineteen.

"What about your grandparents, were they Christians?"

"No, they believe in tribal rituals. They are pagan. What do you believe in?" He wiped his face with one forearm while holding the umbrella with the other.

I thought for a moment. "Do you know how long a light year is?"

"No."

"Well, light travels at 186,000 miles per second or 670 million miles an hour. So a light year would be light traveling for a year at that speed. To get from here to the farthest star we know of takes twelve billion light years. This universe is so old I don't presume to know what it is all about. But I like pursuing its mysteries."

Paul took this in, then told me he was quite sure that I would find God. At the conclusion of the tour, I took Paul's address and promised to send him pictures.

9

WEDDING IN THE BUSH

ROM THE VICTORIA FALLS I flew to Harare and checked into the Backpackers Connection near the airport. Two dollars a night for a bed in a four-person room, plus access to a lounge with a pool table and bar. I was discovering that cost was all-important to travelers because it afforded more time to travel—and time was king. I was proud of how little I paid for things, despite having money. It wasn't so much a Scrooge complex as enjoyment of a simple lifestyle.

That evening in the lounge, a paunchy, strutting South African, with glasses perched below his narrow forehead, introduced himself to everyone as Ruben Hendriks. He added a challenge: pool for a hundred Zimbabwe dollars a game. No one accepted, which was lucky for Ruben because he wasn't that good. In the end, I played a few games with him—without a stake.

"Travelers are all alike," the wide-faced, lightly bearded Ruben scoffed. "They go from hostel to hostel, never really tasting the real Africa, the people. They isolate themselves." He cleaned his spectacles and handed me a Castle beer. "Take a chance. I'm leaving for a little village near Masvingo after sunrise tomorrow and wouldn't mind some company."

His feet pointed slightly to the outside when he walked and his tanned hand constantly cradled a beer. While the balls clacked and dropped into pockets, I watched how Ruben stroked the cue, talked, drank beer, and even smiled to determine if I could trust him. I also interrogated him a fair bit.

He had been evading South Africa's draft for four years and didn't intend returning to his country until the government changed. Currently, he worked for an NGO in the south called Zimbabwe Unemployment Benefit Fund, ZUBF—pronounced "zoo-biff"—for short. They helped train unemployed Africans grow their own food and get jobs. He was in Harare to pick up a guy called January and take him to the village for training.

I decided to take a risk and go to the village with them.

At eight the next morning, Ruben and I sat in the front seat of his pickup, with January perched behind the window in back, amid what looked like Ruben's entire possessions. January was a bored black employee at Backpackers Connection who wanted to join Ruben working for ZUBF. I felt guilty about the segregation, but stifled any comment. I also felt guilty about my cynicism towards Ruben—despite that *Trust* card deep in my daypack.

Driving south along the outskirts of Harare, large posters of a solemn-looking President Mugabe hung every hundred yards from newly constructed lampposts. "These guys are all alike," Ruben complained. "They win a revolution then drum who's boss into the consciousness of little people. Mugabe's a thug." We drove on a graded two-lane highway for two-thirds of the 300 kilometers to Masvingo, drinking bottles of beer all the way. At one point, Ruben stopped to replenish the supply. We parked outside a bar that looked like a wooden shanty. It was dark inside. A plank served as a countertop and cases of beer were stacked behind it. Clientele attire ranged from ragged slacks to sharp, white shirts and suits without ties. The atmosphere was hospitable, not unlike the Slavic bars in upstate New York where my in-laws lived.

Outside, six men surrounded the pickup. Robert, a tall, well-built, friendly guy with an intelligent smile, sunglasses, and deluxe high-top sneakers, introduced himself. He checked out the contents of the truck and asked if I wanted a beer. I declined. What I *wanted* was to empty my bladder.

The loo, as they called it, was outside, eight feet in height, and open at the top. Mud-brown and concrete, it was constructed like a mini-maze. Taking a deep breath, I squashed through the narrow opening, made a sharp right turn, then another to the left. The stench mauled me well before I squeezed into a cubbyhole with an eight-by-four-inch—often missed—hole in a concrete slab on the ground. With all the liquid from breakfast and the

63

beer that Ruben had cajoled me into drinking en route, I required the lungs of a seal to complete the visit in one breath. Not only did the smell make me want to exit as quickly as possible I was also worried about leaving my daypack in the front seat. Trust failing again?

As I returned, Robert was requesting a lift to his cousin's wedding.

"How far is it?" Ruben asked, impatient to be moving on now that he had restocked the beer.

"Not far, ten kilometers maybe."

"I'm in a hurry."

"It will not take long—only ten kilometers."

"Okay, but we can't stay long."

Ten people climbed aboard the pickup, then another four carrying packages materialized out of nowhere. A mile later the paved road turned into a red clay path, which itself disappeared as we rattled deeper into the bush. The "ten kilometers" became twenty kilometers, and our passengers multiplied, too: a grandmother here, a mother and three smiling children there. All going to the celebration. By the time Ruben finished weaving through ponds, over ridges, and around thorn bush and craggy boulders to the wedding site, I counted twenty-five people onboard.

We drove past the wedding party: bridesmaids in pink taffeta dresses with white lace fringes and white gloves, the bride in a white frilly gown, ushers and groom in ill-fitting tuxedos and white gloves. We wheeled through the copper savanna past the scattered guests—men in the same variety of attire as the shanty bar, and women with headscarves and brightly patterned dresses or wraparounds. Finally Ruben parked under the shade of a skinny acacia and the truck emptied.

From behind his mirrored sunglasses, Robert told us that traditionally the wedding party dined separately from guests. He assured Ruben, who was hesitant to stay uninvited, that most people were uninvited. I followed Robert and Ruben towards a group of older men. There was a definite pattern to travel, I reflected—surprises were ordinary.

Robert introduced Ruben, January, and me to the elders (all men), who were congregated outside one of four circular thatched huts constructed of clay and cow dung. Taking time away from serious discussion, the men welcomed us in a language I didn't understand. Smiles revealed protruding, stained teeth and empty sockets. The elders seemed in a dither about what to do with white guys. Eventually they decided to ignore us and go back to their discussion. Though I felt shy and out of place, I was also curious and glad to be there.

While the older men debated, the older women tended the food in six heavily rusted barrels exuding steam, which spiraled into the atmosphere. Chicken and *sadza* boiled inside. Robert did not appear to think there was any point in introducing us to the women and ushered us past to a clearing away from the main gathering. The other guests stared at us. Ruben was embarrassed by our conspicuous whiteness, but after introductions to the bride and groom—and their three children—he accepted an invitation for us to dine with the wedding party.

We sat on a large, flat rock ten yards from the makeshift wooden table occupied by the newlyweds. To the couple's left sat thirteen ushers, to their right an unequal number of bridesmaids. Robert said the bride and groom had already married under tribal law, and that they sanctified their union earlier in the day with a Christian wedding.

I had no idea what would happen next. This was so exciting.

Wearing avocado-green sheaths to protect their pink dresses, the bridesmaids served the meal—men first, as custom dictated. Our communal rock was served by a tall, elegant woman in her early twenties, Shylet, who retained the unrestrained smile of a wholesome teen. While the four of us maneuvered for comfort, she brought three yellow enameled tin bowls: one filled with water, another *sadza* in red sauce, and the third a few slim pieces of chicken to split between us. I never tasted chicken so good and stripped every morsel of meat off the bone, then washed my hands in the water.

We climbed back into Ruben's pickup to rejoin the main party. Shylet and two other bridesmaids sprinted barefoot after us, holding their shoes and waving for us to stop. Ruben jammed on the brakes and Robert and I leaned over the edge of the truck, grabbed the women's arms, and hauled them in like hobos into the boxcar of a moving train. Although there was plenty of room, Shylet burrowed next to me, sliding her warm body the length of my surprised but yielding bare left leg. I looked at her and she flashed a wide grin and winked. Was this heaven or what?

At least twenty kids surrounded the pickup when we arrived. Children are special to me. They make me feel comfortable and wanted, and give me a clue as to the company they're with. To play with a kid, I first establish eye contact, and then communicate at whatever level he or she wants.

Although these children looked solemn, I quickly winked and threw a couple of funny faces their way. The immediate reaction was double takes and toothy smiles. Once I get the grin, I like to follow up with something physical. I tapped a six-year-old boy on the back of the head when he turned sideways to look at a friend. He whipped around to see what was going on. Everyone pointed at me. His face lit up. Next, I tickled a little girl, who had maneuvered into a strategic front position, and made goggle-eyes at her. That did it. The gates of solemnity were blown off their hinges. The kids moved closer to me, made faces, laughed, wanted to be tickled, or got me to tickle a friend.

It was late afternoon. Ruben was anxious to move on. But by now the wedding party had returned from their separate dining area and the festivities began in earnest. The bride and groom stood facing a crowd that easily surpassed three hundred. Some of the guests began to sing and beat drums. The music urged the gyrating mass of people to advance on the couple in rows. They stutter-stepped forward to the staccato tribal beat until their turn came to offer presents to the newlyweds.

Shylet let it be known through Robert, and through her smile, that she liked me and wanted me to stay for the festivities, which Robert explained would last late into the next afternoon—at the earliest. I'd be a fool and a liar to say I wasn't flattered—or uninterested in what would happen. Still wearing sunglasses, Robert tried to convince Ruben to stay, but he was adamant we reach the village before sunset. Robert gave Ruben his final word on the subject: "If you like, first enjoy the dancing, a quick fuck, and then go." He paused briefly. "Do you have marijuana?"

Ruben declined Robert's graphic suggestion, but did roll a joint for him, and loaned his camera to an acquaintance to take what might be the only photos of the bride and groom. I followed Ruben back to the pickup. I admired the trust he showed with his camera, but my main emotion was disappointment at having to leave.

Ruben chuckled. "Robert told me that Shylet was very interested in you, mate!"

"Yeah, how about that? Just natural charm, I guess."

"Well, don't get a big head. Remember she sees 'white and rich.'"

"Thanks, Ruben, I needed that."

10

Village Life: Down with the Sun, Up with the Rooster

As we drove, Ruben explained why he was on the run from his home in South Africa. "The bastards treat blacks like shit. I refused to join their army. I escaped to Switzerland, spent four years as an engineer, got married, divorced, then smuggled myself back into South Africa undetected."

"Why return if you felt the way you did?" I asked, munching a banana.

"I'll tell you, mate, I could never get used to the Swiss. And I bloody well missed Africa. The style of living in the West is too fast, and for the most part too impersonal. In Africa, life is slow and easygoing. Hospitable, despite the bigotry. When I returned home, the government tracked me down. So I had to split sharpish!

"At the first Zim village me and this pickup hit, I met this bloke, Godfrey. Turned out he was the head man at ZUBF. Bloody disorganized group! But I thought, bugger it, and offered my services. Godfrey accepted my offer, grateful for the help. He could barely offer me a roof over my head, but that was good enough for me."

He unwrapped a pack of cigarettes with one hand, and banged it against the steering wheel to pop one out. He pushed the box at me. "Cigarette?"

"No, thanks. Haven't smoked a cigarette in twenty-five years."

He lit up, took a long drag, and washed the taste down with a slug from the brown bottle of beer. "I like the people at ZUBF," he confided, "and I need a home."

When we stopped for petrol, I confessed that I felt uncomfortable sitting inside the cab while January sat outside.

"Don't be, mate. January would feel more uncomfortable sitting with the two of us blokes. He wouldn't be in the conversation. Besides, this is the way Africans travel. There aren't many vehicles here so they hitch a ride." Ruben often stopped to pick up locals walking along the side of the road. They hopped in back after paying Ruben a token fee. "People shouldn't think they're getting handouts. It doesn't do much for their self-esteem."

Before we left the petrol station, Ruben took a moment to mix hash with tobacco that he removed from a cigarette casing. Then he stuffed the mixture back into the hollow paper. "How about this? Do you smoke this stuff?"

"I smoke, but I don't inhale!" I laughed. He didn't.

"That's a political joke in America," I said and changed tone. "Yeah! I smoke grass, although hash would be a first." I took the restocked cigarette as the pickup chugged into the hills. One advantage to being older and smoking pot, I mused, is that no one would ever suspect I was stoned, just thoughtful.

Godfrey lived in a valley, within a six-house enclave of teachers. He greeted us without fanfare and grabbed the beer that January handed down from the pickup. A dignified man, he lived in a small, green, three-bedroom, concrete house, with his wife, Sunday, his sister, his three children, another teacher, and the teacher's son. We popped a few tops under the shade of a lonely tree in front of the house. Across the red dirt road an eternity of unfenced savanna melted into purple mountains. The surreal sky made the red soil glow—as if the state of Montana was in Godfrey's front yard.

Dusk was descending over the plains. Ruben had taken off his shoes and socks and, trailed by Godfrey's three kids, crossed the road to find an open space to test a gigantic kite he had taken from the truck. He was one of those people that couldn't sit still. It wasn't long before the four figures blended into the landscape as if in a painting. Ruben carefully explained kite aerodynamics to a growing crowd of kids that suddenly materialized as if he was the ice-cream man. This was perfection: the lonely wind, milky-rose glow of the setting sun, the vast expanse of savannah, and the eager curiosity that only children's faces can wear.

When the sun went down, we ate dinner by candlelight, there being no electricity in the basic house. The living room had a dining table, nondescript couch, and the only record player in the village. A cable ran from the player, out the window and into a battery inside a beat-up 1964 rusty green Volkswagen.

Sunday served food in the same kind of painted tin bowls as at the wedding. Plain-looking and in her mid-thirties, she had intelligent eyes and a rarely flashed, stunning smile. First, she brought water to wash our hands, then *sadza*, cabbage in tomato sauce, and the tiniest piece of chicken. The food had been cooked outside, over a glowing wood-fed hearth dug into the ground.

Godfrey sat solemnly at one head of the table, Ruben at the other. January and I sat next to each other and faced the barren wall. The children must have already been fed and put to sleep, while the women were conspicuously absent. They ate huddled on their haunches in a dingy kitchen no bigger than the size of a generous bathroom. I expected them to eat with us, after all, Godfrey had been educated in the US and Sunday also taught school.

Conversation at the table proceeded at a respectful pace. Except for the scooping of *sadza* and the rural sounds of insects, silence filled the void between sentences. Speaking softly and slowly, Godfrey recounted his two and a half years at a small Massachusetts university where he'd studied for his master's degree in third world developmental organization.

He leaned his prematurely balding head forward. "After finishing my master's," he said, "I traveled around the United States for six months raising money for ZUBF. That was four years ago. The money is running dry." Ruben interjected that ZUBF needed to be organized, and that he was just the man to do it.

What struck Godfrey as the biggest difference between his culture and the United States, I wondered. He slouched as far back as a person could in a simple wooden chair.

"Two things," he concluded, "the pace of life and the apparent lack of friendliness of the people. Maybe these two are connected. I am not saying that people in your country are not friendly—because they are—it is just that there is so little time to be wasted. In Africa, time is what we have in abundance and little else.

"Yes, and also black people in America disappointed me. They seemed always to be complaining while accepting welfare checks. There is no welfare in Africa, and since we have so little, there is little to complain about."

"You don't have to be old to be Wise" by Judas Priest blared from the record player. Anxious for the black viewpoint after the Halseys and their friends at Lake Kariba, I asked how he felt about whites now that fifteen years had passed since liberation.

Godfrey lifted his head from picking at the chicken, washed his fingers slowly, and matter-of-factly said: "I really do not spend time thinking about whites."

Could that possibly be true?

He was reluctant to talk about his government's politics, but did say that there was a drain of white farmers who he felt, because of their expertise, were an integral part of maintaining a healthy level of food production in Zimbabwe.

I woke, along with nature, to the high-pitched screech of a rooster. A stark realization hit me. The world only recently—in the big scheme of things—had use of electricity. Here we slept when it got dark and rose with the sun. My mind boggled that I had never thought of it before.

Sunday and I chatted briefly while she cooked breakfast outside. She and her husband taught in different schools, and she dreamed of the day they could teach together. She dreamed of working with him, yet couldn't eat a meal with him.

At breakfast, hard-boiled eggs and tomato puree with bread, Godfrey and Ruben went over their ZUBF plans with me. I sort of committed to do my best to help them when I returned to the States.

Afterwards, Godfrey's ten-year-old daughter, Lilly, took me to her school. With a purple ribbon on the back of her head, she led me with quiet authority down the deserted red clay road. The school was surrounded by a flimsy fence and had an entrance that required students to walk up three concrete steps, traverse a four-foot wooden platform, and down three steps again. "Why the steps?" I queried. Lilly gave me a "who knows?" shrug accompanied by a "seems pretty dumb to me" scrunch of the eyes and face.

We became buddies touring the one-story school, which consisted of an administrative building, five small functional concrete classrooms, and a sixth that looked as if it had been in construction since before independence. All the windows were either missing or broken. Beaten-up blackboards were inlaid into dirty and chipped, pale green walls, and timeworn wooden desks with inkwells stood on concrete floors. Latrines were outside. No maintenance engineers here. On the way back, we played catch with a stone, but quickly switched to soccer once we entered her yard and encountered her twelve-year-old brother and his new "ball." I have never had so much fun with a plastic bag tightly wrapped in twine.

I spent a couple of days doing nothing but getting to know my hosts. However, soon the time arrived to return to Harare and catch my flight to Nairobi. The plan was that Ruben would drive me to a bus stop at the roadside shanty bar where we had stopped on our way to the wedding. But first Ruben needed to buy a pair of goats.

He wanted goat's cheese and milk to eat and drink, but also to learn how to raise the animals so he could teach the unemployed. Godfrey and Ruben decided to drive to the home of a woman who knew of goats for sale and could also help negotiate the fee. The black Africans would bargain together, while the two whites (and January) waited at the woman's hut. Godfrey and January climbed in back of the pickup. I offered to switch places, but neither of them accepted.

After fourteen kilometers of bouncing along a dirt road, we made a sharp right and abruptly stopped in front of a small corral built from one-inch branches tied with string. Inside, cows and a couple of bulls, complete with fierce white horns, milled aimlessly. On the other side of the road, clay-and-cow dung huts baked under the sun. Melancholy sunflowers and a field of corn bordered the huts. A woman and seven barefoot children husked a tall pile of white corn stalks. They tossed the corn into buckets and then poured it on to a clay slab where it would dry.

The woman looked sixty, but was probably about forty. Her gaunt face showed the years tilling the soil and bearing children. A brightly colored kerchief covered her small black head, protecting it against the blazing sun. Her deep forehead ridges and elevated cheekbones made her eyes look as if they'd been chiseled into her face. Leathered skin surrounded her flat nose and deeply flared nostrils. Her teeth reminded me of decaying timbers jutting out of a broken mineshaft. But her eyes burned brightly and tenaciously.

Without much discussion, we piled out of the pickup and began peeling corn. After a while, Godfrey and the children's mother left in the pickup. Ruben, January, and I worked along with the children, peeling corn to the last. Once we'd made sure there wasn't a single husk in evidence, we all stood around and admired the pile of discarded stalks. The skinny but healthy siblings, all with big, brown, welcoming eyes, used sign language to invite us to view the four thatched huts that constituted their home.

We first visited the cooking hut, a dark, musty-smelling structure boasting a hearth and an assortment of enameled tin bowls and pans lying neatly on the dirt floor. Except for the entryway there was no ventilation. I wondered how anyone could stand the smoke. Next we peered into the separate huts for males and females. The fourth served as storage for dried corn.

The tour completed, I tickled the kids, who now numbered nine. Ruben showed them how to hypnotize a chicken by placing its head under its left wing. He told them the chicken would stay in the trance forever unless physically disturbed. The kids sat on their haunches and leaned their heads towards the chicken, equally hypnotized. Only ten minutes later did one of the curious boys lift the wing and break the spell. He looked as startled as the hen, which suddenly glanced around and squawked frantically away.

Just then Godfrey pulled up in the pickup with the mother, two goats in the back, and the goats' owner. The petrified animals had their feet bound together with twine. The female accepted her fate, but the male whined and struggled. Money quickly exchanged hands, and we were off once again.

At the roadside shanty bar, Ruben, who didn't seem the type, embraced me. After such a short time, I was surprised to find that we had developed a bond. I threaded my arms into my daypack, gave my farewells, and boarded a 1940s-style, dirt-scarred bus bound for Harare.

The air inside was dense with human odor, and even though the bus was packed like a New York subway during rush hour, for the first fifty kilometers no one sat in the open space next to the only white person. To mitigate my self-consciousness, I buried my nose in a book, acutely aware of the people around.

Primal instinct caused me to look up. "JESUS CHRIST!" I screamed. The bus was hurtling down the two-lane road as if it was out of control. Was the bus driver crazy? Or drunk? Or both? I clutched my seat and watched through the window as he passed buses, trucks, and even speeding cars. A pattern developed. First, he stalked his victim vehicle, like a lion moving in on its prey. When he was within reach he would weave in and out of the oncoming lane to assess traffic for a passing move. If there was no chance, he would inch even closer to the vehicle, until we could clearly see the faces glued to its back window.

I remembered a word that an eighty-year-old friend and experienced world traveler gave me for just such an occasion before I left: *inshallah*, God (Allah) willing. As I gave myself up to God, I surveyed the other passengers. Everyone but the most hardened sat red-knuckled in their seats, wide-eyed like me.

Somehow we reached Harare. After many an *inshallah*.

UGANDA

MATRIARCH

11

AHMA'S INSPIRATION

J IN BULAWAYO, PUT ME ON to the Ssese Islands, a remote chain of eighty-four isles in the northwest corner of Lake Victoria in Uganda. "It's an experience for one who wants to take the road less traveled," he said. "The mosquitoes are as thick as a rising of locusts, but they only bite cows. When you get there, stay at the Ssese Scorpion Lodge at Luku on Buggala Island.

"Take the train northwest from Nairobi to Malaba, and walk across the Kenyan border half a mile to Uganda. Take a van south to the capital, Kampala, a *matatu*—it's also a kind of taxi, but you'll find out—then to Musaka, and another to a small fishing village called Bukakata.

"But get there before dark," he warned, "and catch a fishing boat to Luku. The Scorpion Lodge is primitive. They speak only one or two words of English, but the fish is good."

What was I getting myself in for? A jungle in the middle of nowhere? Just one or two words of English? And the only thing I knew about Uganda was that in the 1970s the Israelis staged a daring hostage rescue from pro-Palestinian hijackers at the airport in Entebbe, in defiance of Uganda's brutal dictator Idi Amin. Maybe this excursion *was* too much too soon, but since there was no one to dissuade me, I made arrangements.

In Nairobi, I purchased a Ugandan visa and a train ticket to Malaba. I also phoned home and eventually reached Kathi. She was attending my grandmother's funeral. She gave me the details of her death. As I hung up, a vacant feeling washed over me. Yet I sensed a lingering presence.

My grandmother's nickname was Ahma. I admired her. She was my buddy. We played canasta when I was a kid, fighting and laughing over the cards. By telling her how young she looked and feeling delighted and rakish at her aroused vanity, I learned how to charm women. It wasn't a surprise she died; the last time we talked cogently was five years ago when she was ninety-four. She had said to me, "Denny, I'm scared. Parts of my day disappear and I don't know where they've gone. My friends have all died and I'm ready, but my body does not know how to quit. I'm afraid it won't let me die with dignity."

A sense of security seized me—the sensation that she had joined me on this adventure. Well, Ahma, come along for the ride!

I slid open the wooden door of the sleeper compartment where I would spend nearly a whole day. A leftover from the British, the train from Nairobi to Malaba would take twenty hours to cover just 400 kilometers. At present, I was alone in the compartment. I placed my dusty backpack and serpent's head handled stick in the storage bin below the army-green vinyl bunk beds and stretched out. Army-green, I reflected, had to be the most popular seat color in Africa.

We inched along out of Nairobi's inner core into its seething skin, a shantytown without electricity or covered sewers. For two hours, the train crawled through this four-mile slum that housed political refugees from surrounding countries devastated by war and rural refugees from land incapable of providing for a growing population.

Pulling aside the curtains, I felt like a voyeur as I observed the activities of everyday life in this human bazaar, which stretched for miles in every direction. Tin- and rag-roofed shacks and mud huts were stitched together by a maze of foot-worn, copper-colored paths. Privacy was non-existent. The women walked gracefully with burdened heads. They cooked, carried suckling babies, and tended clotheslines that crisscrossed the community like telephone wires. A rooster proudly pecked a scurrying hen that had dared compete for a scrap of garbage. Bony livestock and scrawny, half-dead dogs and cats looked on. Gargantuan armies of kids laughed and smiled, cried, and pissed. They ran alongside the train waving their hands and squealing with delight.

Finally, the train came on to the golden plains of the Rift Valley. Fifty million years ago, earthquakes ripped away the northern part of the continental land mass, creating the Middle East. Viewed on a map, the Middle East looks like a piece of a puzzle that would fit snugly into the eastern edges of Sudan and Ethiopia. This wrenching of land created a seam, the Rift Valley, which runs down East Africa as far south as Kenya and Lake Victoria. It became known as the cradle of mankind after the Leakeys, the renowned family of archaeologists, found three-million-year-old hominid remains there.

Out the window, women and girls weeded and tilled fields of maize. Mothers bent over at the hips. Their stomachs and faces parallel to the earth. Their hands in it. The apparent idleness of the men and boys made me wonder what my grandmother would have thought of the division of labor.

Though we called her Ahma, my grandmother's friends called her Dolly because as a child she looked like a doll. She stood about five-one, but her electric personality and passion for life made her buxom, Gibson-girl body quite imposing. She wore high heels and moved fast. Her jet-black hair was always bunched in curls at the top of her head and was supported in back by a Spanish comb. Her rosy cheeks created appealing dimples when she smiled or laughed, which was often. And she loved to repeat certain phrases: "Mark my words," "Your word is your bond," and "To thine own self be true, and it must follow, as the night the day, thou canst not then be false to any man." What I remember most about Ahma was her eyes. Those black eyes could sparkle or pierce steel depending on her mood.

My eldest brother, Dave, was her clear favorite. She gave him ten dollars for his birthday. The rest of us got two. But Ahma thought that I would go places. "Look at the way you dress," she'd say, "those bright colors. And the way you walk. There's destiny in that walk." And she never tired of telling the story of my grandfather's birthday. "Denny wasn't hip high," she'd say. "He had a mind of his own even then, and when no one was looking, he decorated Papa Joe's birthday cake with feathers just plucked from the goose. My word, what a mess!"

She told family stories with great authority and vigor. There was story after story about the importance of family, about how we reached way back before the French Revolution, and how, coming from royalty, we had a legacy to live up to. She embellished the tales with a bevy of colorful family characters, such as her great-great grandmother who escaped the guillotine in France, fled to America and spawned a family of adventurers. Unfortunately, the great lady's wealth was lost in America because she neglected to tell her descendants that her stash was hidden in the posts of her bed.

"And my mother could shoot a rifle as well as any man," Ahma used to say in a voice as definite as her spirit. "She was so good at reading palms that within six months of leaving my father she had furnished the rented flat for my brothers and me. My mother was a lady—and a lady is a lady, even when she's cleaning garbage cans."

Her grandfather, meanwhile, was a Sandy Hook pilot who was swept overboard and drowned during a storm as he was guiding a ship into New York harbor at the ripe old age of seventy-five. This just a week after siring his seventh child by his third wife.

Ahma started in business aged fifty, after the family lost their wealth in the Great Depression. I can hear her saying "No sense crying about spilt milk." She opened her house to boarders and later traded antiques. She specialized in dolls for the last twenty years of a career that ended when she was ninety-two. Ahma was a prototype modern woman, and a great inspiration in my vision of family. Of the values she instilled in me, such as a sense of equality, the most relevant now was that at fifty (or forty-eight, in my case) you could begin a new life.

I had been joined in the compartment by a single fellow traveler. Bill was a short, thin Kenyan student studying to be a teacher of African history at Nairobi University. He told me he lived in a little village a couple of stops before Malaba and belonged to the Luo tribe, the second largest in Kenya. He spoke three languages: English, Swahili, and Luo. His father worked for the railroad as an accountant before retiring, so he seemed to be the person to ask why the train went so slow.

Bill scratched his head and replied in a prematurely husky voice. "My father says the tracks in Kenya are usually repaired rather than replaced. So the drivers increase speed only on the straight sections they are sure of. He says that fixing the railway is not a priority for the government. They have no funds. In January, the Mombasa to Nairobi train fell off the tracks into the river. The rails did not hold."

I offered Bill a chunk of Cadbury's chocolate, which he graciously accepted. Cadbury's was a treat for me—a reminder of home. As we ripped into the candy, Bill said how excited he was to be going home. It had been almost a year. Perhaps to relate his country to mine, he pointed out that Kenya was about the size of Texas. "But Texas," he added as a punch line, "does not have seventy tribes!"

That evening, Bill and I fought the laws of physics as we struggled along the wiggling, clanking train to reach the dining car. It reminded me of an old mystery movie where the evil killer—armed with a pistol, of course—and the good guy wrestle for supremacy as the train sways and groans. The dimly lit dining car was devoid of frills. Its eight booths had a simple wooden table covered by a faded red tablecloth. Bill carefully laid the contents of his brown lunch bag on the table—a banana and a container of *maharagwe* (kidney beans in a spicy sauce). We shared this bounty along with my purchases: chapattis, rice smothered with stewed vegetables, two bowls of turtle soup, and two large bottles of beer.

I wanted to make the most of dining with a history major, so began to ask questions as we ate. "How did the English get Kenyans to work their farms?"

Bill studied me for a moment, bit off a hunk of banana and chewed it slowly. "The English introduced the concept of individual land ownership, on the model Cecil Rhodes had used. Get cheap labor, charge rent for the land they live on, and levy taxes. To live one must pay. To pay, one must work. That is it!"

"Interesting strategy. And how did you Kenyans get your land back?"

Bill straightened the sleeve of his shirt, which like his slacks was meticulously clean. He spoke quietly in precise and formal English. "Let me tell you a story about my country. There are two great tribes besides my own, the Masai and Kikuyu. The Masai are pastoral and fierce, everyone leaves them alone. They care about cows, not politics. The largest tribe in Kenya, the Kikuyu, occupied much of the better farming land around Nairobi before it was lost to the colonials. Jomo Kenyatta, the father of our country, was Kikuyu. He raised money from the Indians and communists, and ..."

"Hold on a minute! Do you mean the Russians?"

"Yes."

"Are you saying that the Russians financed the revolution?"

"Of course! They brought Kenyatta and other African leaders to Moscow to teach them revolutionary tactics."

"Huh! I never knew that!" I slouched in thought, draining the beer and occasionally looking out the window as a waiter cleared room on the table for fresh bread. The setting sun cast its deep red hue on cows and chickens outside and a gentle crimson light on our table.

Kenya's Mau Mau rebellion occurred when I was a kid. Though it was crushed, it ultimately led to independence from Britain. From what Bill said, it looked as if communists and capitalists waged an ideological power struggle by fueling these wars. China and Russia backed revolutionaries in Zimbabwe and Kenya, while the West represented the establishment. I made a note to myself to study other countries in Africa to determine how many were caught in this ideological vice.

"Didn't the Mau Maus take a secret oath to kill every white in the region? It made great copy for the tabloids—savages using machetes to hack off limbs, white women and girls ravaged. Is that true?"

"It was an effective technique for encouraging white people to leave, was it not?" He frowned. "But the newsprint was misleading. Some say as many as forty thousand Africans were killed. Only a couple of hundred whites."

"Do people dislike whites now?"

"I do not believe so. After the war, the British were magnanimous. They gave Kenya monetary grants, lent us money to buy out white farmers. However, we lost expertise. We were self-sufficient in grain before the revolution. Five years later, we had to import fifty percent. Farming with hoes and sickles does not produce enough food to feed the population, yet modern equipment puts people out of work."

An article I read said Kenyatta's regime made Kenya one of the most stable countries in Africa, but that he and his successor, Daniel Moi, also kept the Kikuyus in political power by getting rid of the opposition.

"I hear that both Kenyatta and Moi have been accused of massive corruption. Didn't a former Mau Mau fighter say Kenya was a nation of ten millionaires and ten million beggars?"

Bill's frown deepened. He looked around the dining car suspiciously. He leaned towards me and confided in a voice not much louder than a whisper, "Kikuyus have violently manipulated the government since independence. However, it is not safe to talk about such matters. Some bad people, workers on this train, chopped off heads in tribal disputes only last year."

Carrying a skimpy duffel bag, Bill disembarked in the night two stops before the border between Kenya and Uganda, but not before cordially extending an invitation for me to visit his home. He wrote the "address" on his lunch bag: his father's name and the name of the village.

12

THREE GREAT DANGERS
TRAVELING IN THE THIRD WORLD

O N A WINDLESS MORNING, THE train reached the border
town of Malaba. In step with six other travelers laden with
backpacks, I passed through the Kenyan checkpoint and
then walked the seventy yards to its Ugandan equivalent. Both
were mustard-colored sheds not much bigger than telephone
booths. A yammering throng of barefoot youngsters accompanied us, aggressively selling black-market Ugandan shillings. It
challenged my financial acumen to follow their "math." Let's see,
that's 1100 Uganda shillings to the dollar and 70 Kenya shillings
to the dollar. How many Uganda shillings for a Kenya shilling,
again?

After showing our passports, we crossed a dusty street, entered an even dustier parking lot, and then packed into a van
heading for Kampala. The driver, all of fifteen and head barely
above the steering wheel, drove about four blocks on the main
road, and then turned left down a narrow dirt path through a
neighborhood of hovels overflowing with children and wide-
bodied women. The van stopped at one of the hovels and two
scruffy teenagers emerged, lugging plastic gas cans. Off went
the gas cap and in went the gas. The honcho doing the pouring
dangled a lit cigarette from his lips as if he was chewing a blade
of grass. OH, JESUS! This is it, I thought. When the van blows,
I'll get a memorial for the long on spirit and short on body parts.

When the tank reached capacity the guys rocked the van to squeeze in every last drop of fuel—the cigarette bobbing up and down with each jerk. The young driver relinquished control of the wheel to an older gent with a thin, gray mustache and a flowing, white gown. An Arab-style kaffiyeh topped his head, giving him an air of dignity that had been absent in the boy.

The remainder of the trip to Kampala turned out to be relatively boring, despite the occasional roadblock staffed by smiling soldiers with machine guns, and a roadside sign that read: *The pouring of petroleum products on the road is prohibited.*

Kampala is situated around the capital of the pre-colonial kingdom of Buganda. Buganda was ruled till the late nineteenth century by a monarch called the *kabaka* and a parliament, the *Lukiiko*. Buganda was said to have one of the most sophisticated governments in Africa before the turn of the century, although when I read about its system of punishments I had my doubts. Charles Miller, author of *The Lunatic Express, An Entertainment in Imperialism,* a book about building the Mombasa to Uganda railroad, described justice in action, saying criminals were dismembered before being roasted alive over slow fires for capital offenses ranging from wearing a leopard skin, which was high treason as the leopard was the royal animal, to stealing a cow. Lesser offences were punished by slicing off lips, ears, noses, eyelids, and hands. My skin crawled when Miller described the punishment for more serious crimes which called for cutting away a person's entire face, except his eyes. On his first visit to Uganda in 1890, Frederick Jackson was shocked at seeing one such victim, without lips or cheeks, and both rows of teeth exposed.

In Kampala, we entered a lot the size of five football fields. It looked like the LA freeway at rush hour, but it was jammed with *matatus*. Let me introduce you to the *matatu*. *Matatus* are mini-buses, vans, or stripped-down cars that pack people inside so tightly one person's arm slips and slides on the sweat of another's body. The driver's sidekick, the moneyman, herds people in and out of the vehicle like a shepherd. And, like sheep, you obey. When it's time to go, the moneyman pounds on the roof because the driver ain't got a clue. That's a *matatu*.

In the seething activity of vehicles, touts, travelers, vendors, and dust, I barely had time to get my bearings and say goodbye to the other travelers before a skinny tout grabbed my backpack from the van. "Where you go?" he asked.

"Musaka."

He turned and bolted, with me in hot pursuit, chasing my backpack through the ferment. Before I knew it, I was sitting in the middle of the middle seat of a sedan that closely resembled a Californian low-rider. Incredibly, they rigged the battered, old car with three rows of seats and enough room in the bulging, twine-laced trunk for luggage and chickens. Before entering, I noticed a lug missing in the right front wheel.

I was the eighth passenger, and assumed no one else could fit and that we'd make it to the island before dark. Yet we had to wait another hour as the touts found four more adults, one with a baby, to pack in. All the while, jabbering juvenile vendors hawked warm cokes, watches, popcorn in small plastic packages, peanuts, and other goodies. They delivered their goods and collected money from the waiting passengers as if we were spectators at a baseball game, passing everything down an assembly line of hands.

As I waited to leave I found myself prey to shifting emotions. At first, I was mainly aware of being squeezed like a hotdog in a bun, then I felt conspicuous as the only white person. I became fascinated with the activity outside, before finally being overwhelmed with impatience to get to Ssese. Who knew what to expect in Bukakata at night, wherever that was? It was now two in the afternoon.

I was relieved when the driver eventually squeezed into the front seat, along with three other people and the baby. His slight upper torso and hips, which would have suited a jockey, were pressed against the door away from the pedals and steering wheel. To drive he had to keep his feet and hands at thirty-degree angles to the rest of his body. He looked like Plastic Man.

The relief at setting off soon evaporated. Hand on horn, Plastic Man careened down the one-and-a-half-lane road at 140 kilometers an hour. I feared for the livestock and humans in brightly colored garb who wandered the road. I feared for me. This guy was fucking crazy! At first, I relaxed when he slowed down behind another vehicle, until I realized it was just part of his Russian roulette art of passing. The real terror wasn't so much that he couldn't see what was ahead of him, although that was frightening, it was that what was ahead of him was usually a truck coming directly at us. "I'm dead!" I thought realistically.

Fortunately, soldiers stopped the car three times in the first fifty kilometers. The third time, I mouthed words very slowly to a robust, wide-faced matron to my right. "Why ... are ... soldiers ... stopping ... us?"

"We are overloaded. It is custom," she said.

"What ... are ... they ... saying?"

She looked at me with a slight frown. "He is paying them!"

"Wouldn't it be less expensive if he took less people?" I wondered aloud.

She shrugged.

To take my mind off the road, I calculated what the driver would need to save in bribes to offset three or four fewer people. Still my stomach churned every time I thought of the driving and the condition of the aged, rattling car. I held tight to my daypack with the *Trust* card inside and commenced the mantra—Inshallah! When this had little effect, I looked around for support from other passengers to get this rooster to slow down. No help. Almost everyone was asleep, and the rest sat with the bored demeanor of rail commuters. This couldn't be normal, could it?

Around four o'clock, the driver pulled to the side of the road at a small *matatu* way station a few kilometers short of Musaka. He wrenched my backpack from the overflowing trunk and laid it on barren ground. I was never so glad to exit a vehicle. I checked for the money-belt around my waist while uncorking my water bottle. I breathed new life and guzzled water deeply. Before I could even wave goodbye to my fellow survivors of what seemed like an experience dreamed up by the Marquis de Sade, a teenager appeared and hoisted the backpack on to his shoulder. He schlepped off in the direction of a blue pickup on the ruddy dirt road to Bukakata. I was the thirteenth person to climb into the rear of the pickup. What luck, I thought, even on this road we should be able to cover the twenty kilometers to Bukakata and catch a fishing boat to Ssese before nightfall.

Fat chance! Another hour was spent cramming new arrivals. I counted twenty-seven in the back and four in the cab—plus, sacks of food, satchels brimming with personal artifacts, tires, green bananas, an upside-down rooster with feet tied and eyes darting, and a ten-foot cylinder of rolled aluminum fastened to the back of the cab like a mast on a sailing ship. Seatbelts were used to tie banana branches! I strained my neck to check out my luggage. It hung over the tailgate, but was tied tightly.

Bandana around neck, sweating from humidity, and again the only white, I had been shoehorned between a craggy-faced, mustachioed man with a white shirt, and a tall, very handsome Adonis wearing an oxford sports-shirt and tailored slacks. A portion of my derriere rested on rimless tires, while the remainder hung over the edge of the pickup so that my feet dangled above the road. Nevertheless, after the death-trap ride from Kampala, I felt at ease, cozy, and adventuresome bouncing along this narrow dirt road, which sliced through wide-leaf trees and bushes. The pickup scaled gorges and sides of hills. This land had the expansive feel of the Australian outback, only it was Africa. Africa!

The port at Bukakata was bustling with men in bright shirts and husky women in brilliant pinks, greens, and oranges. There were wooden shacks selling fish, with some beat-up bikes leaning against them, a couple of pickups, and a rather diminutive looking dock that wasn't quite up to being called a pier. I was looking for the serpent's head stick, which must have been left behind somewhere, when a studious-looking young man with round sunglasses tugged at my shirt and pointed toward the dock. "Boat is leaving," he said, "Must hurry!" Apparently, everyone knew the white man's itinerary.

Under a fading blue sky sheathed with a faint milky-white, the air carried the enlivening smell of a large body of fresh water. The cluttered boat was long, narrow, and deep, like a dugout canoe, and had a small outboard motor. It reeked of fish and was covered with grime. There were three fishermen and eight passengers. The fishermen laughed and jostled each other, looking at me while pointing suggestively to the young woman beside me on the plank seat. I ignored them and stated my destination. "Luku."

13

SSESE ISLANDS: FEEL OF PRIMITIVE

A N HOUR LATER, THE FISHING boat left me and an old woman on the exceptionally lonely dock at Luku and motored away to the next island. While I watched the boat shrink amid the dancing light sparkling off Lake Victoria, the woman disappeared into the dense, green jungle. I was left alone in a clearing the size of a football field. I dropped the pack on the ground and stared at the green. So this was the Ssese Islands.

Thirty paces ahead to the left, there were several vacant huts, which looked like an abandoned set from a jungle movie. As if from nowhere, a local appeared and pointed a drooping finger at the third hut along. It was the registry. Inside, I added my name under the most recent entry on the moist paper:

23/04/93 Denis Hickey, SF, California, USA
F1 978886532 American

I stepped out of the registry and stared into the jungle. What was I getting myself into? I was nervous, didn't speak the language, and dusk had descended. Jesus! A jungle and me alone. Would any other travelers join me, or would I be a single shingle? A fish eagle drifted on the thermal above. It looked like an omen, but of what I didn't know.

There was only one route in—a narrow, amber road that sank into the mass of trees and vines. Up that road I hoped to find the Scorpion Lodge before dark. I thought *what the fuck*, secured my backpack and water bottle, and pierced the jungle. After a quarter mile of lush vegetation and hordes of non-lethal mosquitoes, I

89

came upon two gray brick structures with flat tin roofs. One had three adjoining rooms that looked like monastic cells. The other was longer, with a separate cooking hut in back, which belched fire and smoke. The yard was equal parts grass and patches of dirt. A weather-beaten wooden sign said: SCORPION LODGE.

Relieved, I unbuckled the backpack and let it slide to the ground. In due course, Mary, a sturdy, barefoot woman in her late twenties, greeted me. She had the rounded look of a mother. She showed me to a dark cell with a single cot, kerosene lantern, and an old wooden chair with a coarse towel folded neatly over the back, and then pointed two fingers to her mouth questioningly. Starving, I nodded "Yes!"

I sat outside on the ground awaiting dinner and absorbing the buzz of the jungle and emergence of stars. As I began to wonder whether it was *food* that I agreed to, Mary returned and led me to the main quarters. She pointed to a chair and commanded "Sit," then to a tin bowl on the table for me to wash. She brought in *matooke* (steaming mashed green bananas in tomato sauce), a slab of cooked white fish, and a cup of chai. *Matooke* was a basic starch—occupying a similar place in Uganda's diet as *sadza* did in Zimbabwe's—but the fish tasted better than anything served in the finest French restaurants.

I spent two days exploring Buggala Island, which was alive. *Everything* moved and wiggled, flashed, croaked, cried, sang, talked, or screeched. Across the path from the lodge, hundreds of storks strained the upper branches of an ancient leafy tree. Egyptian geese, yellow-billed egrets, and white pelicans took turns flying overhead. Monkeys and pigs scampered. Larks and swallows swooped. And a million varieties of bugs conducted their daily business. The place was creature heaven.

On my second evening in Ssese, I strolled a few miles deeper inland. Along the way, teenagers were chopping firewood with machetes. We exchanged salutations—hello in Swahili, the rest in English. *"Jambo!* How are you?" I replied, *"Jambo!* Fine, how are you?" I nodded pleasantly to guys talking and drinking warm beer outside their huts, and passed tiny grocery stores sparsely stacked with bananas and nuts. I tipped my panama to the village women in sash dresses who were busy cooking, nursing, or cleaning. And I turned and teased the little kids that followed me. I took a fork in the road and found myself back beside the water

At the lakeside, a ballet of chatting and giggling women, skirts hitched to their thighs, filled plastic jugs and washed clothes and tin plates. Bare-chested, young men in cutoff pants watched, flirted, and heckled. In the setting sun, the sludge of Western overload drained from my memory to be replaced by the smell and feel of this green goddess Ssese. In my mind's eye, I left the sandy road and waded waist-deep among the girls. Women who tilled the soil, cooked *matooke* in sizzling juices, and suckled their young. I laughed with the hunter-fishermen who related stories about times past.

I was still in this vision when I felt an insect crash into my left eye. Stunned and temporarily blinded, tears leaked down my cheeks as I stumbled around. Locals poured from their huts and surrounded me. They stretched my eyelids to see the damage and then removed the dead creature from my milky mucus. Though I was touched by their kindness, the dream bubble was broken.

The next morning, Mary served a breakfast of porridge, fruit, and chai in the Spartan dining room. Her coal black skin shone in her pink blouse. I compared the African women with my grandmother. They had lots of kids, family close by, did things slowly, and were highly subservient to men. Ahma had family close by, but a lot fewer kids. She also had extraordinary control over her life. She said once that a sense of self-worth puts you in the driver's seat. Sitting on the toilet in her bathroom, I often noticed the brittle, brown newsprint with her amendment to the Declaration of Independence tacked on the mirror's molding: "We hold these truths to be self evident, that all ~~men~~ are created equal."

After breakfast, I sat bare-chested, barefoot, and in a baggy bathing suit as I wrote in my journal. An industrious wasp busily built a mud nest on the concrete floor to my right. Drums sounded in the distance. And I was being watched, maybe stalked, by a gargantuan spider. It was creeping languidly just outside the single redbrick step leading into the hut. Every so often, I checked its progress. Soon its two-inch legs, which supported a green and yellow bulk about the size of a generous jellybean, began feeling their way up the step. Mary's four children played quietly in a mud hole outside, compliments of pre-dawn rain. The sky was still gray and angry. The spider made several attempts before it conquered the step. It checked me out, and then gradually, with only a hint of forward progress, began to scale the face of the wooden door before stopping—perhaps in diabolical ambush.

As I was mulling over the spider's intentions, I heard the shuffle of hiking boots outside and a backpack hit the clay. On the other side of the open window a man was scratching his balding head as he looked around. He peeked in.

"Doctor Livingstone, I presume?" he said. "G'day, mate. Name's Andrew. Comfy little place to rest your bum, isn't it?"

At that exact moment, a rooster strutted to the doorway, stretched its neck, plucked the spider off the door, and without so much as an "excuse me," swallowed it whole.

"That was a bloody big spider!" Andrew exclaimed. "Wouldn't have wanted him getting into my knickers."

I laughed—as much at the audacity of the rooster as at Andrew's comment. While we exchanged our life statistics, the busy wasp flew in and out of the hut carrying mud like a mason to plaster the walls of its nest only inches from our feet. Andrew was from a little town in New South Wales, Australia, and had been traveling Africa for six months.

"What's the price of this resort?" he inquired. "Just the bare essentials, I take it?"

"A dollar a night and a dollar for each meal. Landlady's name is Mary. She's a sweetie, but she likes cash up front. And only knows a few words of English."

Though I treasured being the only foreigner on my part of the island, I enjoyed the immediate camaraderie that travelers share. Later that evening, Andrew and I wandered to the dock to catch the setting sun and find out when the island pickup made its thirty-two-kilometer run to Kalangala in the center of Buggala. Near the dock, we found another new Aussie arrival, Peter, resting his head on his backpack, chewing on a blade of grass, and staring at the evening sky.

Peter looked to be about six feet long and in his early twenties. His wiry body was draped in loose pants like sweats, but thinner. He wore a dark pullover and a woolen cap to protect his stringy brown hair from the sun's rays. He used words carefully, as if he had a daily ration. But when he smiled his face lit up and his brown eyes sparkled. This contrast with his serious nature created charm. A straggly, silky beard combined with shoulder-length hair and pleasant face gave him a look like Christ in the holy paintings from when I was a kid. I felt an immediate connection with Peter and much more a sense of ease than with Andrew.

We talked Peter into spending the night at the Scorpion Lodge instead of under the tree. And after dinner, we chitchatted on the stone doorstep in front of the now fully booked lodge. Peter said he was an artist and a throwback to the hippie era—he traveled in search of knowledge and wisdom.

"My dream," he said solemnly, "is to travel the world, then visit the Hopi Indians in the United States to learn their culture and put it on canvas."

"Why the Hopis?" Andrew asked.

"Because they don't believe in violence. And they have a history for predicting events—dead accurately—and I want to understand why."

Andrew figured that, at twenty-eight, he would soon be married with family and wanted to sow wild oats before departing the single life. "We Aussies have a tradition of traveling for long periods. The general opinion of most blokes is that we're so far removed from our ancestors that we need to visit our roots. What do you reckon, Peter?"

"I reckon!" he said. "Anybody have paper to roll up?" From his pants' pocket, he pulled a brown tobacco-leaf pouch—cannabis. "I picked it up in Kampala for half a dollar US. I'd share with you blokes but I haven't got any bloody paper." At that, Andrew disappeared into his room and returned handing an ultra-thin sheet of airmail paper to Peter, who brushed back his hair then rolled the joint with practiced fingers. "Cheers, mates!" he said, passing it around. We sat on the doorstep casually getting stoned under the darkening veil of dusk.

Across the courtyard, flames danced inside the cooking hut, smoke slowly rose to merge with the seal-gray of approaching night. Near the hut, a pig snorted around a clucking hen. Mary cooked while her sister swept the family abode with a short broom of sliced papaya leaves tied with twine. The thin-legged children played house with imaginary props, and storks settled in the front trees. Blips of light from fireflies and the peaceful smell of evening evoked childhood memories of early summer nights in New York when I chased similar flashing pinpricks, jailing them in a mayonnaise jar. I asked blissfully: "Can you guys think of anyone back home who has looked at something like what we're looking at?"

Andrew, chin on hand like Rodin's *Thinker*, smiled slowly, "Are you kidding?" he said. "No way!"

"Can't think of anyone," said Peter.

We laughed like old buddies. An observation made by Jeff in Zimbabwe flashed into my mind: "The middle of nowhere to us is the heart of somewhere to someone else."

The next day, it was off to Kalangala, but not before taking a picture of Mary and her family, all washed and dressed for the occasion. Mary wore my panama hat over her crew-cut, and Andrew snapped while I joined the group. Afterwards, Mary's sister showed me how to balance a pail on my head while Mary wrote her address to send copies of the pictures to. She used her husband's name. It reminded me of letters addressed to my mother: Mrs. John Hickey. I added "MARY" to the address, then gave her sister a San Francisco postcard. She smiled broadly and held the card close to her chest while the whole family gathered around as I attempted to explain the location of San Francisco on a small, plastic, blowup globe of the world that I carried for just such an occasion.

Andrew, Peter, and I circumnavigated the world, like Magellan, giving a geography lesson from San Francisco to Lake Victoria. From there we traveled to the North Pole where we got bogged down explaining to the rapt audience the concept of ice. With a limited vocabulary and the lack of anything cold in their environment, explaining ice was like conveying *War and Peace* in charades. Finally, Peter, displaying the patience and talent of a mime, picked up a pail of water and a stone. He poured the water and pointed to the stone. "*Ice* ... like ... water ... to ... stone." A glow of recognition exploded into Mary's eyes and she squealed: "*Ice* ... like snow?"

14

PETER'S DILEMMA OVER WOMEN

AT THE DOCK, NEAR THE tree where Peter sat chewing grass the day before, we met two Peace Corps volunteers on their way to Kalangala. Both American, Sue was about my height with brown hair wrapped under a cap and Don was slightly taller with red hair and lots of freckles. They were fresh from completing a tour of duty in Lesotho, a small, landlocked country in the heart of South Africa. We all plopped on the grass and very soon Andrew was in the midst of a story about a twenty-hour bus trip across Tanzania that stretched into fifty-eight hours.

"Our bloody bus driver picks up this bloke, who tells the driver about a shortcut. The driver decides to follow his directions and turns the bus around. I'm thinking we're going the wrong way, and, sure enough, after two hours of cliffhanger driving, the bloke we picked up thanks the driver and gets off near his home. Bloody hell! It goes from bad to worse. Because of the detour we run out of gas in the middle of nowhere. Then the bus breaks down three times and the driver gets drunk...."

Travelers bond with stories. I told the tale of my trip to Musaka, and Peter wove another yarn about a drunken bus driver that passed out at the wheel. But by far the most thought-provoking anecdote was Sue and Don's ride through Tanzania.

"We hitch a ride in this truck going north," Don said. "About three hours later, the truck driver hits and kills this old woman. The thud shot through me." Sue's body twitched at the word "thud." "Then the guy continues driving. He leaves the scene! We ask him: 'Aren't you going to stop?' He looks at me like I was a lunatic and says: 'If I stop, the people of this village will kill me—and maybe you. What shall I do?'"

"What happened?" I asked, picking at the grass and wondering what I'd do.

Don shrugged helplessly with a touch of guilt. "What do you do?" He said this like he needed to hear a response, but we all treated the question as rhetorical. "And then the truck was too far away from the scene to go back. I still don't know what was right. Africa is such a trip. It's not like a normal world."

"Either that or we are not the normal world," Peter quipped, munching on a fresh piece of grass as we all hopped in the back of the Kalangala-bound pickup—with a full complement of locals and livestock. We bumped along the soft, red road farther into the jungle and emerged after a couple of hours to an unusual sight—a hotel that consisted of a corrugated tin roof (on the left), a hacienda-style concrete verandah (on the right), and a roof (in the middle) elevated above an aqua-green and canary-yellow canopy, which extended over a porch. The building was a bonanza of color. A white and blue sign with an arrow read ANDRONICO's MALANGA LODGE. Another sign indicated CAR PARK, while a third, leaning against a flowerpot, reiterated LODGE. The porch steps were alternately painted white, navy blue, and army green, and the building was baby blue on one side and jade green on the other. White bougainvillea partially shielded a lattice porch railing, and a white picket fence surrounded the front. The *pièce de résistance* was an inscription painted in bloated white letters on the canopy above the stairs:

ANDRONICO'S LODGE: WELCOMES ++ HIS ++ HOLINESS +
** POPE* JOHN** PAUL* II ++ VISITORS ALSO WELCOME

Andronico, a diminutive older gentleman with an entrepreneur's indomitable spirit, greeted us warmly and energetically. He stroked a narrow, gray mustache as he instructed us in flawless English to sign his guest book, and after we settled in, to sign in with the police down the road. Then he escorted us to a maze of connected shacks in back—the guest quarters. Drifting through these catacombs, Andronico assigned rooms while informing us that he was a former teacher in the village, and that his place was in the *Lonely Planet.* "Many important people come to visit Andronico," he asserted.

The rooms echoed the Scorpion Lodge in size and furnishings. Outside a barrel trapped rainwater for our use. And whiffs of rich, fresh fragrance greeted us from three portable toilets on high ground in the rear. These "Chic Sales," as my grandmother used to call them, were painted in Andronico's favorite colors and labeled according to constituency: WOMEN, MEN, and, in huge letters, OFFICIAL USE.

Sleeping arrangements settled, Peter and I lit out in search of the registry. We strolled down a burnt sienna street that ran the length of the village, whose earthen homes housed about two hundred people. At the north end, we found two mud-brick administrative huts with thatched roofs. We knocked, peeked inside, and then entered the first one. Its tarnished sign said "CID." Sitting behind an ancient wooden desk, an official in a white shirt glanced at our passports and cried: "This is not the registry office! To register, go to police building next to CID. Come!" He rose and escorted us to the next hut. On the way, Peter asked what CID meant.

"Criminal Investigations Department," the man replied.

"Ah ha!" Peter and I simultaneously exclaimed. I leaned his way and whispered out of earshot: "With your long hair we're in deep shit."

"No worries, mate. I'll wager this guy will go around the back door and be sitting behind the desk when we arrive." Peter then paused to grab a cigarette stuffed behind his ear and lit up.

At the registry, two other officials greeted us, one in an army-green uniform and black beret and one in civilian garb. Fanning the pages of my passport in full view of a growing crowd of townies that strained their necks looking through the window, the guy in the beret said wistfully: "You have been to many countries. Someday I want to travel to your country." He handed back the passport. "But very difficult for Africans to obtain visa." Then, flashing toothy grins, they both thrust out their hands to shake. Black beret said: "Welcome to Ssese. Maybe you sponsor me for visa to America?"

That night, in an alcove between the main house and the cata-combs, two girls in T-shirts shyly served dinner. Andronico introduced the girls as his daughters, adding that he had thirteen children. Then he took me aside and pulled a Mafiosi-sized wad of bills from his pocket. "How much do you want to exchange? I save dollars to go to the United States to tell people about my hospitality." He changed my fifty-dollar bill at a fair rate.

After the meal, I scooped water from the rain barrel and, for the first time traveling, ran it through my six-ounce filtering pump, mixing a few drops of iodine to kill viruses or bacteria. Fortified with water, I again walked the dirt road through the village. It was very dark, no moon. The huts were candlelit and the hearths burned wood—flickering lights piercing the black of night. Kicking at the dirt and looking up at a crowded sky of sparkling stars, I listened to sounds of laughter break the silence. On that lonesome road, I felt detached, like an alien, while the very human sound of laughter filled the black space around me.

After the walk, I stopped to say hello to Peter. Sucking on a joint, he slouched on his bed and bemoaned a frustrating relation-ship with a woman he met at the Modern Green in Nairobi—the bar Jeff said had been open twenty-four hours a day since 1967. I recalled Jeff's exact words: "It's a place where women hit on guys. Watch your balls if you go there or some woman will grab them!"

Peter's voice was pensive and his Jesus Christ eyes sad. The goatee on his face looked like blades of grass struggling for ma-turity on a newly planted lawn.

"I was there with another traveler, a guy named Trevor," Peter recalled. "That's where I met Janice. You should have seen her! She's black and beautiful." He shook his head, "She wasn't a prostitute, mate. I mean, she never asked for money, just wanted to know me. I'm sure she wasn't a prostitute."

Jeff's voice came to me again. "The Modern Green is a trip, man! ... I don't think most of the babes are prostitutes. Just want a white body to hold because we're different, superior maybe in their view. Or maybe they want a nice place to stay for the night."

Peter used the flickering candle as a torch to take another toke. We probably looked like a couple of hobos in a shack near the tracks. The room smelled musty with a faint odor from the nearby loo. "No, I don't think they were sluts," he said. "At least

Janice wasn't. Anyway, mate, Trevor and I took Janice and this other girl to Lamu. It's on the east coast of Kenya? *Great* place!"

He passed the joint. I sucked it deep and watched the smoke mingle on exhale with the candle flame, feeling a tingle creep through my body.

"Janice and I got along great. We fought once in a while and I reckon she was possessive. I really liked her. But after a few days in Lamu, we got into an ugly fight over some trivial issue. Trevor and I split. The next day, we saw them with two other guys. Just like that! Couldn't believe it. I thought she really liked me and she turned out to be a dirty slut. And she was so pretty. It bothers me a lot." He looked into space. "I don't know why!"

I remembered when I acted like an asshole in the back seat of a car at eighteen. Hadn't guys matured since then?

"Jesus, Peter!" I said, with more than a hint of exasperation. "You meet two women at a bar. Pay to bring them to Lamu. What did you and Trevor have in mind?"

"Well, I reckon Trevor wanted to get laid—and he did. He told me he doubled up on the condoms … you know, because of AIDS. I was nervous about AIDS, too, so I didn't fuck. I just wanted to talk, be friends, you know … to hold her. Yeah, I was bloody lonely, but I didn't want a sordid affair."

"Does doubling up make a difference?"

He stopped his story to consider. "He seemed to think it did."

A moment of silence.

"It sounds like everyone got what they wanted," I summarized, with an edge to my voice. "Why was she 'dirty'? It doesn't sound like the purpose of the trip was a long, intimate relationship."

"Whoa, mate!" he said, leaning back as if repelling an attack.

The room was stuffy, and I was irritated by the status of women in Africa. "I hope this doesn't offend you, but I'm tired of the words 'slut' and 'dirty' in reference to women. To me those words reflect such hypocrisy. We desire what women have, then abuse them for it." Both of us sighed deeply. "I've done the same, so I can empathize with you. Later, I felt like an asshole, too."

Peter ran his fingers through his hair as we focused on the burning candle. Why does hair carry with it an obsessive need to be stroked and preened? Then he stared down at a wad of hair in his hand. "Look at all this! I don't know what's happening. It comes out in bloody chunks!"

"Looks healthy." I shrugged, took a swig of water, and leaned back into the groaning chair.

"I'm really worried, mate. Is it normal to lose this much hair?"

"I don't know. Maybe it's the malaria pills? They're pretty strong."

Sensing Peter was tired of the conversation, I suggested we call it a night. Back in the cell, I crawled into my sleeping bag on the grungy bed, wishing we had finished the discussion. An hour later, there was a rap on the door.

"Denis, are you up?"

"I am now."

"It's Peter! Can we finish our conversation, mate? Would you mind?"

I lit the lamp and opened the door to his bedraggled face. "It's okay. I'm glad you came over."

With eyes aching for understanding, he opened up. "I've really been affected by what you said. Been running it over in my head like a broken record. I'm not saying you're right, but I've been bothered by how I think about women for a while now. You know what I mean, mate? I get my knickers in a knot when I try to decipher women and—"

I laughed. "You Aussies have a vocabulary all your own. But I know what you're saying about deciphering women."

He snickered; inched up on the chair he was straddling, and put his chin on its back. "You seem to have respect for women, mate. And I think of them as 'sheilas.' Deep down there's something wrong with my thinking. I don't know where. I've seen enough in the eight months I've been traveling to know that women have a way ... I don't know, I reckon they're different than us. You know? I know I sound confused right now. I get angry at women because I'm confused." He took a deep penetrating breath. "What's your take?"

"I've been married for twenty-six years and have two girls, so you'd think I'd know a lot about women. The truth is that the best thing I've learned about women is to put the toilet seat down."

"What? Wait!" Peter said laughing. "What's that about toilet seats?"

"Hey! If you've ever experienced the fallout from a woman hitting water at three o'clock in the morning, you'd know exactly what I mean."

"Cheers, mate! That's a handy thing to know."

What *was* my take on women? "I guess I've been lucky in life when it comes to women, starting with my grandmother. She died recently."

"Sorry to hear that."

"Thanks. You treated my grandmother with respect, you know. I remember playing canasta on her kitchen table next to this great iron stove in her three-hundred-year-old house. 'Denny,' she said, 'I've competed with men all my life. It's not that hard.' Then she leaned her face towards me and, with the authority that only my grandmother could muster, added, 'And I expect them to treat me like a lady.' Then she laughed. She had a great sense of fun, my grandmother." My eyes moistened at the thought of her.

"I grew up with women who demanded respect, not verbally, but through their body language. My Aunt Virginia was an artist like you. She earned her master's and married one day shy of forty. Always said she married in her thirties. My Aunt Jody was a head-nurse at twenty-six and built her house from scratch because the bank didn't lend money to the average woman in those days. My mother worked full time as a nurse, too, and had five kids. They passed along to me the idea that women were inherently powerful."

I looked at Peter. He was the sensitive artist trying to understand how he could treat beauty like shit. "In my family you had to respect females or your life was in serious jeopardy. When I had daughters, I wanted them to be like the other women in the family. Society often breaks girls down as we raise them, and they grow up thinking little girls are inferior to little boys. Look at Africa, it's a boy everybody wants."

"So it sounds like what you're saying, mate, is that if I want to understand and appreciate women, I need to respect them first. Right?"

"You got it."

Peter and I talked into the wee hours of the morning before he returned to his room. Long after the roosters belligerently announced a new day, and the ample collection of birds sang sweet melodies, somewhere around brunch-time, I rolled out of bed, scooped a tin of water from the rain barrel and brushed my teeth. What the hell? A little unfiltered local water wasn't going to hurt. During brunch, Andronico mentioned a steamer that picked up passengers every Wednesday at 3 a.m. and delivered them to Entebbe on the mainland. I woke Peter to go with me and check it out.

We followed a dirt path heading to the lake past a makeshift soccer field till we came to the crest of a long, meandering hillside that merged with low, dense clouds in the distance. A couple of miles off was the sparkling lake and a black dot we took to be the dock. As we got closer, we could see that stretching along lakeside in a thin band, nestled beside reeds, was a primal village of densely packed, rectangular, mud-brick lodges with thatched roofs.

Stepping out of high grass into the village, I inhaled dust and the scent of maize over an open fire. We heard the tinkering sounds of women inside one of the houses and we couldn't help peeking in. Two ladies sat on the dirt floor talking and eating, as a fire spit flames and smoke into the hut's dimness. I felt uncomfortable invading someone's living room, but the people didn't seem to mind.

An old guy, probably my age, with four front teeth missing and sinewy arms, called "*Jambo*" as we passed his hut. Others motioned us to step into their homes. We smiled, looked inside. Once I bowed, getting a hearty chuckle. It didn't take much to get a laugh.

As we emerged from the far side of the village, towards the dock, a bare-breasted, giggling young woman ran from behind one of the huts. She almost bowled us over. She stared at us like she'd seen a ghost and covered her bosom with her hands. Then she fled back in the direction she came. "Nice set of tits," Peter snorted. "Funny how Western media shows African tits on prime time, but not white, eh?"

"They look just as provocative to me!"

Not far from the dock, we stopped to check out an army of ants flooding from the heavy grass on to the baldness of the path. They looked like refugees from an indescribable horror. The black mass rampaged across the path into equally heavy grass on the other side. Peter and I stooped over to watch, mesmerized. "Look at their organizational structure," I said. "Ants are fascinating. Look at those suckers! They never stop. From birth until death, you will never catch an ant sitting under the branch of a tree reading philosophy. They probably think God has ordained hard work as the key to heaven."

Peter shrugged. Then pointed to mammoth soldier ants with ferocious pinchers standing amid the traffic like policemen on horses. At one-inch intervals, these brutes, in a business-as-usual way, herded the swarming traffic.

"We're like ants now, only slower," Peter offered, "waiting in traffic jams and listening to Big Brother TV." Then he laid a three-inch stick with a leaf at the end across the highway, disrupting the flow. The swarm panicked. Immediately, a soldier launched through the crush of bodies to clear the impediment. "Look at the bugger!" Peter said lifting the stick. The brute clung like a pit bull, clutching the stick in its vice-like mandibles. It refused to let go, even as Peter swung the stick in the air.

Four children came over to watch. One skinny little boy, no more than six, carried his naked baby brother piggyback. They got down on their haunches to watch the ants. After a while older boys joined the party. In Ssese, your business is everyone's business.

Peter and I continued our trek to the dock—Pied Pipers leading a pack of Ugandans. Two little girls joined us. I stopped to make faces and tickle a couple of the munchkins while Peter continued with others to the water, where they played pirates inside one of the long fishing boats dragged halfway up on shore. One of the girls in a shabby, blue dress with white lace on the hem ran her fingers through my hair to feel its texture, while I watched the little boy responsibly carry the baby. His mother trusted him to take care of the child at lakeside. Maybe the only difference between children and adults is the level of experience, not the ability to think responsibly. I guess that's why I enjoy children so much. They're on my level of comprehension.

The length of a basketball court, the dock was made of stones planted in a bed of clay. We learned from talking to a dock official that the ship would arrive at 8 p.m. and leave at 4 a.m. the next morning.

At nine-thirty that night, Peter and I convened with the four other Westerners at Andronico's: Don and Sue of the Peace Corps, Andrew, and a young crew-cut Englishman who arrived the day before. We hoisted our gear and trekked back to the dock to assure passage. Sue and I paired up under a dark, moonless sky, inching our way down ravines and maneuvering around obstacles in the meadow. She told me she came to Africa from California because she didn't know what she wanted to do, and didn't want to live like her parents.

"Why?"

"Their life is hectic. All they do is work and get worked-up. I want more balance in my life. I thought I could stall the decision about a career by teaching in Lesotho, and at the same time help people out and learn about life. I found that I want to spend time with my kids like African mothers."

"Time and kids seem to come at a price for women here."

"That's true. But African women, even though they do most of the work, don't seem to be any less happy than women in California. Maybe careers are not what they're cracked up to be."

"My grandmother had family first, then a career."

We walked for a while in silence before she asked, "How about you, why are you traveling?"

I shone the flashlight on a small boulder for Sue to avoid, and wondered what my answer would be this time. Sue had a pretty face and, while she dressed to suit the country, which is to say her clothes were not flattering, I suspected she would have a comely figure under other circumstances.

"I guess I lived like your parents," I said, "and needed to kick up my heels." The answer was simple and short, and felt like a dangling participle. "Where are you going after Ssese?"

"Across Uganda to see the gorillas in Rwanda."

"With Don?"

"No, he's off to Nairobi. I'm going by myself. Want to come?"

"Love to, but I can't. I'm going to Nairobi to meet a friend."

Alone across Uganda, I thought, gutsy lady.

If walking through the lakeside village in daylight was a trip, walking through at night was surreal. Huts aglow, smoke, dust, and firelight, dark faces in dark spaces. The village's residents waved goodbye. I recognized the man I met earlier in the day crouched at the opening to his hut. "*Jambo!*" he called out. "Where you going?"

"To ship," I said, looking back at him in the glow of the firelight.

"When you back?"

I turned around to face him and etch this scene into my mind. I took in the bare flesh, thick lips, flat nose, and deep lines scribbled on his face.

"Sometime. Maybe ten years!"

The steamer was a two-deck, rusty bucket not unlike the one used to transport King Kong in the original 1930s movie. Maybe it was the same ship. Locals boarded carrying chickens, goats, bananas, and sheaths of vegetation. They joined an assortment of people already on board from other islands. Those who could not afford the two-dollar fare for the top deck stayed below. We sat above at the stern and played Minefield, the dice game I had learned on the houseboat in Zimbabwe. As we played we discussed Milan Kundera's *The Book of Laughter and Forgetting*. "Love is an interrogation," Kundera said. Sue suggested that love was more of an exploration.

With passengers stretched on benches and floor, we hooked up our mosquito nets and prepared to sleep as the ferry pulled out. I lay uncomfortably across a bench, feeling the rough churning of engines and listening to snoring all around. It might take the rest of the trip to figure exactly why I left home, I realized restlessly.

Kathi had endorsed this venture, but I saw the fear inside her. We talked and didn't talk when I called home in Nairobi. Our voices had a formality to them. I reflected on what Sue said about love. It had been a long time since anyone explored *my* life. My grandmother used to quote, "Truth is beauty, beauty truth." What is the *un-talked about?* There is so much of it.

Sunrise woke me somewhere among the Ssese Islands, which stretched away across the lake like a string of onyx beads. The steamer had chewed up three hours of the twelve-hour voyage to Entebbe. Raising my head off the air-pillow, I wiped sleep from my eyes and stared round at the snoozing and occasionally farting bodies. An orange sheen began to fill the sky and the swirling clouds. Thicker clouds rose on the horizon like snow-capped peaks in a desert. Geese flew across the bow. Predictably, a rooster crowed on board.

When the boat docked in Entebbe, Sue adjusted the straps of her backpack, said her goodbyes, and strode off to find a *matatu* heading west. The rest of us packed into a van bound for Malaba to catch the overnight train south to Nairobi. Watching Sue's purposeful walk to begin the next leg of her journey, I wondered what she would be like in bed. And if her adventures would lead to her vision of a future family.

15

MISSING, AND MAKING, THE TRAIN

A MATATU DRIVER WITH GRAY HAIR means safety, because gray hair connotes survival. The dude driving to Malaba had yet to acquire a single gray hair. We had three hours to make the Nairobi train. The guy accelerated like a maniac and my patience ran thin. Surprisingly, an annoyed local complained in English about the speed. "I agree!" I added forcefully. "Please slow down!"

From behind, Andrew leaned forward and whispered: "Good on you, mate!" The crew-cut Englishman winced. The driver immediately slowed to forty kilometers per hour, hung his head on the sill of the window, and yawned.

A heated native-tongue discussion ensued as a round-faced grandmother, speaking with the absolute authority of a preacher, defended the driver. She turned and frowned at the *mzungu* (the foreigner, namely me) with fire in her eyes. We missed the train by over an hour.

At the Kenya border crossing, the customs guard said we could catch a bus to Nairobi in town, which turned out to be four blocks straight ahead. The guard called me "Grandpa." Grandpa! He had recently married and I asked him how many kids he intended to have. He said two because of the expense of raising them. Then he changed his mind. "Because of AIDS, I will have four."

On the Kenyan side, we sidestepped the hordes of juvenile moneychangers and asked a local, slowly and loudly, "CAN ... YOU ... TELL ... US ... WHERE ... THE ... BUS ... TO ... NAIROBI ... IS?"

Pointing to our left, he answered in perfect English, "Why don't you take the train?" The Nairobi train, which left Uganda over an hour ago in, stood patiently waiting in Kenya—having traveled the grand total of four blocks. And it wouldn't leave for another hour.

Settled on the train, we each ordered two bottles of beer. Andrew raised his bottle to me, snickering to the others. "Cheers, mate," he said. "Here's hoping you don't give any more instructions to drivers!"

KENYA

FAMILY

16

ALONE ON ANIMAL ISLAND
TALKING FAMILY WITH A
GRIZZLED GIANT ELAND

THE ELEGANT, COLONIAL-ERA LAKE NAIVASHA Country
Club was down the road from the estate of Joy and George
Adamson. In the Fifties, the conservationist couple trained
an orphaned lion cub, Elsa, to return to the wild. The story became the best-selling book (and then movie) *Born Free*. Both
were later murdered—George protecting tourists from poachers.

Towards the lake, at the rear of the hotel, expansive, soft-to-
the-feet lawns were liberally sprinkled with pearl-white tables
and chairs. Vibrant flowerbeds and handsome yellow acacias
added extra charm. The lush lawns stretched to a forest and a
path through the woods leading to a lakeside dock. Nearly two
thousand varieties of birds lived in the lake's surrounding habitat
and were delightful and exciting to the eyes and ears. At the path,
an unambiguously worded sign grabbed my attention:

GUESTS ARE REQUESTED NOT TO PROCEED BEYOND THIS POINT
BETWEEN 7 P.M. AND 6 A.M. MANAGEMENT WILL NOT TAKE
RESPONSIBILITY FOR LOSS OF PROPERTY OR INJURIES
IN THE EVENT OF AN ATTACK BY WILD ANIMALS.

Looking and feeling like Indiana Jones, with a two-day
growth of stubble and a stench that could deck an elephant, I
dropped my pack on the lobby floor and signed the hotel register.

After a week in Ssese, the Club was a welcome treat. There was room service to wash raunchy clothes, a porcelain toilet rather than a hole, hot water to shave, shower, and get the kinks out, a snow-white mosquito net draped over spotless, cream-colored bed sheets, soft pillows.... Oh Lordy!

That night, in the main dining room, I downed two glasses of burgundy and enjoyed a medium-rare steak. The wine didn't need to be French, and a *marchands de vin* sauce sure didn't need to chaperone the steak, but that's what I got.

Was it only six days since I left Nairobi? Railroads, outlandish *matatus*, primitive jungles, no electricity or plumbing, sleeping under the stars on a steamship, intimate discussions—I had to pinch myself to be sure this was not a dream. Six days seemed like a month, people came and went, and tomorrow another experience.

A lifetime ago, I was a workaholic, uninspired by business, dead to nature. Now I could rely on myself in the physical world and the stress of formality was inscribed on faces of the other guests, not mine. And I *saw* people, they were no longer invisible.

After dinner, I dived on to the glorious bed and snuggled under fresh sheets. Getting into bed can be one of the most glorious events, especially when the sheets are silk and the weather hot. At three in the morning, Robert, a hotel attendant, knocked quietly on my door asking if I wanted to see the hippos coming up from the lake in search of grass. These huge critters are just oversize cows and the hotel's lawn was an enticing meal. But their kill record gave me chills—they are responsible for more human deaths than any other animal. I was scared, but really, was this heaven or what?

The hippos came and munched. They looked harmless and, although close, did not make any threatening moves. Before retiring, Robert told me about the game reserve across the lake, on an otherwise deserted island. I could take a boat there and walk the island by myself since the island had no predators. Maybe all I had done since my arrival in Africa and the benign behavior of the hippos gave me an inflated sense of my luck, I don't know, but I told Robert I wanted to go.

Early next morning, I wandered towards the dock. Birds chirped and a small herd of waterbuck grazed just beyond the forest line. Robert took me on the ten-minute boat ride across the lake to the island. Powered by a ten-horsepower motor, the long, narrow boat skirted flocks of pink flamingos and ibis, whose downward curved beaks looked like bananas. We were followed carefully by masses of piggy eyes sitting above wide tunnels of bright-red, mouthy flesh resting comfortably on the water's surface—hippos. There were crocodiles, too. Didn't the latter qualify as predators?

Arriving at a shaky dock surrounded by heavy reeds, Robert said: "I will fetch you at this dock in three hours, Mr. Hickey."

"Call me Denis. Are you *sure* there are no predators on this island, Robert?"

"No predators," he said. He flashed his tobacco-stained teeth and held the boat by the dock for me. "I will come back to fetch you in three hours."

Wide-stepping on to the dock, daypack and camera strapped to my back, I followed a barely recognizable path three hundred yards through reeds, then scrub, eventually reaching a clearing and a shocking sight. Expecting the green compactness of a small island, I surveyed miles of flat, sun-dried savanna painted pumpkin by the early sun. Herds of animals roamed—many just specks on the horizon. No sign of human life—no fences, no telephone wires, no coke bottles.

And no predators? What about the big animals? How dangerous are they? Ostriches, for instance, could be very dangerous. I read somewhere that if you have a branch from a thorn bush, they will stay away because they know what it's like to be pricked by one. I looked around. No thorn bushes in sight. And what if I got hurt, how long would it take for Robert to find me?

Before venturing into the open from the scrub, I noted a clump of acacias as a landmark—a habit picked up exploring woods as a kid. The rush of adventure grabbed hold. Fear mixed with curiosity and the thrill of risk heightened my senses. Waterbuck, impala, and zebra grazed in the open plains and under spreading branches. In the distance, long necks of giraffes looked like moving trees. And far beyond them, the water. I could see forever on this island.

I walked along a shallow gully so that I could see the animals as they looked down at me. I was nervously conscious that each

113

deliberate step took me further away from the dock, further into their world. Occasionally, a grazing zebra bolted, just for exercise. A herd of buckskin-colored hartebeest passed. An impala leaped and twisted in the air, white speckles flashing in the now glistening sun. They all kept their distance from *their* predator. They stared at me. Could they sense the nervousness in my belly? I climbed to the top of the gully, keeping close enough to the tall trees so I could shimmy up in case one of these "non-predators" got it into its head to trample me like a bug.

A herd of warthogs noticed me. I turned towards the adorable, pickle-brained miniature rhinos with tails like antennas. Suddenly one gave me a look that drove me back into the gully for protection. Perhaps they were not so adorable after all.

A herd of forty or so elands came into view. They were most impressive animals—the largest of the antelopes, as big as horses, with magnificent, spiraling horns. The dry air had a thick taste of African sage. Twigs cracked under my hiking boots. The sound attracted the attention of a huge buck with ugly, black scars on his face, and antlers big enough to give anyone a bad feeling. Forty yards away, he raised his great black nose, sniffed the air, and pounded the dirt with massive hoofs.

I got the message loud and clear. Slowly I looked around for the nearest tree, then, I turned back to face him. We looked deeply into each other's eyes. I felt him sizing me up. Intimidated and humble, I tried to mentally convey to him that there was no threat. Would his instinct agree? Would he be gracious? A few zebras waltzed over and gazed down at me. Only one human on this land—and he was defenseless.

The eland females and young were unfazed. They had his protection. Very deliberately I retreated. I backed away until I could no longer feel his power. He watched me till I was a hundred yards off and then went about his business.

With every hurried step back to the dock, I thought of that monstrous eland and the connection we had made. I empathized with the loneliness inherent in his responsibility. Only the savviest got the job. And when a younger, stronger buck eventually overcame him, he'd be out forever.

Robert was waiting at the dock. What a relief! Before long, I was sipping tea English style—with milk and sugar—on the elegant lawn, and musing about what I had just experienced. I couldn't help also observing how tanned my legs had become after I'd tossed aside the toxic sun lotion in favor of gradually browning in the sun.

A fly buzzed around in the soft, warm breeze. Time passed slowly.

Watching the eland buck protect its herd got me thinking about Old World patriarchy and the Kennedy model of great family that I aspired to as a young man. I had wanted to be somebody, own land, have a powerful family, and have fun with them. Maybe this desire came from my grandmother's stories and keen sense of heritage. I foresaw a family of strong individuals with economic clout, and myself as patriarch. I took out a pad and pen from my daypack and put down some thoughts.

INGREDIENTS FOR FAMILY GREATNESS—OLD STYLE:

- Sex is private and primarily for procreating, producing lots of kids.
- Grandparents, cousins, aunts, and uncles all tied together by economics and tradition (storytelling, singing together, celebrations, respect for age, marriage forever).
- Males protect the family, resolve disputes, and set family philosophy.
- Females raise children, organize the family, nurture, and execute the family philosophy. If the man was the head, they were the neck turning the head.
- The needs of individuals are subservient to those of the family.
- Inheritance by the eldest male child.
- Power!

Ten years ago, my family developed this family charter:

BUILD A FAMILY OF INTEGRATED INDIVIDUALS
WHO UTILIZE DEFINED PRINCIPLES
TO POSITIVELY INFLUENCE OTHERS AND LIVE HAPPILY
AS INDIVIDUALS WITHIN A FAMILY UNIT.

I compared the "Old Style" list with our charter. What a difference! In grade school, the nuns taught sex existed primarily for procreation. If you happened to enjoy it, well, that was a side benefit. I never quite bought that point of view. When I thought of sex, I got consumed with the side benefits. Sex as recreation. Early on, I wanted lots of kids. Later, I subscribed to the *replacement* concept—two kids, a stable population, less environmental pressure. But two kids sure limits the influence a family can achieve. And my whole sense of male and female changed when I had girls. I tried to focus on them having healthy self-esteems like their grandmother, so they could compete on an equal footing with men.

My grandmother kept family history alive. Who was going to be the reservoir of family knowledge when I died? There was nothing about history in our charter. Even though I grew up in a matriarchal family, I knew I was destined to be the male inheritor of family power. But the females in my nuclear family expressed only passing interest in the philosophy of family power, so it never became a major factor in our lives. Although the concept of family first and marriage forever was present in my youth, the focus now was on individual achievement—and the two did not fit together. *Individual* by definition was a selfish concept.

Where I came from the individual was now the focus and, as in business, success comes from where you focus your time. Munching on a butter cookie that came with tea, it became clear as a cloudless day that my old dreams of "great family" had been altered by the number of children I'd had and contemporary emphasis on the individual.

My family had given me an advantage over many ambitious men, because when I went home at night I could release work pressure by playing with my kids. Young people brought out the little boy in me. Now, almost suddenly, everyone in my family was going their own way. I felt like the only one attached to family greatness.

It was a lonely feeling to lose this sense of oneness with the three loves of my life—my wife and daughters. And once this oneness was gone, what was left of my destiny? Me trying to cope with the speed of society and wondering how much was enough to buy my way out of it.

I relaxed, listened to the sounds of the birds, and wondered if the Kennedy model was dead. Was world unrest the result of the enormous philosophical gap between poor countries with strong family values and rich countries that put the individual first? When I watched news on TV, the fighting was always in poor countries. I raised the family of my dreams, but what was a "great family" in today's Western context?

17

ALICE, WAIT! WE JUST MET

FROM LAKE NAIVASHA, I HITCHED a ride from a guest to the Nairobi airport, where I would catch a taxi to the city. The next day, I was to meet a family friend, Carmen, at the Norfolk, a four-star hotel near the University of Nairobi. Figuring I could move into the Norfolk the next day, I looked in the *Lonely Planet* for a hostel downtown for the night. Just before the listing of hostels, I noticed a warning about taxi scams at the airport. So I was suspicious when a driver showed me to his beat-up, smoky-blue station wagon. There was no picture on the license inside, only blurred print reading "Taxi" along with a name and number that I memorized.

"The New Kenya Lodge, please."

"That is not a good place," the driver said. "I know a better one close by."

"Then how about showing me both?" I said, suspicious. I tossed my pack in the back seat of the cab and climbed in front. We drove through barren countryside for about twenty-five minutes, then into a seedy maze of streets known as the River Road section of Nairobi. Thousands of Africans lived and worked in this dingy, littered enclave of low-end commerce and housing that faintly smelled of mildew.

The driver stopped at his choice of hostel, which, after a cursory inspection, I rejected. It was the kind of low-budget experience for which I wasn't quite prepared. A couple of policemen sauntered over to the driver's side and began chatting with him in Swahili. They were dressed in army camouflage, armed with automatic weapons, and had very penetrating eyes. They made me uneasy.

I nonchalantly squeezed my head around the driver, searching for official badges. They leaned on the taxi, hands against the roof and guns dangling menacingly from straps across their shoulders. During the chitchat, one of the soldiers eyed me. A long scar ran from the outside edge of his left eye to the jawline. Then, without a word of explanation, the two stuffed themselves in back of the cab and laid their machine guns across my backpack. The two men didn't smile or talk—just eyeballed me with serious, official looks.

Now I vividly recalled another travel guide warning about scams pulled off by thugs dressed as policemen who find fictitious passport violations.

Terrific! I hadn't been in town more than half an hour and I'd already been caught in two classic scams. Apparently, the "cops" were going to accompany me on the drive to the New Kenya Lodge. We drove in uneasy silence. What an experience! Whether or not I liked the New Kenya Lodge, I was getting the hell out of this cab.

"Hey, this place looks pretty good!" I said, as soon as I caught sight of the broken-down hostel. "You can let me off right here."

I got out, quickly opened the back door, and eased my pack from under the machine guns, all the while waiting for the proverbial other shoe to drop. The guys in green grudgingly lifted their weapons, staring at me with menacing expressions. Grimacing inside, I waited for the order to produce a passport. Maybe it wasn't a good idea to wear a pink body shirt. I hoisted the backpack on to my shoulders and gave them a nice smile. Sweat dripped under my armpits.

The passport order never came. The guy with the scar locked eyes with me and grinned—the type of grin that was too short to convey any friendliness.

The New Kenya Lodge was a three-story, wooden structure with steel-braced doors and barred windows. Three young travelers sat on an old couch in a tattered recreation room, talking and laughing in animated discussion. I relaxed. The friendly receptionist smiled warmly. "Welcome to the New Kenya Lodge," he said. "Put your backpack down and take a load off."

Unfortunately, the next thing he said was that the hostel was fully booked, and I had to go around the corner to the extension.

If the New Kenya Lodge was broken down, this was the pits. Inside, I followed two barefoot, mucus-nosed kids who were trailing their bony refugee parents from Somalia. The family led me to the manager, who showed me to a single room with thin walls and a door that could barely stand up against a cough from one of the kids. Staring at a naked bed and soiled mattress, I imagined an infestation of tiny, black bugs with crimson eyes licking their chops. Although tired, and despite my experiences in Uganda and the desire to understand a small slice of what it's like to be a refugee, I promptly hoisted my pack, said goodbye, and grabbed a taxi straight for the Norfolk.

The Norfolk greeted me with a swank, royal blue carpet in the lobby. Followed by a splendid room—twin beds and a hot bubble bath, in which I sipped decadently on a glass of port while taking care to avoid splashing bubbles on my book. *To Become a Man,* written by Masai author Henry ole Kulet, told of a young boy's struggle in the Fifties to break tradition and enter the modern world as a doctor. The Masai did not take kindly to mingling outside their culture.

That evening, I broke my new tradition of taking public transportation and flagged a cab to Buffalo Bill's—an upscale version of the Modern Green, the all-night bar Jeff had enthused about and where Peter met Janice. Temptation had been on my mind.

On the bottom floor of a three-star hotel, Buffalo Bill's ignited my voyeuristic curiosity for a forbidden world—one created by myth and a stereotyped sense of novelty. After scarfing down a chicken dinner under the awning of Buffalo Bill's outdoor restaurant, I shyly peeked into the adjoining lounge. An oval, mahogany bar captured nearly two-thirds of the available floor space. Intimate booths surrounded the bar. Pictures of America's Wild West hung from the walls. In between the bar and the booths, there was just enough room to stand for a drink.

The difference between this bar and any of a number of similar drinking fountains anywhere in the world was that it was filled with beautiful, dressed-to-kill, black African women. White chiffon and sleek, black cocktail dresses tightly hugged their dark bodies.

I sauntered in and sat at the bar, intending to drink a quick beer and check the place out. In other words, the normal misguided attempt at fulfilling curiosity without actually partaking. An uncomfortable feeling took hold each time I looked up from the bottle I nursed. Everywhere there were eyes intent on inviting my attention. Ogling eyes, suggestive eyes, soft ones, defiant ones, wild eyes, submissive eyes, mischievous eyes—they all beckoned. Even women sitting in booths *with* men were not safe to gaze on. So this was what it was like to be a woman in a bar dealing with men's eyes.

Several women sashayed next to me. "What is your name? Where are you from? What do you do?" they asked, sliding their hips unambiguously along my side. "Buy me a beer?"

I enjoyed the flirting. Except I felt deprived of choice. I was being sequestered by the most aggressive women I had ever met. It hadn't occurred to me before that a preferred choice of partner might be shy and slow off the mark. How many women married guys who didn't suit them just because those men were the first to ask? How many stayed with aggressive suitors because they didn't know how to say no? I bought another beer.

Then Alice introduced herself. Though it's a cliché, she could have been a work of art. A classical sculpture made flesh. Beneath her braided hair, her wide eyes shone like silver and her full lips curved wide.

We exchanged banal comments. Alice came across as petulant, with a "I'm not that kind of girl" attitude. However, through the course of the evening, I learned that she turned emotions on and off like a faucet, and had a haughty attractiveness that demanded attention.

Before I knew it, Alice and I sat snugly in a cab heading back to the Norfolk. The power of nature at work. She said she was a secretary and gave me her card. I really didn't have a clue how I would handle Alice at the hotel. It had been two months since I had touched a woman. My blood was fired up, to be sure—and there is no fire like lust. But "Be careful of AIDS," kept coming to mind. And Peter's comment in Ssese made more sense: "I just wanted to hold her." A serious debate raged between my conscience and reckless lower body.

The cab ride through deserted, dimly lit streets seemed to go on forever. She nudged close in the cab, sending a shiver through me. In a resonant voice, she asked, "Denis, what you do?"

"I am a traveler."

She leaned close. Her lightly applied perfume filled my nostrils. "Where do you travel?"

"Around the world."

She stopped fiddling with her bracelet, and, wide-eyed, repeated, "Around the *whole* world?"

"Yes. By the way, Alice, that's a lovely dress you have on."

"It is my most good dress." She beamed and played with the frill lace on the fringe of her brown bodice. Her ample breasts rose and fell. "I wear it when I go to club."

"Why do you go to the club?"

"To meet interesting people—like you."

I paid the driver, then walked around to Alice's door and opened it. Slinking through the posh lobby of the Norfolk, I felt all eyes were on me. But Alice flowed by the receptionist obliviously. After shutting the door of my room, she flashed her big, brown eyes and began to relieve me of all responsibility for determining my fate.

"What now, Denis?" she asked, standing two inches away and moving me towards the bed by the window with her glance. Her full lips gleamed with the coral lipstick she'd applied in the cab.

"I'm taking this step by step, Alice."

"Denis, how long you stay in Nairobi?"

"I don't know. I'm meeting someone tomorrow who will be traveling with me."

"Man or woman?" she demanded.

"Woman."

"Woman!" she exploded jealously. "You meet *woman*! Who she is?"

"Alice! We just met."

"I want to know!" She pouted and tapped her foot on the floor. "Why you with other woman?"

"She's a friend." I laughed sheepishly. Any response was irrelevant.

She pushed me on to the firm bed, and then pinned me down with her legs and heaving chest. Alice had stopped talking and was letting her hands do the walking. She ripped two buttons off my only button-down shirt, and went for my chest hair. She was a tigress playing with her prey. God, this was fun!

"Now, easy, Alice. Wait! Let's just sit up for a while." I chortled at the role reversal.

"WHAT?"

"You have to take it easy on me, Alice." I couldn't believe I was saying this. I could say that through a superhuman effort I resisted her onslaught, but more accurately my sexual drought meant that nature took its course prematurely. I thus settled for delightful touching and playful chitchat.

Soon Alice fell asleep. I covered her with the top sheet, and then slept in the matching twin bed. I thought hard about what I was missing. At around five o'clock, she crawled into my bed with her panties on, and I held her in a spooning position. Barely awake, she turned and whispered, "Denis, you should have taken my dress off and folded. It is my good dress."

Cradling her, I again recalled Peter's words. "I just wanted to hold her." I guess Alice needed someone to hold, too. I felt grateful.

At eight, she slipped out of bed, showered, and put on makeup for work. When she came back into the room I was propped on an elbow in bed. With a towel wrapped around her goddess body and a sweet expression on her face, she said: "Thank you, Denis. I have one of best times. You good man to be with."

I was thinking hard about unraveling that towel, but what a nice thing to say.

18

Old Friends
Reminiscing in Nairobi

CARMEN WAS COMING FROM CALIFORNIA to be maid of honor at the wedding of a Nairobi University classmate. She had spent her junior year here in Africa in order, she said, to broaden her horizons and feel what it was like to be a minority. Now she was twenty-six-years-old. I wondered where the time went.

Since high school, Carmen had been a regular at the girls' many parties at our house. Parties at which I enjoyed parenting, since my kids were the only real hobby during my climb up the corporate ladder. Work and family, that was pretty much it. Kids kept the little boy in me alive and separate from the hard-nosed businessman, although Kathi always tried to get me to integrate the two.

When Carmen graduated from college and moved to San Francisco, we got together for lunch or a drink every few months or so. I guess it made her feel mature to have an older friend. Of course, I was aware of the married man-younger woman assumption on people's minds, especially with Carmen's long, glistening, brown hair and good looks. None of the married men I knew had a friendship with a woman other than their spouse, much less someone younger. But it had been my intention from the beginning to eventually convert my own kids to friends—a notion I inherited from my grandmother, who accurately assessed that she would outlive her peers. Carmen was happy to meet me in Nairobi and travel together, and that was good enough for me.

I wouldn't have dreamed of telling Carmen about Alice. Somehow I didn't think she'd understand. I would be another father falling off the pedestal with a resounding smash. Funny, I'd have told a traveler. Travelers will give a person the time to talk without judging. I didn't feel guilty about Alice. It didn't mean I loved my wife or family any less. Rather, apart from the risk of acquiring some disease, it did not have anything to do with them. How did other men feel? It would be hard to tell because we were such liars when it came to sex and family. Or we'd clam up. Wouldn't it be the ultimate intimacy if, instead of getting slammed, we could have real dialogue about our sexual activities?

Just as I was beginning to dissect this question, Carmen, backpack strapped to her shoulders, ran over screaming: "Denis!" She rushed into my open arms, and we hugged as if we hadn't seen each other for years.

"Let me drop my pack somewhere and chill out for a while," she said. "Do you have an extra bed in your room? I'll be staying with my friend Ruth the rest of the week, but tonight I thought we could catch up. And if you want, I could take you on a tour of the university. Did you know it was right across the street? I know I'm babbling but I'm *so* excited to be back in Africa, and so happy to see you."

Carmen had that Californian youthful zest in her voice. She was excited and moving fast. I was excited and moving slow, glad to see someone from home after two months on the road. Her plan was to spend her first week in Nairobi assisting Ruth, the bride, with the wedding. After the ceremony, which I was invited to, we would both travel to the Kenyan coast.

We got something to eat, bought a few bottles of beer, and retired to my room. Carmen brought letters from the girls, one from my former business partner, which tied up details of our former partnership, and four letters and a care package from Kathi, including homemade chocolate chip cookies. Devouring the cookies, Carmen and I talked well into the night. About her job caring for adults with disabilities, her boyfriend, their plans, her memories growing up.

"Remember the time you were walking across the El Paseo parking lot going to the movies and a bunch of us were coming in the opposite direction? You said: 'Where are you guys going?'

And we said: 'To your house.' 'There's no one there!' you said. And Mike shot back: 'That's okay, we know where the key is.'"

"Yeah, you guys sure made yourselves at home."

She leaned over and tugged my growing curls: "What a little hippie you are!"

She continued reminiscing. "And Kathi used to place that box of animal water pistols on the ledge by the front door for water fights. And then the guys started to bring bigger water guns, but you always had the biggest."

"Kathi let me stay at the leading edge of firepower. She didn't like chaos, but supported my need for it. I remember when Jerry Fasig cornered me in the kitchen with a water pistol while I was pouring a glass of water. Not smart! The guys were easy pickings until they figured out they could physically abuse a dad."

Carmen chuckled. "I can't imagine myself as a parent. I still find it strange to see myself as a woman. But I've been thinking about having a family lately.

"How did you ever survive our high school drinking years? Shannon and Chimene are such party animals."

"The golden rule—whoever drives doesn't drink. I think you guys lived up to that rule pretty well. Also, I tried to keep in mind how I was as a kid." I laughed recalling Chimene's high school, on-off boyfriend. "I remember D'Atilio opening the front door after midnight as we were entertaining friends. Chimene was clutching his shoulder, her face blue.

"'Don't blame me for this!' D'Atilio said defensively, as Chimene staggered to the bathroom. 'It was her idea to get drunk! I'm leaving.' When Chimene closed the bathroom door, our friends asked if we were going to punish her. Kathi said the porcelain she was hugging would probably do the job for us."

Carmen and I giggled together.

"It was cool being at your house," she said. "We could be ourselves. But you had clear guidelines. Remember when Durf broke your basketball net on the garage?"

"Yeah."

"You let it be known that whoever broke it better fix it."

"No one fucks with my basketball equipment! They must have gotten up at three o'clock in the morning to replace the rim."

"Let's talk more about the philosophy of raising kids when we travel, okay?"

126

Carmen had to spend the bulk of her time helping with wedding plans, but we agreed to meet twice a day. That gave me an opportunity to kick around Nairobi. Downtown Nairobi was small, but the skyline could be confused with Phoenix. It even had a movie theater with reserved seats. Unlike Zimbabwe, Kenyan blacks walked confidently. Was their posture the result of a longer period of independence or due to their different tribal culture? The women wore braided hair. Rust colored teeth were the rule. And street hawkers sold everything from shoeshines to budget safaris. On street corners, women with clinging babies and a small army of barefoot young boys in tattered shorts, Somalian refugees, begged the tourists for handouts.

Ah, the realities of poverty. I remember my early twenties living in New York City. How quickly I became acclimatized to stepping over the sodden bodies of drunks, not really seeing their faces, their personalities, or their humanity. They were simply lumps of flesh on the ground, to be ignored in the hurry of life. On this journey, I decided to shitcan those values and look into the faces of beggars. Part with some money.

I quickly discovered, though, that there had to be a method. For instance, a street urchin, with a lifeless face, pencil-thin body, and swollen stomach, dogged me for blocks like a persistent puppy chasing after its mother. Only there wasn't anything cute about it. I gave him money. He wanted more. "No!" didn't work. Neither did walking faster. He chased me pointing to his pathetic tummy, his hand clinging to my shirt. I tried using people on the street as picks to lose him. I tried reasoning. "Look, I gave you money. Go after that guy. Go!" I tried anger—and it wasn't an act. Murder in my heart, I looked down at him and in a hard voice thundered: "OKAY, LET'S GO TO THE POLICE!"

The threat worked. Like a tick burned by a match he was off. However, my "gentle human" persona had shattered. I walked like a machine with a stony look that told beggars: "Don't bother me." Guilt set in. I had to resolve how I would deal with beggars so that I could return to a mellow equilibrium. I made a decision to give money or food to women with babies and beggars with a sense of humor who showed signs of life rather than death. The others I would be polite to, occasionally ignore, and outpace.

19

Dinner with the Masai:
Politics, Population Growth,
Circumcision, Multiple Wives,
Lost Virginity

ONE EVENING, CARMEN ARRANGED FOR me to dine with a college friend and a Masai—a tribe that had always excited my imagination. Ole Kina had just passed the Kenyan bar exam, no small feat for the son of a cow herder. Earlier in the day, Carmen attended the ceremony in a courtroom. She was honored by the invitation, but amused by the white wigs black lawyers wore in Kenyan courts, remnants of British colonialism. However, the sight of Africans sauntering down Nairobi streets in Western business suits challenged my National Geographic-inspired ideas of the continent just as much as the wigs.

Her hair wrapped in a bun exposing silver filigree earrings, Carmen led me towards my dining rendezvous—an outdoor meat stand next to a bar on River Road.

We walked along concrete sidewalks worn thin in the middle. It was hot and muggy. I was breaking-in a blue shirt that Carmen picked out for the wedding. It was a world apart from the tailored oxfords I wore in boardrooms. Meant to be worn outside the pants, it had swirling, white lace embroidering its hem and neck. Orange flowers exploded over its surface, connected by blood-red vines and yellow dots.

"This is your chance to pump him about Africa," Carmen teased as we arrived.

Four men waited at the meat stand. She introduced me to Ole Kina, whose blue, striped suit and white shirt barely contained his six-two frame and shoulders looking like he wore football pads. Ole then introduced his elder brother, John, and two friends, Kuto, an accountant, and Robert, who was short in comparison to the others, an economist with Barclays Bank. All were in their mid-twenties and Masai, save Robert, a Kikuyu. With the introductions all in order, Carmen politely split to attend to her wedding chores.

Ole examined several slabs of beef dangling from hooks on dingy racks at the meat stand. Flies buzzed and suckled the juice. To my relief, the butcher cut off the leanest and reddest piece indicated by Ole—a slice big enough to feed a starving lion. He wrapped it in newspaper and handed it over. The five of us strode into the bar next door to the butcher.

It was dimly lit and dank smelling. A slight scent of urine drifted from a bathroom in back whose walls did not quite reach the ceiling. The bar's fifteen or so wooden tables were stark and unadorned. There was no music. People sat quietly sipping their drinks. Women mixed freely with men, unlike the club I had visited in Zimbabwe.

I hung my daypack on one of the scrawny chairs. SLAM! The chair hit the floor. It must have been made of balsa wood. I smiled sheepishly, righted the chair, and slid carefully into it, hanging the daypack behind me.

Placing his big body easily into his own chair, Ole Kina ordered a round of Tusker beer. However, a national labor strike had cut the flow of the country's prize brew, so we had to settle for alternatives. At the same time, Ole handed over the newspaper-wrapped beef to the waiter. "One simply brings the beef into one's favorite bar," he explained in firm, Queen's English. "The barman cooks the meat over coals and delivers it to one's table."

Staring at me through puny round glasses that looked out of place on his big round head, Ole opened the conversation.

"Do you drink blood?"

Was this a joke for my benefit? No one laughed. "*Blood!*" I cried, squirming in the chair. "Oh! You mean, blood?"

"I mean raw blood," Ole clarified, cracking knuckles as big as a stevedore's.

"Not that I can recall. Steak juice! Are you serious? Do the Masai drink blood?"

"Yes!" John joined in. "We mix it with warm milk squeezed from the udder of a cow. For Masai, blood is a daily staple that provides protein."

"How do you get it?"

"We bleed cows," Ole answered, cracking the last knuckle. "You should try blood in milk sometime. Once one gets used to it, it is really quite good." Behind the glasses, his eyes sparkled with genuine candor.

Why not blood? People can adapt to anything. After all, I was getting used to the aroma from the toilets. A moment of silence ensued and the drinks arrived—Guinness, coke, gin, and vodka, the alcohol came in plastic packets rather like airline snacks. Unable to break free of my American discomfort with silence, I asked, "What do you guys think of the strike?"

Kenya's inflation rate in the last year was over 200%, so the national organization of labor unions, COTU, demanded a 100% wage increase for workers. President Moi's government refused, the union organized a strike, and its boisterous leader landed in the clink.

"Africans follow their leaders like cattle to the slaughter." Ole shook his head in disgust. "But I believe the strike is successful, in that it marks a beginning of massive resistance—on a scale we have never experienced before. Maybe it will provide the spark that forges a true democracy."

Now everyone leaned forward into the conversation.

"What about Moi?" I asked. I looked around at the quiet faces in close quarters. With all the land in the world, we were scrunched together like sardines in a can. "His face is everywhere—on your currency, every building and shop, in newspapers, on TV. Doesn't he ever smile?"

John fiddled with his glasses. He was a poet and aspiring entrepreneur, who dreamed of promoting Masai culture internationally by touring the world with a troupe in full ceremonial dress. His eyes blazed and his voice trembled. "Moi is a brute!" he raged. "He does not have to smile, he is in control. Do you know, Denis, he is one of the richest men in the world? How did

130

a former schoolteacher get that much money? He and his cronies skim their share of every shilling the government receives."

"That is the payoff for winning a revolution," Kuto the accountant offered quietly, puffing a cigarette and gesturing softly with his hands as if we were prisoners planning a breakout. "Killers become war heroes, and then claim the rewards off the people they liberate. Are we better off?" Scratching his mustache and looking around the table, he answered his own question. "Yes, to be sure. We are not servants anymore."

"Economic slavery is no different than physical," John piped in.

Robert, whose handsome features reminded me of the young Muhammad Ali, sipped a Guinness and coke. He looked intently at the rest of us, but said nary a word. The lone Kikuyu at the table, he was part of the tribe that had held the staff of power in Kenya since liberation.

The cook arrived with steaming meat, chips, and a junior machete, with which he chopped the meat into morsels on the heavy wooden table. He poured a pyramid of salt beside the mass and left us to it. We picked at the chips and bite-sized chunks of beef, eating communally with our hands.

"What caused the inflation?" I asked. "All over Africa the symptoms are the same—rampant inflation, deteriorating infrastructures, social unrest. What's going on?"

Silence.

Robert wiped his mouth with his forefinger, took his suit jacket off, and draped it on his chair. The chair remained upright. He spoke with the authority of a banker and the infallibility of an economist.

"It is a tough question to answer simply. I believe the inflation is not because Africans cannot eventually run their own countries. Let us face facts, we are new to the world of high finance. We are beginners at governing and administering in the modern era. How long did it take the West to learn? Is it not true, Kuto, that when a country's resources, its wealth, are sufficient to supply the needs of its people, there is stability in prices? Instability and inflation must inevitably come when a country, such as ours, spends resources it doesn't have." He looked around for confirmation.

Although Robert had directed the question to Kuto, Ole answered. "If the Kikuyus are in power, they must bear the brunt of criticism, Robert, but I agree that we are only beginners." He looked at me. "I think what Robert is saying is that we do not have an abundance of wealth: some minerals, a limited amount of industry, agriculture. We rely heavily on safari tourism."

"We never needed much!" John interjected. "Most Africans live in dirt huts, use wood for fire. When the land did not provide, people starved or migrated. Times were simple."

Meanwhile the beef was politely under attack and disappearing fast.

Jabbing John in the ribs good-naturedly, Robert said: "For the Masai the world is simple—they need only cattle, and what cattle they don't have they take."

"Like tax proceeds belong to the Kikuyu," said Ole Kina, laughing. He flipped his head in Robert's direction. "Robert knows that cattle are no joking matter. God proclaimed to our sacred forefathers that the Masai are the chosen ones, the rightful owners of all the earth's cattle."

How impressive and well informed these young men are, I thought. If there are enough of them to go around, the future of Africa is in good hands.

Robert resumed his analysis. "Look around Nairobi. What you see is Western-style dress, cars, oil for cars, entertainment, housing, war materials, medical tools. The white man brought us civilization and his products, but not the means or technology to produce them ourselves. If our wealth is enough to sustain us and no more, then anything we buy from the West, or any currency that is smuggled out of the country, creates inflation. Instability and inflation come when a country spends what it doesn't have."

"If you can't afford to buy Western goods, how did you get the money?" I asked.

"In the past, the West lent us the money. Now our credit is bad," said Kuto. "To acquire foreign exchange for imports we sell the food we grow, and then petition the United Nations for charity to feed the starving."

I grabbed one of the last choice pieces of meat and a few French fries then licked my fingers while the impact of this socioeconomic mess sunk in. "Is the debt to the West the reason the International Monetary Fund is so persistent in Africa?"

"The debts held by Western banks are totally worthless," Robert, said. "The IMF is using the promise of more loans to leverage Moi into creating a functioning second party to achieve democracy, followed by a market economy so that the West has a chance to get its money back. Market economies are all the rage, as you say, but how it benefits the average African is not clear."

I stood up to go to the bathroom. SLAM! The damn chair did it again. This time everyone laughed.

When I returned, John was breaking open a packet of vodka and pouring it carefully into his coke. I tore into my second Guinness and coke as the conversation evolved into a discussion of the Masai.

Ole explained that they were pastoralists—meaning they herd cattle, sheep, goats, and donkeys. He said that much of their culture is intact because they didn't succumb to English-style dress and habits. John added that he and his brothers are unusual in their level of education and desire to leave tribal life. He said the Masai were independent and fierce, to the extent that even today the politically dominant Kikuyu steer clear of them. I recalled reading what the adventurer Henry Stanley once told a London audience: "If there are any ladies or gentlemen this evening who are specifically desirous of becoming martyrs, I do not know in all my list of travels where you could become martyrs so quickly as in Masai."

The guys told me that Masai males wore a red woolen cloak slung over one shoulder and averaged over six feet in height. They were raised to be fearless warriors. Circumcision marked their entry into manhood and, if chosen, into a fierce fighting force called the Moran. To become a man and prepare for circumcision, a young warrior in times past was required to kill a lion. To this day, they said, lions steer clear of the color red.

I was curious about the circumcision. Robert said that in some tribes a boy must stand in front of the villagers while the foreskin is cut from his penis, and sometimes the knife was not so sharp. If he showed emotion, he shamed himself and his family. "These are very old ceremonies," Ole Kina added, I guess to explain the apparent focus on an individual's humiliation.

I asked if clitorectomy was still prevalent within the Masai.

"Clitor-what?" John retorted. They looked at me with blank faces.

"We call it clitorectomy. The removal of the clitoris, the most sensitive portion of female external sexual organs."

"Ah!" was the group reaction. Silence and straight faces ensued. With no one else offering, Ole said: "We call that female circumcision."

"Why do they do it?"

"The Masai often went on cattle raids because, as I've said, the cattle of the earth were considered property of the Masai. Often these raids kept the men away for many weeks. I was taught that the female circumcision ceremony marked a girl's entry into womanhood. But from a practical point of view it also was intended to keep the wife faithful to her husband while he was gone, and avoid tribal conflict when he returned."

I wondered what the women would say. I always hated this practice. A major part of my sexual pleasure was the woman's enjoyment.

"People in the United States think this tradition is sadistic," I said, trying not to preach, "because it is painful and the woman loses her enjoyment of sex." They listened, interested. "You are saying by performing this operation the woman would be more faithful because she wouldn't be interested in sex?"

"I do not know," John said. "Women perform this ceremony and I have not asked a woman. It is different in Africa from your country. We live close together in huts and do not wear many clothes. You have birth control and a different attitude toward sex. Here children are the primary reason for marriage, and very important to a man. If a woman is not a virgin, or has sex with a man to whom she is not married, it often causes family shame."

"If America cares, the tradition will eventually be changed," Ole added. "However, controlling birth is very important to the Masai also."

They didn't seem to be offended by my views.

"As a matter of interest," I asked, "while we are on the subject of virginity, how old were you guys when you first had sex?"

There were a few chuckles. Quiet Kuto almost fell off his chair. What would the crazy American ask next? We went around the table. Of the five of us, one lost his virginity at seven, two at eight, one at ten, and one at eighteen. Guess who?

"Nah!" I chuckled. "You guys are kidding, right? Can you do it at seven?"

Since there was no answer, I steered the conversation on to our first times, which we described. The African girls were nine to fourteen. Ole said a girl he knew came into his hut and told him to take his clothes off. Robert remembered an itching sensation during intercourse. He was caught by his mother who ran the girl off and lectured him about the consequences of violating God's trust. Even though I was a late bloomer compared with these guys, I recounted my own loss of innocence during a confusing night in a car so small our legs were sticking out the window.

I asked them about the inconsistency of easy sex and families shamed by pregnancy.

John threw up his hands: "In Africa, what else is there to do?"

"What about polygamy?" I loved these conversations.

"I can only answer for the Masai," Kuto replied. "Marriages among us are often arranged, and are for the purpose of having children. You see, the number of children determines a man's security in old age. Polygamy you ask? A man can have several wives depending on his wealth." He looked at me with furrowed brows. "Do you have only one wife?"

I gave the standard answer: "One's enough for me!"

They all laughed immediately. "Maybe you are wiser than the Masai," Kuto said. "We are polygamist out of respect for women, to give them time between children. A Masai cannot have intercourse with his wife when she is pregnant, or when she is nursing. He marries other women to fill his need and increase the size of his family."

"But the old traditions are breaking down and the population is soaring," John added. "I don't know what it will mean to us."

I made a mental note to revisit this relationship between birth control and survival in Africa.

We polished off the last of the Guinness and the packets of gin, and then the guys walked me through the darkness of River Road till I found a taxi to take me safely to the Silver Springs Hotel, a cheaper one I had moved to. They warned me that Nairobi had become dangerous at night because of the influx of refugees.

As the taxi drove down Kenyatta Avenue, I reminded myself to thank Carmen for introducing me to these extraordinary young people. I thought again about the question of overpopulation. It was becoming clear that unless something was done about population growth, the West would be forced to choose between supporting African welfare or watching endless scenes of famine and war on TV. The key lay with treatment of females because they bore the children. Elizabeth Cady Stanton once said: " ... a woman's place in society marks the level of civilization." And once you raised the standard, it occurred to me, the number of children would go down.

20

SECOND AFRICAN WEDDING: "CUT THE TETHERS OF FAMILY OWNERSHIP ..."

T HE WEDDING TOOK PLACE ON a bright and sunny day, one
of the three hundred or so that Kenyans struggle through
each year. It was held at the All Saints Church, a big modern
stone structure with a red shale roof. Carmen met me at the entrance in tears. Her camera had disappeared and she asked me to
make sure I took lots of pictures with mine. Then, after a squeeze
of my arm, she swaggered away in a form-fitting, knee-length,
cream-colored dress that the ladies worked on during the last
week.

Following Carmen's athletic stride through the gathering crowd, I noticed that many of the men wore suits and ties
while I was decked out in the blue shirt with swirling flowers. Bridesmaids looked stunning in amber satin dresses and
lace gloves. Ushers, who didn't usher, wore tuxedos and white
gloves. And eight of the cutest flower girls, aged two to nine,
were dressed all in white—frocks with matching veils, stockings,
gloves, and shoes. They filed into the front row of the bride's side
mahogany pew in order of size.

The bride, Ruth, who was four months pregnant, gracefully
walked down the aisle wearing a white, fluffy dress and lace veil
that covered her light brown face. Carmen followed her making sure the long, flowing train of the dress didn't get dirty or
snagged. She stood beside Ruth at the altar, while the minister

heaped on the bride and groom, Willis, all the blessings, warnings, and promises that a long-standing relationship in Christ would invariably need.

The wedding scene looked purely Western, with three noteworthy exceptions: the brilliantly colorful dresses and headscarves that many of the women wore; that the babies present didn't cry, a phenomenon I witnessed throughout my travels in Africa; and the third was the audacity of photographers.

Photographers can be aggressive in the West, it is true, but aggressive was too puny a word to describe these guys. They stalked the couple like wild dogs on the hunt. Wires from floodlights squirmed like snakes along the altar of this spacious, simply decorated, stone interior.

"Do you—" *click, click, flash, flash!* "—take—" *click, flash!* A videographer stuck a microphone between the faces of the minister and the couple. "—to be your lawful wedded husband?" *Flash, flash, click!* Inaudible sounds. "I now pronounce you man and—" *click!*

No one seemed to mind.

When the ceremony was over, a group of women chanted tribal songs in the courtyard outside All Saints Church, while others showered confetti on the newly married couple. Carmen wormed her way through the crowd and grabbed my hand. In a much better mood, she introduced me to Samuel who was going to escort me to the reception. He introduced his Indian friend Nigel, who wasted no time informing me that he managed a branch of his father's import business. Meanwhile, a shy woman stood unintroduced ten feet behind Samuel. She didn't look part of our group, and just hung around the fringe trying to figure out where to put her eyes.

Nigel spoke incessantly. I tried to draw Sam into the conversation, but Nigel would have none of it. He moved closer to me—close enough to see his eyes behind the copper din of his sunglasses and blocking Sam from view. Nigel was giving us a lift to the reception and it was only when we got into his Toyota Corolla that I learned why the shy woman was hanging around. She was Sam's girlfriend, Anne.

Nigel dropped us at the Milimani Hotel, and drove on to another commitment. As we stood in the long, slow queue to enter the reception room, Sam picked up where Nigel left off. Now he did the talking and ignored poor Anne. She waited patiently on the outside. Finally, I leaned around Sam to ask her questions. No dice! Samuel answered as if she was invisible. Meanwhile, inside staccato African wedding chants beckoned those outside to come on in.

Sam said he was completing his master's in psychology. His thesis was on the plight of pregnant women in Africa. He concluded, with dignity and all seriousness: "The problem of pregnant women is unsolvable because of our culture. Women want children as companions and to protect the family assets. Also, there is social pressure to have children." Anne nodded at the "social" part, and snickered when I asked if men had something to do with the situation. Sam ignored the question.

The reception room inside the Milimani was the size of a very small church. With its low, acoustic-tiled ceiling decorated with looping party streamers, it barely accommodated the three hundred guests. Packing that many people in was akin to squeezing Fat Albert into Madonna's Levis. The guests stood or sat in rows all the way from the back wall to the head table and the two subordinate tables, where the 'elders' sat. The three tables were draped in floor-length, white linen. At the head table sat the bride and groom, three ushers, and Carmen. At the right-side table sat the bride's family and honored guests, characterized by their diminutive and humble parish priest. On the left table, the groom's family, including his powerfully dressed mother and father, were seated.

The groom's father was handsome. His round, shaved head, muscular physique, and somber, forceful eyes contrasted sharply with his passive-looking son, Willis. Ruth's mannerisms, however, spoke of confident ease and leadership. A person would naturally wonder how she and her new father-in-law would get along.

Matrons squeezed through the crowd serving food and drink. According to the custom, males were served first. Food was accompanied by short speeches from the elders at the tables and a few audience members—groom's side first, then bride's. No one at the head table said a word. The speeches were delivered in Luo, the tribal language of bride and groom, while a translator rendered them in English. Only men on the groom's side spoke, their speeches like sermons. They spoke of Willis as a good boy who studied hard and didn't visit the girls' huts (laughs from the audience). Equally, Ruth was a good girl who studied hard, didn't get into trouble with boys, and praised God. The overall message directed at the young couple—delivered in old-folk talk with lots of formality, a touch of old-time religion, a few smiles, and rare jokes—was follow Christ, be good, and above all *keep the house open to the family.*

The only woman to speak, other than Ruth's mother, was her heavy-set aunt, who appeared to be in her early thirties. As she rose from the audience, a tense hush rippled through the air. Observing her confident, almost combative demeanor, I wondered whether she was highly respected or a "black sheep." Whichever, one thing was abundantly clear, there were rock-of-Gibraltar genes in this family, which nourished Ruth and her aunt. The aunt held a rope. With a firm grip, she stretched it in front of her like Moses holding up the Ten Commandments. The rope taut, she looked first at the in-laws, then at the newly married couple, and in an iron voice, she commanded the couple to "cut the tethers of family ownership, and put your happiness first."

I looked around. People were frozen except for the groom's table, who had hardness in their eyes. Gradually the tension passed.

Carmen noticed that the women serving food avoided me, so she gave me a "come up here with us" nod. I obliged, honored to sit at the head table. My white friends in Zimbabwe said that in all the years they had lived on the continent, they had only been invited to one black African wedding. This was my second.

After Ruth had cut and helped distribute—men first, of course—the triple-decker cake, we had gift-giving. Women lined up single file to present their offerings while chanting tribal songs, swaying and foot-stomping towards the married couple in a way similar to what I had witnessed at the Zimbabwe wedding.

At the head table, watching kids play around the remnants of the wedding cake, I wondered whether Ruth's aunt was the new order trying to break the hierarchical rope of family ownership. The new model put the individual in the driver's seat, swapping extensive family ties for independent kids and the chance of divorce.

21

TRAVELS WITH CARMEN

AFTER THE WEDDING, CARMEN AND I flew to Malindi, a mostly Muslim town on the coast of Kenya. We spent six days at her favorite resort, the Silversands. A mile south of town, the place was a charming enclave of huts with petite concrete porches and steeply sloping thatched roofs that nearly touched the ground. Our hut was not much bigger than a two-person tent, with barely enough space to fit the beds with mosquito nets. Nevertheless it was cozy.

At quarter past six each morning, we woke—thanks to the loudspeakers at the local mosque—to the brooding, orange sunrise and sweep of fast-moving clouds. By eight, the sky had always cleared and we began our Malindi routine. First, we relaxed in armchairs on the red porch, like Ma and Pa Kettle, sniffing scents of jasmine and gazing at sprawling bougainvillea, coconut trees, and glistening, white sand framing the sparkling Indian Ocean.

Breakfast was taken nearby at a 7–11 and fifties-style hamburger hangout—with menu written on the wall and zesty Zambian music. In late morning, we sat under the shade of a coconut tree watching fisherman pound the water to herd fish into submerged nets at low tide. Old men dug holes in the sand searching for crabs. Local kids stopped by to chat, fondle Carmen's hair, and sell their wares. In the afternoon, we snorkeled or climbed over rocks along the coastline, checking out tide-pools. Some days, we'd sample exotic fruit drinks at a fancy Italian resort. Or rent bikes and peddle into town, maneuvering around huge stacks of pineapples at crowded markets and passing women in colorful saris, wraparounds, and black, head-to-foot dresses called *buibuis*.

One day, we sauntered over to the Indian section of town to shop for clothes. As in Nairobi, Indians owned many of the businesses. Carmen bought cotton string pants, and I picked out an orange *khanga*, an East African sarong, with red and green parameciums printed throughout.

Carmen was comfortable to be with: charming, well rounded, with a good sense of humor. The type of person that remembers where a conversation got sidetracked and brings it back. Her knowledge of Swahili, which she said Arabs introduced to create a common language, constantly endeared her to the locals,—a mixture of African, Arab, and Indian, with a smattering of Italians driving big cars.

On the last evening, we curled up in chairs on the porch, smoking ganja while entranced by the sounds of surf and the rosy glow on the horizon.

"You know," I said, "being outdoors I'm realizing how much we live within walls back home. Maybe we see the squirrels and birds outside, but we can't hear them."

"I love the culture of the outdoors!" she said. "So relaxed and friendly and interesting. Ever since I could remember I watched TV about Africa and dreamed about coming here and feeling the energy of this place. See animals in their natural habitat. It's the thought of something untainted, primitive—pristine, I guess.

"I took a class about healing dance with a teacher from the Ivory Coast. His stories about Africa did it! I looked into exchange programs. I wanted to shake things up in my life. You know what I mean, Denis?"

"Absolutely!"

We passed the joint back and forth leisurely. She watched its smoke swirl. After a while, she asked: "Hey, were you concerned about the girls and drugs when they were young?"

"They *still* seem young, but, yeah, of course. We talked to them about it early."

"How early? How old were they?"

"Well, I guess Shannon was seven or eight."

"So young!"

"We were big on educating them early. I trust the intelligence of kids. Parents in Africa trust their kids at four and five years old to take care of younger brothers and sisters. We felt children have the capacity to understand, they just lack experience.

"Anyway, back on the ganja. One night, we had friends over for dinner and afterwards smoked a joint. One of the topics we discussed was whether to tell our kids we imbibed. Our friends would never tell. The next day Shannon saw the stub of a joint in the ashtray, and knew we didn't smoke. She was a bitch for days. We couldn't figure out why. But the only thing that made sense was that she thought we lied about smoking.

So we sat her and Chimene down and told them about marijuana, and alcohol, the laws, and our position on the laws. Simple communication. We didn't have to hide anymore, and the girls loved talking to us when we were stoned."

"How about them? When did you first know they smoked pot?"

"Oh, let's see. I guess, Shannon's high school graduation party. I walked outside by the pool to talk to a few of the guys. One of them had just taken a giant hit and tried to hide it by holding in the smoke. I waited till he turned blue, and then said something like 'You better let that out or you'll keel over.' Then I went inside and made a peanut butter and honey sandwich on toast, my favorite. A couple of guys watched, making goofy comments, so I tripled the peanut butter and honey and asked them to try it. One bite each, then silence. So I went around the house asking everyone to take a bite. The place went from loud chaos to quiet. That's when I knew for sure."

Carmen giggled loudly. "I remember that night! Our mouths were glued shut from lack of saliva. You were such a rat!"

"When Shannon figured it out, she pointed at me laughing hard, but of course without any sound." We giggled and giggled at the image before sobriety drifted in.

"I wanted my girls to visit the cliff but drive down the middle of the road. The wild kids I came across growing up either had too many restrictions or too little."

"I don't know about that kind of frankness so early with kids," Carmen countered. "Certainly my parents were never that way. Chas and I have been thinking about having a family. Family provides purpose, you know! Anyways, it's caused me to reflect on how I was raised. Techniques, good and bad. Did you think about raising a family when you were young, or when you got married, or what?"

"My grandmother told stories about the family heritage. But my dad probably provoked most thoughts of how to raise a family." I pictured his hard belly hanging over his belt, his wire-rim glasses, big cigars, and redness in his cheeks. "We must have fought since I gained control of my vocal cords. Dad could tell a funny joke in at least ten different brogues. He had a natural talent and a booming laugh. He had the sweetest Irish tenor voice. Tears would roll when he sang *Danny Boy*. Yet he didn't have a clue about what went on inside someone else's head. We'd fight, and I'd tell myself 'I'm never going to do this or that to my kids.' But then I also started thinking about what I *was* going to do."

"Did he abuse you?"

"Maybe in today's terms, but I was mentally stronger. He had a good heart and always apologized after a fight for the names he called me. Actually, his apologies taught me empathy, because I had to decide whether to forgive him or not. I'm thankful to my dad. He caused me to reflect on how to raise children of my own. It got so I could visualize their laughs, their personalities. I wanted my kids to be happy and teach me to do things I couldn't do naturally."

"Sounds like the habits of your dad created the father in you." Seeing my quizzical look, she added: "I mean those things start you thinking about being someone different. I think that way sometimes."

"I see what you mean. It's true. My dad triggered habit changes when I saw myself acting like him."

"It's like, like my dream of Africa," Carmen said. "The more I wanted it, the more I thought about how to get here. I could see it. Seems like what you do the first bunch of years of your life sets the stage for the next bunch."

Thoughts like this cause you to look out to sea.

"You said you could visualize Shannon and Chimene's laughs," Carmen continued. "Did you see their faces?"

"It was so long ago. I don't recall."

"What about their character?"

"I remember wanting them to have a strong self-esteem to handle my domineering ways, you know, be happy with who they were. I'd think about teaching them things I couldn't do myself, so that they could role model it back to me. Like you said—to become someone different. And then, thinking about my future kids' qualities led me to qualities I needed in a wife."

"Sounds manipulative," she said, nudging my foot.

"It is!" I said, nudging her back. "But visions work."

"We're all manipulative in our own way," she said. "I want to enjoy my kids, too, but I don't know whether I could be as liberal as you. Like, I want to develop a philosophy. It's like driving with a map as opposed to winging it. So what's your philosophy?"

What was it?

"We wanted informed individuals who would become our friends when they got older. So we emphasized communication and a friendly attitude."

"I don't know about having my kids as friends. Where's the line between parent and child?"

"I think Kathi would agree that we never had any problem with that line. The kids had one vote each, and parents two each." She laughed. "We disciplined the girls, not always in the mainstream way, mind you. Like we used Gandhi's approach on occasion. They were seven and eight and *we* went on strike for two weeks because they weren't doing their chores."

"Shannon told me about that! She said she didn't get allowances or rides to school, and that she had to learn to cook her own meals. I think she told me the strike wasn't over until she and Chimene gave you guys a piece of paper with your issues written on the first half of the page, and solutions on the second."

"That's about right. I would add that the girls had the opportunity to state their issues, too. Our friends thought we were mean. You hate not giving your kids things, but I didn't have to yell at them about their chores during the strike, and in the end we all gained an intimate understanding of labor negotiations—from the management's and workers' point of view."

"So getting back to philosophy, what were those family meetings all about?"

"Umm, they sort of evolved. After New Year's, Kathi would arrange a three-day weekend trip to talk about things that happened to us during the previous year, and write resolutions for the coming one. Shannon and I had an almost ritualistic fight before the meeting. Two talkers clearing the air, I guess. Then we'd all sit on the bed, or pillows that Kathi brought to the hotel, and discuss character traits and family dynamics. We eventually developed a method of listing qualities on a flipchart—"

"What kind of qualities?"

"Oh, things like communication, patience, or charity. There were about thirteen of them. Then we'd discuss how each of us individually fared relative to each quality. The rule was whoever was being talked about had to listen and not defend themselves. That took a day and a half. On the Saturday night, we'd go to a really good restaurant and have fun blowing a bunch of money. Then on Sunday we'd assess the chart, figure out where we needed to improve and write a New Year's resolution."

"That's really cool. I need to give some thought to my own philosophy. It's a new world for raising children," she said, shaking her head. "The old rules are probably good, but they need a lot of stretching and a lot of thought."

Since it was our last night before returning to Nairobi, we made an effort to go to bed early, but I had a hard time sleeping owing to the humidity and buzz of mosquitoes outside the netting. I saw Carmen moving under her sheet.

"Hey, are you awake?"

"Yeah! All sorts of thoughts are running through my mind. The nets don't let in much of a breeze in this humidity. I've been wondering, Denis, how can you leave Kathi for a year? I could never leave Chas. I'd feel like I was deserting him."

This question! Why did I have such a problem answering this question? *To heal a wound* came my heart's resounding response as I thought of the frustrations that led to my first separation from Kathi four years before. We had learned to communicate as a family, but not as a couple. In her family, they avoided conflict at all costs. In mine, argument was a way of life. The attraction of opposites.

"I needed to be on my own for a while," I said, trying again to come to a sensible answer. "The first bunch of years we were married, I hated to be away from Kathi and the girls. Then things build up. I needed to get those things out of my system. It wasn't only Kathi I left. It was my partnership, business, the pace of life in general. These things I thought I had control over, actually, I realized, controlled me. The more you control, the more you are controlled. Am I making any sense?"

"I think so. That's a lot to think about."

Back in Nairobi, Carmen's vacation was almost over. She would carry the originals of my journals home, along with letters and gifts for the family. We spent the afternoon at various offices setting up my travel arrangements: a safari to the Masai Mara and the Serengeti, a trip to the coastal town of Lamu, and then Zanzibar. On our last night together, I treated Carmen to dinner at an Italian restaurant recommended by Ole Kina. Over pasta and wine, we got into an ardent discussion about marriage. I felt honored when Carmen asked what I thought was important to consider in long-term relationships—my favorite topic. "Good communication, tenacity, a sense of humor, and trust," I said.

"You left out fidelity."

Although she was in a good mood, as usual, my long-standing philosophy about fidelity made me uncomfortable discussing the subject with her. But I gave it a shot.

"I think infidelity presents a tremendous risk to a relationship," I opined, "but I don't believe strict sexual exclusivity should be the cornerstone of marriage if you are in it for the long-term—especially in today's world."

Carmen's body stiffened, color fled her face. "I hope my husband *never* messes around with another woman," she said, flashing me one of those *I am disappointed with you* looks.

"Lots of things happen in a relationship that we can't always anticipate, Carmen. People grow differently, have different needs—"

"I would feel betrayed," she cut in righteously. "Don't you think adultery is wrong?"

From here I could only be a villain. Her tone identified infidelity as a violation of common decency. But I was a decent person. Kathi and I discussed the subject of infidelity many times, and concluded that we might need intimate contact with another person sometime during the arduous road to old age.

"Wrong is a strong word, Carmen. If it wasn't for infidelity, *People* magazine would be out of business." She wasn't laughing.

What could I say? To me the word "adultery" smacked of moral storm troopers raiding someone else's life.

"Don't misunderstand me, Carmen, I believe fidelity is critical to building a bond during the first several years, but for me it doesn't have the flexibility needed for the long term. I can think of more noble aspects of a good marriage, like inspiring each other to think and grow. Or raising children that are fun to be with."

"What you say sounds practical, but honesty and trust keep intimacy alive," she said, turning the glass in her hands, perturbed. "And you can't have intimacy with infidelity."

She had that Katharine Hepburn in the *African Queen* righteousness. I should have tried to change the energy right then, but I didn't know how at the time. My experience had been that the honest discussion about our sex lives was the most intimate of my marriage.

"I agree about honesty and trust," I said. "But if you categorically disavow 'adultery' for the length of a relationship, how do you maintain honesty? Or trust for that matter? How do you fantasize together? And shouldn't *trust* assume the other person is doing what is best for them, and ultimately the relationship?"

"It's a matter of respect," she said calmly. "You think adultery can ever be good for a relationship? Adultery affects more than just the two doing it. The impact of broken homes on children damages their abilities in relationships—sometimes for life. The adultery of two people ends up affecting generations."

"You have a good point about how it affects families. I feel very strongly about marriage for life. That ideal helped Kathi and I stay together. I also believe that when you make a commitment to have children, you should commit for at least the time it takes to raise them. That means no love affairs outside of marriage. Love just gets deeper. But I firmly believe long-term relationships need flexibility. Advertising and movies soak us with sexuality, then our society requires fidelity from us. Like sexuality is some sort of a test. Well, for me there is a huge difference between risking the family by falling in love, and a discreet fling in the hay."

"Did you feel this way before you were married? Huh?" The "huh" came like a dagger thrust.

"Yes, I did as a matter of fact. I wanted honesty in our marriage, so I told Kathi that I probably wouldn't make it through the rest of my life without sleeping with another woman. That I liked women too much." This was the truth. I was just being honest before the big commitment. But I doubted honesty played very well at this point in the conversation.

"Well, how can you determine the risk? And speaking as a woman, I prefer a deeper, meaningful relationship over a roll in the hay! My boyfriend would never say that to me, and I wouldn't want him to. How can you have a healthy loving relationship when one or both parties are sleeping with someone else?"

Embarrassed, I sensed the blood seep into my face. I was the cynic throwing mud on the world's greatest institution. And that "speaking as a woman" comment bothered me, as if women are innocent. I peered into the sparkling wine, annoyed, searching for the right articulation.

"A loving relationship to me," I said, "means understanding why a person does something and equitably adjusting for it. For instance, what if after a few years one partner wants sex and the other doesn't? Or one wants to travel or go dancing, and those activities are not the other's priority? Or one partner gains a significant amount of weight and the other likes *thin* people? I think unilateral decisions like those affect fidelity."

"You can rationalize all you want, but I want to live my life exclusively with Chas. He's the man I love." She put her fingers in a pyramid and then to her lips, with a look of finality. And that was the end of the discussion.

My *good parent* bubble had burst for sure, proving the old adage that reputations take a lifetime to build and a moment to lose. I resented her lack of respect for my thoughts or the longevity of my relationship, and wondered where she would stand on the issue after twenty-five years of marriage. On the other hand, maybe I was rationalizing my own behavior. Maybe the difference in point of view didn't matter. Why should one person's view of life be the same as another's?

22

MASAI MARA AND SERENGETI

CARMEN AND I PARTED THE next morning at the office of Sovuku Tours, the budget company that would take me on a five-day camping safari to the Masai Mara in Kenya and the Serengeti in Tanzania for $150. You don't have to find a safari company, they find you—with an army of touts paid commission for every customer hooked. In Sovuku's paltry office, I met two mates in their mid-twenties flirting with a female clerk—Lee, a lanky Englishman with spunk, and Dan, a husky, good-looking American with an appealing sense of humor. Carmen took one look at the pair and quipped: "Looks like I'm leaving you in good hands."

A Sovuku van with an opening at the top for gazing at animals was ready to go. I gave Carmen a last hug and kiss, and boarded. As it pulled on to Kenyatta Avenue, I waved until she disappeared from view. My heart pulsed with sadness, but I was filled with anticipation at what the next slice of life had to offer.

Outside Nairobi, we traveled along a one-lane road with holes the size of moon craters. It was obvious that the infrastructure the British built was retreating to nature. There is a saying in Africa that if you drive in a straight line, you must be drunk. And our driver had to maneuver up land banks with the vehicle pitched at impossible angles, not to mention weaving past a cow hit by a truck and left to die.

We stopped for sandwiches at Narok, a Masai town near the entrance of the Masai Mara reserve. Narok had a butchery, bar, fleabag hotel, and curio shop loaded with ebony caricatures of animals, hefty women, and long, skinny men with bubblegum stomachs. I traded my belt for a white and blue-beaded Masai one and gave pens I had bought for the occasion to local kids who had just started attending school.

The Masai Mara and Serengeti game reserves are neighbors on the great savanna of eastern Africa. The Masai live here. It was where Ole Kina spent his youth. There were then about 380,000 Masai. Pastoralists that have resisted the urge to adopt a sedentary lifestyle, Masai routinely ignore international boundaries as they move cattle across the open savannah with the changing of the seasons.

In the Mara, we drove under the big sky through endless golden grasslands with animals roaming free. At a rare waterhole, graceful impala lined up single file, like kids at a grade school water fountain. The herd posted lookouts for protection. Standing under an acacia at water's edge, the patriarch nervously scanned the surrounding area, while metering drinking time. He tapped each individual on the back when its time was up. Predators, knowing drink was a necessity, added monumental risk to even this simplest of needs. With crocodiles beneath the brown water and land predators everywhere else, the biggest risk an animal faced must be quenching its thirst. What must it feel like to slurp the water knowing at any time the huge mouth of a crocodile might rise up from beneath the murky surface and rip your head off?

The first night in camp I was woken from a sound sleep by the raking of my tent and growling of a large animal. I was genuinely alarmed—until I recognized the species the growls came from. Human. I unzipped the front flap and ran out to catch Lee and Dan busting a gut and intermittently clawing and growling at me. But suddenly, seized by a haunting presence, they stopped laughing and the three of us turned around slowly in the eerie dark. Not more than a hundred yards away, two sets of luminescent eyes as big as coconuts watched. Probably hyenas thinking the dumb humans would make a tasty meal. My heart really raced this time, and we scrambled frantically back inside the comfort of our tents—making sure we zipped them tight.

During the week, our driver, George, took us to view animals. We saw four of the "Big Five"—lion, elephant, rhino, and brooding herds of buffalo—as well as giraffe. All that was missing was a leopard. Baboons walked with their butts high in the air, or sat calmly combing the fur of the young for parasites. We saw lots of lions wandering the plains or resting with their family amid the clumps of bushes. At the Masai Mara, lions are so accustomed to humans that they often use the Land Rovers as shields to stalk their prey. There were ugly-but-cute warthogs, kneeling on their front legs to munch grass, hippos marauding in muddy water, and sneaky crocs. George told us that when a male lion takes over the pride of another male lion it kills all the young ones. A harsh illustration of "survival of the fittest."

Before dinner, we'd play volleyball with the Masai attendants and their friends who lived in a neighboring village or kraal. It was the *mzungus* against the Masai, who ranged in age from seventeen to twenty-six. The Masai were handsome, with elongated noses and gaping holes in their ear lobes. The games were close but only because the Masai squabbled so much among themselves. With their tall, thin bodies they could have easily beaten the Westerners if they had any discipline. During breaks in the action, several of the Masai would place their arms down along their sides, hold their feet close together, and jump up, as if they were trying to scrape the sky with their heads. When I asked Ole Kato, a thin wiry man of about twenty, why they jumped, he said, "We always do it!"

Watching the guys jumping, I couldn't help think about the fuss made over genetics in the United States. People had similar facial characteristics as their mother or father, so why couldn't the genes store leaping ability or other physical skills—or anything? There was plenty of room. I knew that by the end of the century we'd have a silicon chip no bigger than the edge of a person's fingertip that could store a billion bits of information. And that was after fooling around with electronics for only fifty years. The human body had been engineered over four and a half million years.

One afternoon, we hiked five kilometers across the plains of the Mara to the kraal where the attendants lived. The weather was hot and dry and the clouds sparse and big against the clear blue sky. Ole Kado guided us. A muscular man with hard features, he wore a red cape, and carried a spear easily eight feet long. The upper end of the spear held a two-foot blade and the lower end was fashioned to a point like a javelin. I had heard that lions feared those with the cape and spear as much as they feared the elephant. It gave me some comfort on this journey into the wild.

"Hey, Ole Kado, can I carry your spear?" I asked, as the dry grass of the savannah crunched under my hiking boots.

"Yes, but you must give the spear back to me if a lion comes."

"That's why I want to carry it."

He laughed. "Believe me, you would want *me* to have the spear if a lion comes."

During the walk through the bush, Ole told me he developed his earlobes by inserting larger and larger objects, ultimately graduating to a plastic Kodak film container. And during rest breaks, as they did during volleyball, Ole and his buddies would jump in the air.

The kraal was shaped like a stockade with a circular wall of skinny trees—in form not unlike the stockades in cowboy and Indian movies. Men and boys catered to cows outside. Ole told me that cows are rarely killed, but can be traded or sold to settle debts.

Beyond the gates of the stockade, the interior was nothing more than brown dirt with a few tufts of grass pounded flat from use, with thirty or so flat-roofed huts surrounding the inner stockade. Sticks framed the huts and were plastered with mud and cow dung. Hens and chicks pecked and scratched for food.

In the center of the stockade, brightly colored bead necklaces, wrist and ankle bracelets, breast coverings, and drumsticks that looked like mallets lay spread out on the ground in a straight line for presentation to visitors. Tall women with a variety of red and red-striped capes, buckteeth, and large holes in their ears, which looked like two halves of a wrinkled pepper, sat beading on the dirt. They had long foreheads and short-knit hair like a wool sweater. One woman wore blue, red, white, and green beads the diameter of yarn that were stitched in homogeneous patterns. Some had pellet-sized holes in the top of their ears that dangled beads like tinsel on a Christmas tree. Everyone was barefoot and tolerated the pesky flies that sucked on the mucus that seeped from the eyes and noses of the little children.

While the women blandly displayed their beadwork to the rich whites, three scantily clad children delightedly showed me

153

their hut. It was dark inside, musty smelling, and devoid of any sign of personal identity, such as pictures on the wall. The kids were proud of their home and happily played outside. There were no cars to worry about, no forms, licenses, appointments or appointment books. The major possession was a large cask for lugging water, and the major source of wealth looked to be the cows and beaded trinkets. I didn't see anyone drinking blood mixed with milk that Ole Kina mentioned, but then it wasn't mealtime and people didn't snack.

This way of life was rich with time, family, and community, but poor in almost every other way. And looking at the skimpy closeness of the huts, I could imagine how difficult it was to keep virginity, fidelity, and community harmony intact.

23

Muslim Life in the Ancient City of Lamu

AFTER THE SAFARI, I FLEW on a six-seater to Lamu, a string of islands hugging the east coast below Somalia. A remote, self-contained Muslim city of ten thousand, it is Kenya's oldest, dating back to the thirteenth century when the Persians traded for slaves, ivory, and rhino horn with tribes as far inland as Uganda. They introduced Islam along the way. Later the Portuguese, Arabs, and British battled for control of the coast. Lamu has been described as a place of fantasy wrapped in a cloak of medieval romance.

The front-page headline of the newspaper I was reading on the plane proclaimed: PRESIDENT MOI BEGS FOR $34 MILLION IN FOOD AID—IMF HOLDS FUNDS. Moi also warned the striking government employees to "stop this disloyalty." No women's faces in the news, only sober-looking males. The paper cited debates about whether the West should compensate Africa for the twelve million slaves transported to the Americas and the twelve million who died along the way. Or if blame should be directed at the Muslim middlemen, or the tribes who sold their brethren into slavery. On page four, an article described the lynching and burning of three sorcery suspects who allegedly kidnapped and beat a girl and forced her to eat rotten meat. Dispersing the villagers, the police chief warned not to take the law into their own hands. Another article was entitled:

Policemen Flee from Urchins,
by Ngugi wa Mbugua

Six plainclothes policemen, on Tuesday night, were forced to flee after a group of street urchins they were trying to arrest near the city market smeared two of the policemen with human waste. The five boys had been confronted by the police outside a public toilet on Tubman Street around 8 p.m., when two of the boys disappeared into the toilet and scooped the waste into their hands. As one policeman floored a resisting urchin, the boy shouted at his companion: "Mureithi thii urehe mai (Mureithi, go get some feces)!" Seemingly uncomprehending, the officer went on struggling with the shouting boy until he was smeared with the waste. Another officer who tried to intercept the boys at the entrance of the toilet had his suit soiled and quickly took to his heels. Four other policemen who stood nearby watching the early evening drama took the cue and also fled in the direction of Koinage Street.

The plane touched down on a rutted asphalt runway with grass growing between the cracks. This was Manda Island, part of the Lamu archipelago. Hunching under the doorway of the plane, I was struck first by the smell of honeysuckle. Then I looked down and saw a swarming crowd clamoring to carry luggage off the befuddled passengers. A skinny, bare-chested local grabbed my backpack and quickly merged with the crowd. "Hey, come back here!" I shouted.

My eyes followed the backpack bouncing like one of a string of barrels down the river. It disappeared into the moving swarm.

"Do not worry," said a deep voice, resounding with mellow trustworthiness. "This is not Nairobi. We are not here to rip you off. If you have a place in mind, we will take you there. Worst case, we carry your luggage. You need only to relax and enjoy Lamu." The owner of that voice was tall, handsome, and confident. His demeanor assured the backpack was safe. He had tranquil eyes, skin the color of a coconut shell, and thick, flowing muscles like those of a running back in American football. The first "chief tout" I ever met, he walked with me empty-handed over sand and spindly grass to a small dock, where we loaded into a fishing boat. The sole purpose of Manda Island appeared to be as a landing strip.

"Can you take me to the Peace Hostel?" I asked the young chief.

"As you wish."

He introduced himself as Jamal, told me he knew a better hotel not far from the water, then paused to stare at my head. "I like the hat you are wearing. Maybe you trade with me?"

"I'm kind of attached to it myself. I'll think about it."

The lesser touts stowed the luggage under the bow of the fishing boat ferry, and we were off, bouncing atop white-caps in a brisk wind. Legendary Lamu Island was in sight—fifteen kilometers away. Dipping my hands into the warm water and smelling the sea, I felt born again.

The boat docked at a bulkhead that framed a honey-colored sidewalk of packed sand, which ran along the waterfront. This sidewalk—in reality, a pedestrian road since there were no cars on the island—provided access to a half-mile of restaurants, textile shops, fisheries, a few dusty, two-story, concrete hotels with aged colonial décor, and a bank that looked like a Spanish hacienda.

The place reminded me of Venice. Water lapped and slapped against the bulkhead and narrow, musk-smelling alleyways connected a medieval maze of dwellings. Except in Lamu, the alleyways were dirt and the dwellings tin-roofed, concrete houses side by side with thatched-roof, mud huts braced with twine. Jamal said the narrowness of the alleys provided shade to cool homes during the blazing heat.

He talked me into booking in at the Brosuis for seven dollars a day. The dark-stained wooden room had a queen-sized, four-poster bed with animal figures carved into the wood, a canopy, and a white mosquito net, which was draped halfway down and tied until bedtime when it could be unfolded to encircle the bed. Three windows gazed dreamily over the quaint town, where coconut palms surrounded tightly knit homes and splotchy-white buildings on the waterfront. The city looked ancient from these windows. Two dhows, fishing boats with oval, billowing sails, rocked in the windy seas, as if they were waving at those onshore.

Back in the vestibule, I tipped Jamal thirty shillings. He motioned once more towards my panama, soiled with the dust of travel. "What about the hat? A trade?"

I had been thinking about his proposal. Maybe it was time to shuck some tired-looking clothes. "Okay, I want one of those long, loose pants with string tying the waist."

"I will meet you tomorrow morning at ten o'clock on the waterfront," he said, "in front of Bush Gardens Restaurant. We will make a trade." Then he walked off with the suppleness of a cat.

In my room, I unpacked, checked my valuables and passport, and counted my money. I loved money. When I was six, I stole dollar bills from my mother's pocketbook and gave them to my unsuspecting grandmother, who patted me on the head and deposited the cash in a bank. With interest, the account grew to twelve dollars over four years.

Dressed in shiny, blue sweatpants, which clashed with my wedding shirt, I donned my panama for the last time and stepped into the narrow streets. The adults dressed quite differently from mainland Africa. Sometimes, I even felt as if I'd walked into an Old Testament flick. Men wore *kanzus*, white, ankle-length tunics, and traditional caps. Although others tucked modern sport shirts into their brightly colored *khangas*. A few fingered prayer beads. Half the female population wore vibrantly colored dresses that almost glowed they were so bright, while the other half were wrapped in black *buibuis*, some with veils. All the kids ran wild.

Towards evening, I scrambled back to the Brosuis, rubbing a welt on my calf. Mosquitoes! I needed to dress in long pants and splash some DEET before dining out. One chomp from the wrong mozzie (as the Australians called them) could send me vomiting to the nearest hospital with high fever and chills. In the worst case, my blood could turn black and I'd require a transfusion.

I was beginning to learn the habits of this pest—and about the malaria parasite it could carry. Mosquitoes make their home in stagnant water, and hunt for blood between four in the afternoon, when the sun cools, until just after daybreak when the heat returns. The female is a flying vampire who uses blood as food and to produce eggs. It finds blood by sensing the carbon dioxide and other organic substances emanating from its victim. Then it lacerates the skin, but its mouthpieces are so fine we often don't know the mosquito is around until it's too late. It gorges on the victim, transfusing blood into an exterior sack reminiscent of a sweet potato.

Worse, species in the genus *Anopheles* are infected by and transmit the villainous malaria parasite during this transfusion process. The parasite matures inside the mosquito, then finds its way into the salivary glands. When the mosquito bites into a subsequent victim, the parasite slithers with the saliva into the innocent veins of the host, and on to the liver. There it quickly reproduces to mount an attack on the red blood cells. I was shocked to learn that three hundred million people a year become infected. Many hundreds of thousands die. Even scarier, the parasite quickly develops an immunity to new drugs.

After dining at a restaurant by the dock, I climbed the four flights to the top-floor patio of the Brosuis. The patio resembled a tenement roof in Brooklyn, high enough to look over the city and quiet enough to sit and ponder life. I rolled a joint. The ganja had been acquired from a suspicious-looking gent in the fading light—enough for one joint, which fit my moderate tendencies. As smoothly as evening turned into night, the ganja melted me into a soothing calm.

I was reading one of Kathi's letters a second time. She reminded me how long I would be gone. A feeling of loneliness arrived. Except for our one-year separation four years before, I'd never been away from home for more than six weeks. Even during our separation home was close. How would distance affect our relationship? We were almost formal to each other when I had the opportunity to call home these days.

Kathi and I were opposites when we met, needing the other to make us whole. She started with perfection and hated conflict. I strove for perfection and thrived on conflict. Nine months after we were married, Shannon arrived, redheaded and sassy. A year and a half later, Chimene, big-eyed and cautious. We were so happy to be married and have our New Age family. Kathi proved an intimate friend—loving and being loved in return. Sleeping with her head on my shoulder added a glorious dimension to life—knowing that at the end of each day I would snuggle up to her sweet scent and warm, soft flesh. It made insecure times earning a living bearable. We promised to love forever. And the longer we were together, the deeper I fell in love. Ten years after the wedding, we walked the beaches of Tahiti like honeymooners, not able to touch each other enough.

I looked out across the city and sea. No streetlights, only the dim rays of waterfront cafes and creeping light from homes. A cat wailed, its voice blending with the whoosh of palms in the wind.

Downstairs, I untied the knot of the mosquito net and climbed into bed, entombed in a cozy but stuffy shroud. I sent "thank you" messages to Kathi across the ether. Thanks for her organization and support for my journey, for her trust and courage, even for the thoughtful gadgets she sent with me. Breathing the night air deeply, I thought how nice it would be to share these experiences with her and the girls. We all love to travel. It was always the four of us and the world.

At half past four in the morning, a magical tropical breeze woke me. Chants from loudspeakers hooked high on the city's main mosque pierced the dawn calm. The experience was charming despite the hour. At six, chants again called the faithful (very faithful, I thought) to prayer. They almost drowned out the roosters' wake-up calls, serenading birds, and rasping sounds from donkeys. Background male voices chanted throughout the city at smaller mosques. This routine was followed five times each day.

The wharf in front of the Bush Gardens Restaurant, a small, thatched-roof eatery that smelled of fried potatoes and samosas, had a gentle busyness. Dhows would dock with their ferried passengers. An old fellow with a massive, flat nose would pick himself up from the wall he sat on to help tote the baggage. Nearby, teenage boys took turns hurling their cinnamon bodies off the wharf into the swirling coral water five feet below. Little, barefoot girls, with white and purple dresses and close-cropped hair, grabbed their skirts and wiggled in anticipation each time one of the young men revved his arms and legs for the plunge.

"I take you on tour of Lamu," offered a man, who had also been observing the action. "Show you everything. Very cheap!"

Why not? We made tentative plans. When the guy left, the old fellow summoned me to the bulwark with a jerk of his head. He bent towards me and said in kind of a growl: "Do not go with that man. He is no good."

Just then Jamal showed up dressed in sandals, slacks, and a bright yellow shirt rolled to the elbows. Speaking with control and influence, the chief tout exchanged a few words with the old man. Jamal motioned me to follow. "Say *jambo* to Mr. Bill Clinton," the old man yelled in parting.

Once we were on the sandy street by the shops, Jamal confided with an air of finality: "The old man is right about Arif who offered to show you Lamu. Let me tell you a story. Last month, a rich Italian bought heroin from Arif at a bargain price. However, Arif turned the Italian into the police. A person could get twenty years in jail for possessing heroin. Instead the Italian paid 40,000 shillings, nearly five hundred dollars, as a bribe, and Arif got his heroin back as part of the deal. He is no good. Now, the hat...."

Passing a scattering of locals and a few tourists, I asked him how his English got to be so good. "I have a Dutch girlfriend. I visit her in the Netherlands, so I must speak proper English to communicate."

"That's a long way to go to see your girlfriend. What about the local women?"

"They are Muslim girls. If you want to raise a family, you marry a Muslim woman. European women are much more liberal, and to my liking. We talk about lots of things. She visits me three times a year. Come, pick out your pants."

We turned into one of several huddled-together waterfront shops, where Jamal whispered something in the ear of the shopkeeper. He came over to where I was fumbling through clothes and picked out a pair of pants resembling pajamas. They were made of blue cloth and had vertical, yellow streaks and white stripes. No money exchanged hands.

"You do not have to pay for the pants," he said. "It is taken care of."

Strolling off with the panama on his head, he seemed to have everyone in his hip pocket. Local boy with charm makes good.

By now, the lively Zambian music and smell of shellfish were enticing me inside the Bush Gardens Restaurant. Wicker lamps dangled above tables with bright orange tablecloths. I ate shrimp curry and sucked a mango shake as people sauntered—what a silky smooth body the mixture of African, Arab, and Indian produced. A full-size cat, no bigger than a starved rat, jumped up on the chair next to me, put its paws on the table and stared with iridescent, hungry eyes. Sensing no objection, it inched across the table, gaining confidence with each step. It shot me one last glance before pigging out on the remains of lunch. I didn't mind. The cat was so thin a strong wind could blow it away. In fact, if you weighed all the cats in Lamu, they probably wouldn't total one donkey.

And donkeys were everywhere. When off duty from their role as beasts of burden, the vast population of these hacking and wheezing creatures foraged for discarded garbage in dusty passageways—competing with the cats, goats, and chickens. Next to a drainage canal in the street, one donkey ate soot from an old fire and another chowed down on fruit peelings thrown between two wooden handcarts.

Donkeys knew protocol. They knew if they walked in the way of a human they got whacked with a thin whipping-stick made from a tree branch. When a human was in their path, they cast down sad eyes. Their demeanor reeked of insecurity. They stopped moving to get a sense of the tormentor's direction, so they could get the hell out of the way. Females were lowest on the totem pole, the males would take out their inferiority complexes by biting and kicking them. The only solace a female had was the jerky-rough suckling of her young. Though often a nursing mother, little one hanging on her teat, couldn't get out of the way of a teenage boy quick enough before she and the little one got whacked in the face. Men and boys were equally tough on donkeys.

In the maze behind the waterfront, hordes of barefoot children played an endless variety of games with sticks, stones, yarn balls, and bottles. They stopped and stared at me. Then began to giggle, exposing snow-white teeth.

"*Jambo.*"

"*Habare?*" I answered with the Swahili for "how are you."

"*Habare!* Ha ha, hee hee," they teased, as if a *mzungu* is not supposed to know even the most elementary of terms. "*Mzuri sana* (very good)," they squealed,

The ladies of the maze dickered with merchants, or chatted together. Some retreated inside dark, utilitarian homes as I approached. Those wearing veils covered their faces when I approached, like turtles hiding in their shells. When the eyes above the masks smiled, it was enchanting. After an hour or so of wandering, I came to the town's biggest mosque, which was being renovated to add a second floor. A small man, with a thin mustache and thin lips, took it upon himself to show me the interior, which was void of silver and gold, just circular walls, large stone columns to hold the place up, and a ceiling of mortar.

"We build a new addition upstairs for women to worship," he said in a friendly way.

"Why?" I asked.

"This will make them more faithful."

"How come they don't worship like the men?"

He explained that Muhammad exempted women from going to the mosque because the job of taking care of many children never ended.

Lamu was not unlike the world of the eland—extended family living close together, but men and women hanging out separately. I was told in Zimbabwe that in some tribes it is believed that a man living close to a woman for too long begins to atrophy. Back home, men and women hung out together in consensual partnerships, but clung to Old World ideas of ownership that left little room for mistakes. The result was if we did make a mistake, we were then exempted from the "lifetime commitment."

Snaking around Lamu for miles, I emerged into wide-open spaces with soccer and volleyball fields, and ... wait ... a basketball court and bouncing ball.

There's no game like b-ball. Leaving the ground for the air, the feel of the ball rolling off your fingers after calculating the arc and distance, returning to earth and watching the ball's trajectory. Will it or won't it? At twelve years old, I took Reynolds aluminum wrap, rolled it up into a ball, and shot into a wastepaper basket for hours. Sometimes I'd be a New York Knick or better, a Celtic. "Two seconds left, Hickey spins towards the basket. He shoots ... it's good!" As I got older and played in real games, I always knew that if I got the last shot, I could make it.

Here was a full court. Thin asphalt sprinkled with clumps of grass and ruts, rusted hoops, and no nets, but, hey, it was heaven! Four locals in their early teens, looking like skinny shot-putters, wildly chucked a pathetic ball, before the first team showed up—complete with a hotshot.

"Where you from?" the hotshot asked.

"America."

"America! President Clean-ton!" squealed a lanky bloke. "Michael Jordon!" shouted a skinny six-footer with a coal-black face and deep inset eyes, who tried unsuccessfully to slam-dunk. That precipitated a pre-game slam dunk contest. After a buzz of jabbering and finger-pointing, one of the players walked slowly to the sidelines and placed a palm leaf over my camera so no one would steal it. One of the dudes handed me the ball and the game was on.

The guys had good inside games and ran up and down the court barefoot with the ball sticking to their fingers. Still, the only shots that drained from the outside rolled off my fingertips. They teased and jabbered in a language I couldn't understand, but it didn't matter because we were just a bunch guys playing with a ball.

When I had the stamina to play defense or grab a rebound, I got respect, as if Michael Jordon made all Americans look good. Respect from everyone except the hotshot—cocky, round-faced Magic Junior. He taunted me with his smile and the ball as he juked around me easily on his way to basket. Two games to fifteen points spawned a refreshing competitive camaraderie that ended in handshakes and friendly pats.

After the basketball, I felt more a part of the fabric of Lamu.

24

ALI HIPPY

O N THE WAY HOME, ALI Hippy found me. Ali acquired his name hanging around American hippies during the early Seventies. He still drifted through the streets looking for *mzungus* to invite to dinner and sample local culture. "We eat at seven o'clock," he instructed in an effeminate voice housed within a more than ample body. "Go down two streets from the Brosuis and turn right at the carpet shop. My house is the third on the right. I always look forward to having friends for dinner." He also mentioned a 350 shilling contribution.

With a couple of hours to kill, I washed clothes and hung them to dry on the windowsill, then showered under a spray hooked over the toilet. I found cold water hard to get used to regardless of the heat outside. In the late afternoon sun, I climbed the stairs to the roof to sew a tear in my new pants. As a kid I sewed and ironed because my mother had enough to do raising five children and working full time as a nurse. Mom was small and sweet, with a strong inner lining that she needed with my father and brothers' history of mental disease. My mom was always proud of me. She disliked conflict, so she rarely disciplined me as a kid. We were comrades, really, with my father as our common nemesis.

I thought of my natal family more than ever these days. That was the thing about traveling—time to reminisce and put life in perspective.

Once a person with aging eyes overcomes the frustration of guiding thread through the itsy-bitsy eye of a needle, sewing becomes relaxing. After stitching the pants, I proudly stretched the finished product, feeling its renewed strength.

Standing in an alley in a good mood, I knocked on the rickety door of Ali Hippy's house. Wearing a white floor-length tunic and looking like a chubby Buddha, he warmly welcomed me, and took me immediately to the dining room. Lavish it was not. The room was barely big enough to fit a mid-sized American car. Furniture consisted of thin palm-leaf mats on the floor and the walls were chipped and rutted, as if they hadn't been painted since the Fifties. As we sat cross-legged in a circle on the mats, washing our hands in wooden bowls, Ali introduced the guests to one another: a young, gregarious, crew-cut American from Tucson, an Australian, two German women from Cologne, and me.

"I'm so happy to have you here," Ali gushed. "Since 1972 my family and I have prepared this feast once a week for guests that want to visit a Muslim home. We will start with crab samosas, then coconut rice and grouper fish. Also I purchased lobster at the market for your pleasure tonight. After you dine, my family and I would be pleased to entertain you." He left to get the food.

Ali explained each dish he served. The food was washed down with lemonade. No alcohol. I'd been able to drink water out of the tap, so I took a chance on the lemonade. During the meal, an assortment of family members trooped in and out of a dark adjoining room, where the food was prepared on a small kerosene stove. Meanwhile, we travelers discussed bad roads, wheels falling off cars, buses tipping over, policemen directing traffic around the mutilated bodies of cows or thieves—the normal stuff.

The taller of the two German women, in her late twenties, told of crossing Uganda to see gorillas in Rwanda. "Guida and I traveled through Uganda and climbed difficult jungle trails through mountains to see them. It was an incredible experience, I was almost, how do you say, mangled by a one hundred and eighty-kilogram silverback who thought I was getting too friendly with one of the younger apes. It felt so intimate being with these magnificent animals. They seemed so human."

Danny, the Australian, told of an attack by a black cobra while driving across the Kalahari. "The cheeky bugger refused to give up its position on the road and rose straight up in the air, like the garbage-bin monster in *Star Wars*. It crawled on the bonnet to the windscreen and challenged us with cold eyes and fangs. Then, like lightning, the cobra struck the glass to try to get at us."

After reverential oohs, the feisty American chirped in: "It's good you're leaving on the early bus, the Somalis don't attack early." Somalia, forty miles away on the northern border, was in the midst of a vicious civil war, which included attacking the United Nations force sent to restore peace.

"What?" Danny twitched visibly, and swallowed his coconut ice hard.

"It's probably nothing to worry about," I added. "This guy Jamal told me that in the last several months Somalis have been raiding tourist buses coming out of Lamu. They're after valuables. He said lately Kenyan police with submachine guns ride the buses."

Danny's face flushed. The American from Tucson decided to have more fun.

"A lot of good they do. Police know they're outnumbered by the Somalis, so they stay inside the buses."

Guida added a somber note: "I heard that two months ago they took an African woman off the bus, raped her, and left her by the side of the road at night where a hyena chewed her leg off."

"Don't worry about it, Danny," I said. "Jamal also said they don't attack early buses!" I wasn't worried. I had a ticket to fly.

Ali waddled in with dessert, and caught the end of the conversation. "If they attack, the Somalis treat whites with respect. The Kenyan government would go ape if their tourist trade was threatened." He smiled at the word "ape," a leftover from his hippie days no doubt.

We devoured a cookie that looked like a cake, while Ali's tall, lean, elegant-looking spouse cleared the table. By now I had surmised there were four stingy rooms in the house and counted at least nine other people going in and out of the room with the kerosene stove.

After dessert, Ali, holding a Coca-Cola bottle and a stick, hitched up his white tunic and dropped on to the palm mats. Three sons and a daughter, ranging from four to thirteen, followed him into the room carrying a ratty assortment of five-gallon plastic containers and wooden boxes they used as drums. Together they drummed and sang. Ali rolled his jowls to a smile, translating each song as the five musicians pounded, tapped, and shook. The four-year-old drummer stole the show, while Ali's wife watched from the periphery of the room, swaying fluidly to the beat without moving her feet.

For a week, I traveled in Lamu, exploring the city and its deserted northern beaches. Got heaps of *jambos* from locals, but had a hard time making eye contact with whites. They avoided looking directly, as if it would place a curse on their souls. Young Western women stayed as close to their guys as leaves to a tree, often hanging behind and letting the men make social contact. Traveling alone, I had the opportunity to study couples. Western partners were chained body and soul to each other, and the older they got, the stronger the chain. Africans, around since the dawn of civilization, didn't appear to be coupled at all.

The morning I was to leave Lamu, I was picking at a last salad of mangos, pineapples, passion fruit, and bananas at a sweet little garden restaurant. At the next wicker table, two Englishwomen in their early thirties were engaged in an animated conversation about their boyfriends.

"So how are you and your boyfriend doing lately?" said a pert blond slurping a banana milkshake and staring attentively into the pained hazel eyes of her friend.

"I think it's hopeless. He just doesn't get it. He interrupts me when I speak, droning on and on with that absolute 'air of authority and trustee of all knowledge' attitude that men have. 'You should do this, you shouldn't do that.' He overpowers me and I hate it."

"My boyfriend is the same way, always giving me advice, always right, always knows more than me, always educating."

"Men are so arrogant," Ms. Hazel Eyes agreed, wiping a dribble of mango off her chin. "We're not going to make it. I'm breaking it off. I don't need anyone leading me around by the nose. And I'm tired of always having to argue a point, like we're competitors in a football game, but I'm the one getting kicked! I give up and tune him out."

I saw elements of myself in those guys.

In the boat to Manda Island, on the way to catch a plane to Mombasa and then to Zanzibar, I sat next to a deeply tanned but tired-looking white doctor returning to the United States after three years treating pediatric AIDS in Uganda. I had heard so much about the disease eating Africa alive, but hadn't noticed the bite marks on people in the streets. What was the reality?

"It's not good," she said. "I'd say AIDS has infected thirty percent in the cities, but is lower in the rural areas, probably around ten percent. The worst is along truck routes from Kampala to Mombasa. Almost all the prostitutes along these routes have AIDS."

I asked her what she did to alleviate the disease.

"We treat it and try to prevent it. Our program examined women for AIDS before and after they got married." She sighed. "But the vast majority never came back for results."

"Why?"

"Their husbands wouldn't let them. They didn't want to know." She said that after three years in Africa, she questioned putting funds into medical advances to keep everyone alive, only to have them starve instead of dying at birth. She said the money would be better spent educating women to solve the problems. "There's a saying here in Africa: 'If you want something done, entrust the job to a woman.'"

While my luggage was being weighed in Manda, on what looked like a reinforced butcher's scale, I reflected on the two philosophically linked concepts my trip so far had brought up. How the emphasis on *families* in the Old World had changed to emphasis on *individuals* in the New World, and how that impacted the treatment of women. I admired the way most men in my world adjusted to the changed roles between men and women during my lifetime. And I couldn't help but notice that I was morphing from an unemployed patriarch to an integrated individual spreading my wings within a family unit.

ZANZIBAR

THE NUMBER

25

MONEY—HOW MUCH IS ENOUGH?

F LIGHT 642 DEPARTING MOMBASA FOR Zanzibar at 3:45 p.m. was late. Sitting on a vinyl chair at the single gate where all flights boarded, along with thirty or so other passengers, I watched as the ground crew guided our plane along the runway the way handlers would walk a crippled racehorse off the track. From the way the crew carefully followed and studied the plane, I deduced mechanical problems. An informative announcement, in English and Swahili, came over the public address loudspeakers: "Information update on Flight 642 ... Next information at 4:30."

Did I miss something? Some shred of explanation about why the plane taxied around the runway, then parked sixty yards from us? We all watched the jet and ground crew. Anxiety hung heavy in the air. How safe are airplanes in Africa? That was the question taxiing around my mind. At 4:30, there was a new announcement: "Information update on Flight 642 ... Next information at 5:00."

I had reading material. The front page of the Tanzania *Daily News* proclaimed, "NAM TACKLES DEBT CRISIS—Debt among the 108-Member Group Soars to $1.4 Trillion." The gist of the article was that NAM (the Non-Aligned Movement of developing countries) wanted Western banks, represented by the International Monetary Fund, to forgo a portion of NAM debt in recognition of the obvious fact that it could never pay the full amount back. Western bankers wanted to reschedule payments. The article claimed the debt had doubled in twelve years, and pointed out Nigeria as an example of repayment futility. It would take half of Nigeria's foreign currency earnings to pay its $30 billion yearly debt service. That's roughly equivalent to a business shelling out fifty percent of its sales to repay a bank loan. The situation sounded like a typical troubled company wanting relief from debt on their terms, and a typical banker keeping pressure for repayment as a lever to get changes made. Tanzania was the third straight African country I'd been in where the IMF dominated headlines.

> "Information update on Flight 642 …
> Next information at 5:30."

Similar updates arrived every half-hour until we boarded at 7:30.

The IMF is a United Nations-affiliated organization that normally lends money to promote international trade. It also bails out countries that cannot pay international loans because they had exhausted their foreign currency reserves. Loans from the IMF often buy time to avoid an abrupt halt to imports. Some people said the loans were humanitarian, others said they were protection for Western banks from losses on bad loans, and still others said they were a way to put a country in your hip pocket.

As fate would have it, an expert on the subject sat in the aisle seat next to me. Kevin, a serious, bird-faced American, was a Ph.D. candidate in anthropology and economics at Nairobi University. These dual doctorates made sense, given how societies and economics were so intertwined. How would it be possible to separate "socio" from "economics" and make sense of this world? Nervously rubbing his pockmarked face, Kevin described to me the current evolution of the Western family.

"Anthropologically speaking," he said, "The US will have great problems because older people are not integrated into the mainstream of life. On the one hand, younger people have little respect for the wisdom of age, unlike Africans. So they don't listen to advice and make big mistakes. For instance, witness how people are slaves to credit cards! On the other hand, old people form a strong economic block that simply does not want to pay taxes. They have wealth and voting power, but don't live with young people as they do here. Naturally, spending money for education or fixing the decay in society has a lower priority than medical benefits."

"What can be done?" I asked. However, the conversation paused before Kevin could answer. The engines were revving for takeoff. I was sure he was thinking the same as me: whatever caused the big delay to this plane might still be broken. Somehow closing my eyes mitigated the sense of risk.

"It's airborne," Kevin quipped. "Back to your question, the only way to fix the problem is to integrate society again, to have the community working together."

"Has this integration helped Africa?" I asked.

"In former times, it most certainly did. But things are changing."

I used this opportunity to mention the pervasiveness of the IMF in the papers, and asked if it was a major force in the change. That set him off complaining about the IMF's parent, the United Nations. "It wasted money earmarked for developing countries on the dreams of tyrants. Programs didn't have clear objectives or systems to monitor money, so the tyrants like Mugabe in Zimbabwe pocketed the loot."

"The IMF seems to be a control mechanism," I opined, "to nudge the world into a market economy."

"It's a bank," he said. "It lends money and wants to be paid back—with interest. Meanwhile debt eats away at social programs. Do you know that as a condition for rescheduling debt repayment, the IMF makes 'structural adjustments' that are disproportionately borne by the poor? Through school fees and charges for basic health … things like that. Then school attendance drops, especially for girls, because families can't afford the fees. Debt is a new form of slavery."

I considered the control money and banks have over our lives. In the Eighties, US banks created a mess from their zeal to lend outrageous sums to real estate, leveraged buyouts (LBOs), and foreign countries. The Federal Reserve System, owned by a consortium of banks, bailed out ailing members when they got in trouble by lowering the cost of money to them. The upshot was security-minded investors like my mom watched their interest income from certificates of deposit (CDs) drop 70 percent, since Fed interest rates determine CD pricing. Who pocketed the 70 percent? Banks who increased their margins by lending the cheap cash, gotten from the Fed (read "the people") and security-minded investors, and the very borrowers that caused the problem. The latter received reduced interest rates on their borrowings. Everyone benefited but loyal investors such as Mom. Then the banks made a killing raising, instead of lowering, interest rates on credit cards. The entire interest rate wealth transfer was staggering. And few ever knew. Because money has its own language and culture that the average person finds too tedious and confusing to learn.

"As I understand it," I said, "A market economy means freedom to buy and sell without government interference—"

"And for the consumer," he interrupted, "freedom to borrow money. Credit cards drive the West, and the IMF the rest." The comment came across like a slogan.

"What's so wrong with conversion to a new culture run by big money? Isn't it better than African tribal lords?"

"Well," he said, "what's the long-term purpose of loans that get poor people further into debt?"

"Maybe there's a silver lining. The IMF also pressures countries to lower their birth rate and to have a democratic government. Maybe pressure of this magnitude is necessary. Our culture dropped the birth rate from four children in a family to two in less than forty years. And it worked wonders for female equality, because with fewer kids women could choose a career. Besides, what's the alternative? How can poor countries compete without learning the new culture?"

"At what price? Africans running to catch buses? They may be poor, but 'poor' doesn't have the same connotation in Africa as in the United States, where expectations cause tension and advertising makes us feel so inadequate. It makes you wonder how much a society needs. I mean, how much is enough?"

Descent was such a relief. Kevin's final question had been tugging at me for many years. It hung in the air as we filed out of the plane, happy to be on African soil again. How much is enough?

Guarding the northeast coast of Tanzania in the Indian Ocean, Zanzibar was fifteen miles off the coast of Tanzania. Actually

Zanzibar was an archipelago with two major islands: Unguja (the main island, informally referred to as "Zanzibar"), and Pemba. Zanzibar was once a separate state with a long trading history within the Arab world. It united with Tanganyika to form Tanzania, and still enjoyed a high degree of autonomy within the union. As an important source of cloves, nutmeg, cinnamon, and pepper, it was formerly known as the Spice Islands (although the term was also used to refer to other archipelagos, notably in Indonesia). Zanzibar (the island I landed on) was about fifty miles long and twenty miles wide.

I negotiated a taxi to take me to the southwest side of Zanzibar, to the Kibwni Beach Villa. The driver wound his way through Zanzibar City's labyrinth of narrow, winding streets crowded with age-blackened stone houses, shops, colonial-style buildings, and markets. Dr. James Christie described Zanzibar in 1869 as "a closely packed, reeking suffocation of dirt-caked stone and coral-lime houses, whose open drains, abundant night-soil and busy vermin help erase any image of oriental glamour." At first glance, his rather pessimistic description was still accurate. However, just over a mile outside of town, we came to the clean Kibwni—a block from the ocean, near a naval base housing a collection of World War II PT boats rusting on a pearl-white beach.

The hotel fit neatly into my spending pattern of $20 a day for accommodation and meals. My room sported a bed with a mosquito net, wooden floors, and an overhead fan the size of one of the PT boats' propellers. The kind of fan you'd see in a dimly lit bar in a 1940s South Seas movie with Humphrey Bogart.

After dinning on octopus in a little gazebo in back of the Kibwni, I shared tea and kibitzed with Ramesh, the rather thin and fiery Indian proprietor, and his reflective friend Nadim, a political science professor in Dar es Salaam, the chief port and former capital of Tanzania, across from Zanzibar on the mainland. Apparently, it was my day to meet educators. Nadim's face was black and round as a cannonball. He and Ramesh were the average height of most of the men I'd met in Africa, about five-seven.

The tea tasted refreshing after the long day of travel. It was a typical tropical night with a slight breeze blowing in from the sea. A mosquito hunted for veins as we talked, so I covered my feet with the orange *khanga* I picked up in Kenya.

Nadim asked the stock visitor question. "Now that you have traveled around Africa for a while, Denis, what feelings do you have?"

Rather than spew off a quick response, I reflected. How do I feel? Let's see....

"I feel slow and totally relaxed and close to nature," I replied, "like there was all the time in the world. People make me want to smile. I feel curious about everything. And I have time on my side."

We proceeded to inquire about the status of each other's families, which constituted the standard chitchat in the Third World. However, I wanted to continue my education about Africa's socio-economics, so I used the NAM article as bait.

Nadim scratched his mustache at the mention of NAM, and then folded his arms. "Tanzania is a blueprint for what happens when human industrialization and progressive ideology clash with raw nature. The West made us dependent on their products, and now we will always be in their debt." He clasped his hands with an air of professional intelligence.

Ramesh carefully rolled a cigarette. "The West came here to exploit Africa. So what is new?" he argued comfortably. "All societies are domineering in their way. We need to go forward."

Touching Ramesh's arm with a pudgy, gold-ringed finger, Nadim responded: "How? We would have to change our entire culture to be competitive. Hot climates are not conducive to working hard or planning the future like Western climates where they need to plan for the winter." He sipped tea, and then returned the cup to its plate. "In former times an African put his finger in the ground and pulled out something growing on it. He had no need to plan. Planning and organizational skills are cold climate necessities. Since organization skills create industry, it is a given that Africa will always be behind industrially. Which leaves us agriculture. If we were to automate agriculture, three-quarters of the population would be out of work. So how can we compete and go forward in a way that will reduce our debt? We are buying Western culture without the means to pay for it."

Frowning, Ramesh motioned to his wife, who had just arrived with a teapot, to refill our cups. While she poured, he said: "India has the same climate and they compete. Africans have to learn how."

"When I was in Kenya, I noticed that Indians seem to control many of the businesses there," I said. "Why is that?"

"Maybe it is because India had more people and less abundance," Nadim answered. "Possibly the more ambitious were willing to go elsewhere to find prosperity."

Ramesh scoffed. "India has better universities. Most important, women budget money and teach the young its language. First the language, then control."

After tea, I walked to my room under a sky packed with glittering stars. A dog barked somewhere across the wind. Tucked under a sheet in bed, the whir of the fan above, I watched my mind's video play scattered scenes from my childhood.

My parents had five kids. They both worked, and they argued about money because there was never anything leftover from their paychecks. Once my father bought seventy chicks to save money on chicken. What a mess! We ate oleo and dad froze bread he picked up at a discount from the Wonder Bread factory in Queens. I remembered plastering old-fashioned peanut butter on thawed bread trying not to rip the slice, then searching through brown A&P stamped shopping bags to find one without stains. At school, my bag didn't contain the soft white sandwiches and treats like Dickey Fisher's metal lunch-box. Instead, I pulled out a peanut-butter sandwich discolored by grape jelly. On Halloween, we all went to the rich man's house with an engraved door because he gave great treats. As an eight-year-old, I dallied on his front lawn. I tiptoed to peek through the window at leather chairs and a big television screen, thinking some day I would live in a house like his and never eat oleo or freezer bread again. That could be when I started thinking about a "number"—a target to aspire to, a means to measure, plan, and control money.

I wanted to be someone and money was the prerequisite. It was an indelible desire—like that for a great family. I attributed the drive for wealth to the cash-strapped reality I grew up in. Sure you could be happy with nothing, I reasoned, but I didn't know anyone poor that *was* happy. The number in mind was big enough to drive my vision.

By twenty, my desire for family, money, and personal freedom had through methodical processes evolved into my dream: *a great family and enough money so that no one could pull my strings.* I tucked away my strengths in the core of my being. And with these qualities firmly in place, I could look at the changes in my character needed to achieve the future I desired. Weaknesses were targets to improve.

I told myself that money wouldn't control me. Instead it would frame the construction of my great family and down the pike buy the freedom rattling deep inside. But I never considered, until well into my thirties, how the freedom I knew from going out on my old blue boat on Senix Creek might clash severely with the constant demands of family and the rigors of attaining wealth. This conflict eventually exposed a vigorous struggle for balance between two distinct personalities within me: the ultra-responsible *controller* who drove hard to grow a great family and make money, and the *traveler* who wanted no responsibility and precious few strings.

26

NEAR FATAL ACCIDENT

T
HE CRAMPS ATTACKED ME THE second day in Zanzibar. It could have been the sugar cane ice drink. Who knows? I stayed in bed, a novelty for a guy rarely sick enough to miss work. The next day, cramps and all, I hired a small motorboat and a guide to take me a few kilometers east of Zanzibar to Changuu or "Prison" Island. In the mid-nineteenth century, Zanzibar's sultan, who controlled much of the slave and spice trade on the coast, gave the island to Arab slavers to store their recalcitrant "property" in grimy concrete holding pens. Slaves were purchased from tribes in Africa's interior, and force-marched to the coast, chains tugging and clanking around their heads and feet. They dumped the dead along the way like so much garbage. Fifty thousand slaves transferred hands each year in the markets of Zanzibar.

On Prison Island (named not after the imprisoned slaves but for its unused jail built later by the British), the "pens" had four or five bunks on top of each other. Scrutinizing graffiti on the walls, I imagined the fear these cramped people must have known inside, so unlike their homeland that seemingly stretched forever.

Although slaves from Zanzibar were never destined for the United States, I couldn't help but think about how elsewhere ethnic groups that didn't want to go to North America wound up working there for free, and now languished in ghettos. If you accumulated all the unpaid wages (and interest on those wages) of slaves, the numbers would stagger the imagination.

I toured the island alone, watching three-foot-long giant turtles creep through patches of grass and sand, sidestepping their own droppings, which were as big as howitzer shells. I snorkeled alone in the pristine waters, trying out a European-style bikini bathing suit. The upset stomach lingered, plus, I burned the lower third of my butt using the new suit! The extent of this scorched derriere became painfully apparent the next day when I took a taxi the thirty-seven kilometers to the Tamarind Hotel on the west side of Zanzibar. The plan was that the driver would stay overnight in the car and drive me back the next day. Thirty-seven kilometers didn't seem that far.

The trip started poorly: the driver's age. Hamadi couldn't yet have reached his twentieth birthday, which, as I already knew, meant fast *and* reckless. Hand on horn and foot to the pedal, he spent the first ten kilometers of smooth road making sure pedestrians, animals, and bikers understood Africa's law of the road: *biggest is boss.*

Suddenly, it got much worse. A scrawny old man in tattered clothes walked out in front of us. My foot jammed an imaginary brake, but the car continued to barrel forward. Jesus! My body jerked back involuntarily, but it made no difference. bam! We hit him. As our car sped forward, I turned around and saw the old man using his hands to drag his right leg to the other side of the road. He barely avoided colliding with a motor scooter. Except for the leg, he looked okay. I hoped.

"Are you crazy?" I screamed at Hamadi. "You hit him. Stop the car!" His sandals pressed the gas pedal harder and his right hand grasped the gearshift between us. He didn't speak English. The words of Don, the Peace Corps volunteer in Ssese flashed in my head: " ... the truck was too far away from the scene to go back. I still don't know what was right. Africa is such a trip. It's not like a normal world."

What was normal? How could I help the old man?

Hamadi pounded the steering wheel, letting out a string of what I took to be expletives in agreement with my anguish and alarm. The car sped on, however. And then he glanced over at me, shrugging, sneering, and pointing backwards in the direction of the old man. His body language read: "You're right! The asshole hit himself by not moving faster, and probably dented the car."

We hurtled along the outskirts of town at ninety kilometers an hour, bobbing and weaving around people, trucks, and dogs. I pumped my hands and feet, pointing towards the pedals and screaming: "brake! slow down!" Apparently, driving a car here was a substitute for the traditional puberty ritual of hunting lions.

Finally he reduced speed, but only after I pointed to the gas pedal, then over at my foot releasing pressure on its imaginary equal. I exhaled heavily, falling back against the seat to rest. But my mind wouldn't rest. Why had I justified leaving the scene of the accident? Was it because the old man could walk? Or because I didn't want to get involved in a foreign country I knew little about?

I was shaken out of my thoughts. Literally. We had entered the crater zone. Massive potholes that looked like malcontented locals had set off dynamite charges at irregular intervals to dissuade vehicles. It got worse. Pouring rain blurred the windshield and filled the holes. We were back to swerving and weaving, but this time at a crawl. As the adrenalin eased, I began to notice the full effects of the bathing suit mistake. Each swerve rubbed my lobster-red flesh against the rough seat.

The rain subsided and the weather became clammy-humid. The air smelled of burning leaves and the engine roared each time the taxi slammed a crater. Colors outside the vehicle were vibrant and people ubiquitous.

Standing in streams, riding bikes, selling coconuts, pineapples, and papayas, crowded in the back of trucks, or packed in cars, peeing by the road, or just standing doing nothing. Women wrapped in cotton *khangas* of brilliant pastels carried babies on their backs. Kids without pants stared at us, as did shirtless men wearing kaffiyehs and carrying water and palms. People laughed easily as they talked and walked outside their huts.

We passed swamps and jungles filled with coca-palms, mango, almond, and baobab trees. We saw red monkeys, fields with cows and chickens, and beautiful birds. A woman unhooked what looked like a half-foot millipede from a gazebo latticed with sticks. Cows chewed in garbage heaps. Nobody wore shoes.

Then, we reached heaven—the secluded, classy, and empty Tamarind Beach Hotel. How did it survive? Who else would brave the journey to get here? A restaurant, a bar, and single-bedroom cottages dotted a sandy pathway through Bermuda grass. At the far edge of the grass, palm trees, whose graceful trunks resembled necks of giraffes, projected their shadows on to a narrow strip of unspoiled golden beach.

At night, under a thatched roof, the bartender and I played bao, a game vaguely like backgammon, except there were no dice and the object was to capture the other person's beans. "You sure you never play before?" he asked after three or four games.

This diversion kept me from dwelling on my burned ass, cramps, a headache, and diarrhea. And the old man we hit. I almost forgot him. I still didn't know what to think. Did the years of filled calendars and business crises leave me so callous? Or did traveling this way create such a sensory absorption that as one experience ended, another immediately began and the previous one was quickly pushed into the recesses of memory?

Early the next morning, as I wandered along the beach, squishing fine, soft sand between my toes, my mind returned to the question that had been with me most of my life: How much money is enough? The rich man's house was a distant memory by the time I received an MBA and was walking a high wire between two ambitions—family and wealth. At twenty-two, my belief was that I would run a major American company before turning forty. That self-belief made interviewing for a job easy—ambition is electric. However, I soon realized I didn't have the talent or social background to reach this business objective and enjoy my growing family at the same time. I chose family as the priority, although ambition and money crowded it. It wasn't the money so much, as what it represented: the chance to be my own person out there in the future.

Miniature white crabs, with bulging eyes jacked up like dual periscopes, scampered in and out of bubble-size holes along the beach. The smell of ocean had been so much a part of the early years of my marriage.

Kathi and I had agreed that it made sense for her to stay home with the kids the first two years. My salary was all we had, so I began working the *number*. A register in my brain tracked cash inflows and outflows—in the present and the future. But four years into my career, I lost my job in New York City. It was a terrible shock. How would I ever reach my dream? Kathi always wanted to go to California, so we sold almost everything in our apartment and packed a small U-Haul attached to the reinforced rear-end of our Datsun station wagon. Friends thought we were crazy, that we were ruining the almighty career path by taking such a risk. With the girls bundled in the back seat and twenty weeks of living expenses in the bank, we headed west. We traveled and visited friends across the country for four months, then through a quirk of fate, temporarily settled on the Long Beach Peninsula along the Pacific coast of Washington, living in an old colonial house a block from the ocean.

Winds blew hard along the Long Beach Peninsula, the air laden with tidal smells and drizzle. A sunny day appeared as often as Santa Claus. Fate made me, at twenty-six, a general manager of a small oyster farming and fish-processing company there. The owner of the business was a shellfish scientist who spent the company into trouble establishing aquaculture on the west coast because he was frustrated relying on nature to provide a natural set of oysters each year. He set up an oyster hatchery in California and a nursery in Washington. When I arrived the oysters had been transported to bobbing rafts in unpredictable Willapa Bay. Jack hired me to get him out of harm's way. He disrespected money and ignored its culture, throwing cash at projects as if it was his slave. His strength was working on the bay at his passion, wearing plaid, woolen shirts underneath a rubber suit and contemplating God. I loved Jack.

With an understanding of the language of money, it is possible to tell a story of the past or create a narrative for the future. For instance, while reviewing monthly bank statements, I noticed something fishy was going on—higher-than-normal interest charges. I sifted back through five years of statements, uncovering and documenting the story of our sales agent in Seattle. He had been borrowing from Jack's bank using the company's inventory as collateral, then investing the borrowings in his own side business. Jack's company had been paying interest on these side borrowings for years. Your basic embezzlement. I copied supporting documents, met with our lawyers to determine legal claims and dangers, and drove two hundred miles to Seattle to meet with this agent.

Facing each other across his desk, the agent and I exchanged pleasantries for a while. He was a big man, must have weighed two hundred and fifty pounds. Pleasantries finished, I tossed the bundle of documents towards him, explaining their meaning before demanding reimbursement. Above the plane of the desk my demeanor was cool, but below my knees quivered from fright. You never quite know if you have a person's balls in your hands. He looked angry enough to leap across the desk and kick the shit out of me. He screamed: "Who the hell are you to accuse me?" But I noticed the dew of perspiration building on his forehead. He was caught. I walked out of his office with enough settlement money to keep Jack's company afloat and change its future narrative.

The time spent running that small company matured in me the sense that "how much was enough" was a changing reality, limited only by desire and confidence. More subtly, the journey to Washington itself taught me that my family could be happy and live an exciting life with very little money. On the warm sands of Zanzibar with the tropical wind blowing through my hair, I again felt that security for family while at the same time living on little was a real possibility.

The nice thing about being able to afford all modes of transportation was the opportunity to meet people in every stratum of society to attain a balanced view of a country. Flying back to Nairobi, for instance, I chatted with a soft-spoken insurance adjuster with a build like Woody Allen. He managed the Nairobi branch of a large European company.

"What you need to remember in Kenya," he told me, "is that economic decline brings crime. The government from top to bottom is corrupt. For example, when I asked for an estimate from three construction companies to repair a damaged building, they first consulted the local politician to see who was in line for the job. The bloody politician grants the business license, receiving for his effort a percentage of the construction cost and whatever else he can wring in bribes. The estimates are rigged accordingly."

Relaxed and feeling generous in the turboprop, I bought the guy a beer and listened while he vented his anger about one of his English supervisors that thought Africans were beneath him. "When I think of what our secretaries and adjusters get paid and have to take his crap, it infuriates me. The locals here struggle to get medical care and put their kids through school."

He was equally unhappy about how unsafe it was living in Africa. The superpowers dumped untold amounts of arms in Africa. "The whole continent is armed. I can buy a loaded handgun in Nairobi for three hundred shillings—that's just five dollars. Two months ago, my car was stolen at gunpoint near my house—with my three kids in it! They were petrified."

"Jesus! What happened?"

"Ten streets from my house two blokes jumped in front of the car and pointed a gun at us. Told us to get out and pinched the car. A car can support these men for years. We got off lucky. Last week, thieves shot my friend in the forehead before they took his car."

I had heard all sorts of stories. Reality was always a composite, a kaleidoscope of information. This man handed me his reality. A portion of his truth was now mine.

My reality back in Nairobi was that my flight to Cairo didn't depart till 5:30 the following morning. I decided to find a quiet corner and camp at the airport. Removing pillow and sleeping bag from my pack, I stretched my body over three plastic bucket seats. I felt like a bird trying to figure out where to put its wings. I was on the edge of sleep when a gentle hand shook my shoulder. Coming out of my stupor, I saw two uniformed black women shaking their heads with concern. "It is not good for you to sleep there! You must come with us."

I followed them like a chick behind two mother hens, up a couple of flights of stairs to a door that read Nakuru Tours. It was their place of work—an all-night agency booking trips to game reserves. Inside was a bare-bones desk, three chairs, and a small couch little bigger than a love seat. Lucy and Shanee introduced themselves and asked my name and itinerary. "Denis, you sleep on couch until morning," Lucy said, "then we wake you for your flight."

Not quite believing the scene, I tossed the backpack on the floor, groomed my hair, and spoke gallantly: "I can't take the couch. One of you ladies take it. I'll sleep on the floor."

Lucy had other arrangements in mind. "Shanee will sleep on those two chairs, and I will sleep on this chair and put my feet on the desk. You sleep on the couch. We are used to it." They somehow rustled up a couple of sheets and blankets, while ascertaining my age, reason for travel, how many kids I had, and why my wife wasn't with me. We settled in for the night. "Good night, ladies," I whispered. "Thanks for your hospitality."

"Good night, Denis," they said, and we drifted off into our separate dreams.

EGYPT

MAN

27

SLAUGHTERING THE BULL IN A HOTEL

Y MAP OF NORTHERN AFRICA and the Middle East—a landmass almost twice the size of the United States—was painted mustard. Egypt was nearly engulfed by this color—the color of desert. To its northeast lay Israel, surrounded uneasily by Arab neighbors, and to south and west, the red-hot deserts of Sudan and Libya. Blue dominated Egypt's northern border in the form of the Mediterranean, sweeping down below Greece and Turkey to cool its shores. The Red Sea also provided refreshing blue relief to the east. But within square-shaped Egypt mustard ruled, except for a shady green stripe with a thin blue line running through its middle. The stripe, the Nile Valley, started at the Mediterranean and snaked south. Along it, fifty-five million Muslims ate, slept, worked, and dreamed. I planned to follow the green stripe to the southernmost city in Egypt, Aswan, home to its most orthodox Muslims, and then return in that classic ancient Nile vessel, the felucca.

It was early June. I'd been in Africa for three months witnessing the charm, serenity, and violence of a raw land. My body had adapted to the environment. It was tanned and hard. My hair had bleached blond, a color last seen on this creature thirty years before. I had shed the skin of the businessman, family man, possessor of property. I had passed traveler "puberty," and was now ready to tackle Arabic culture and its religious zeal, which so infuriated the West.

That didn't mean I wasn't nervous. A nervousness that my conversation with Ausar Yazid did nothing to lessen. Ausar sat next to me on the flight to Cairo. He was a rugged dude whose nut-colored face was marred by an ugly scar that ripped along the bridge of his nose and ran clear across his cheekbone. He confidently introduced himself, took control of the conversation, and steered it quickly into a litany of his conquests.

"I have wife in Lamu, another wife and child in Australia, and several other girlfriends. One of them is cousin to me in Lebanon. I am Lebanese you see." He inched close enough for me to smell his musty breath. "My cousin is madly in love with me. I would do anything for her."

He yanked up the sleeves of his shirt and pointed to a series of puffed, ragged ridges across his skin. "Look at these scars! I visit my cousin in Lebanon, in small village in hills. She was fifteen and wanted me so much.

"Bad timing! There was very big fight with Christians in this village. People inside her house—dead all around me. I pull body of her brother on top of me to trick killers into thinking I am dead. They aim machine gun and shoot dead bodies. Bullets go through brother's body and into my arms and side. But I do not cry out. You think I want to get killed?"

As I was thinking of an answer, he lifted his shirt to display his muscular perforated stomach. He winked and said, "My cousin worth it. Very beau-ti-ful! Do you want see other scars?"

"No, that's okay," I said, actually wanting to see them.

It dawned on me that this guy was a scary fellow. He embodied the very qualities that people back home feared. In the US, the voices of political correctness had not quite extended to Muslims. And, despite my growing dislike for the sensationalist nature of the world press, sizzling headlines of violence between fundamentalist Islamists and moderates in Egypt ticker-taped across my inner eye. How accurate was the Western view of Islam? Were they fanatical, militant, violent, polygamous, women-beaters? Lamu was ninety-eight percent Muslim and they seemed nice.

Debarking the Egyptian airliner, Ausar said, "You come visit me at my home in Alexandria. I welcome you."

I thanked him generously, thought about visiting for a moment (such is the challenge of the unknown), but respectfully declined. Ausar's attitude to females had me wondering how women put up with some men's arrogance.

The Egyptian sun was hot and dry, and the desert sands gave off a dusty smell of antiquity and secrets. This was the land of pharaohs, the land of Cleopatra and Mark Antony, the land of the pyramids and the Sphinx, the land that forty-five centuries ago dazzled the world with its sophistication in art, engineering, and military power.

I rode an iron-cage elevator—complete with folding steel door—up to my base for my week in Cairo, the Pension Roma. Near the Cairo bazaar, the pension occupied the fourth and fifth floors of a dusty, turn-of-the-century colonial building, but had a clean, demure atmosphere *and* a phone to call home at the small reception desk. My room was pleasantly tidy and spacious, with mahogany-stained furniture, and two single beds resting on a recently waxed floor. Out a triangular window, I surveyed the jumbled vastness of Cairo, a city whose cacophony of buildings housed forty percent of Egypt's population. Melodious chants to Allah floated across a wasteland of layered rooftops, where anxious pigeons groomed their wings and pranced on ledges carved into cinnamon-colored buildings. Four stories below, children teased and played, spouting fast Arabic in a garbage-strewn alleyway that led to a coffeehouse frequented by men who argued and laughed as loud as my father.

I also had a roommate, Mick, a portly, somewhat scruffy, and definitely self-contained Australian archeologist in his early thirties. He wore glasses that magnified slightly off-kilter, pale blue eyes. Mick specialized in Egyptology and worked at a dig not far from the city.

The first evening, Mick suggested we go to the finest budget restaurant in Cairo—Felfela, just off Talaat Harb Street. While I waited for Mick to get ready, I watched an American soap, *The Bold and the Beautiful*. All the actors were indeed beautiful. But, like the eyes of a snake, their beauty lacked passion. The show portrayed a Stepford society of human mannequins who screwed at the blink of an eye, and who would squash their grandmothers if they thought they could make a buck. I watched mesmerized and shocked at the shallowness of it all. What effect did this image of Americans have on the Muslims in Cairo?

On the way to Felfela, we strolled along Midan Tahir where white-uniformed police with whistles and machine guns directed German and Japanese cars, pick-up trucks, and a swarm of yellow-and-black cabs. Despite the machine guns, continuous honks, and exhaust fumes, Cairo immediately struck me as a friendly and romantic city, a crossroads between Third World charisma and Western materialism.

Exotic women with chestnut skin and brown eyes walked arm in arm with their men. Only a few wore full-body dresses and covered their faces, most modeled silk scarves and mid-calf dresses. Meanwhile, the men had their fair share of rotund bodies and solid behinds, with a mustache commonly found beneath their aquiline noses. They wore slacks and loafers, which stylistically reminded me of the Forties back home, and often held hands with girls with ribbons in their hair or hooked arms with other men. Boys held hands with boys. Music from shops along the way drifted in the warm air—a gentle wailing of voices, accompanied by flutes, violins, and drums. People stopped us. "Welcome! Welcome to Egypt!" And alternatively, "Welcome to Egypt—change money, change money?"

As we squeezed between cars to cross the street, I asked Mick why so many women wore black. "Black in the desert is hard to see, a shield," he informed me. "In the old days, people treated women as chattels. Wearing black they were not spotted as easily. It was a means to protect them."

I'd never met an archeologist before—especially not one who actually dug things up. So, as we sat at Felfela, chewing diligently on tahini with pita bread and a mixture of refried beans, eggs, onions, and minced meat, I asked him how he could really tell what happened from reading hieroglyphics on five-thousand-year-old walls. He laughed. "We can't really, mate. At best, we get an idea of what the society might have looked like. The rest is good fiction."

We left the restaurant and walked along the well-lit Sharia Qasr el-Nil, a main shopping street that reaches from the Nile into the city at an angle. A pickup truck double-parked not more than ten feet from us, and three men dressed in full-length *jellabas* stepped resolutely out of the cab. In the bed of the pickup, one end of a rope tied around its neck and the other secured to the cab, a big, muscular bull, eyes wide and scared, surveyed the busy street.

Mick stopped in his tracks, flipped his cigarette on the pavement, and toed it. We had both traveled long enough to know something unusual was about to happen. The three Egyptians, operating in heavy traffic, unhitched the tail of the pickup, laid down a wooden gangplank, and led the brown bull down like a condemned felon. They pulled the confused animal across the sidewalk in front of a row of retail stores and down an alleyway leading to the rear of a five-story hotel. By now a crowd of nosy locals had gathered to follow the bull and, using a combination of hand gestures and friendly pushes, encouraged us to join them.

The mob herded the beast through the back entrance of the hotel, and down into a basement washroom. While the bull's owners filled a sink with water for a farewell drink, the assemblage vigorously encouraged us to "Look! Look! Come see!" Straining their necks to glimpse the action themselves, several people pulled us forward, stopping us just short of the open doorway. After a light slap at the water with his tongue, the bull stared directly at me with a pleading look, as if I had the power to commute his sentence.

Even while the condemned implored me, the guys from the pickup slipped the noose around its front legs and another around its hind legs. They pulled the ropes outward, slamming the poor thing to the concrete floor. Wasting no time, they slit his throat. The bull let out a spray of urine, drenching the tormentor to his rear, while a jet of blood splattered the open doorway within inches of my face. The beast lay on the floor and life drained from its eyes.

It saddened me to think about how we treat animals we intend to eat. I read somewhere that in the US eight billion animals are killed every year in assembly line fashion, too often under abysmal conditions.

Mick and I shook our heads and solemnly returned to the main street to continue walking off dinner. He told me the meat would be carved up for Eid—the festival that commemorated the willingness of Abraham to follow God's command to sacrifice not Isaac, as Jews and Christians believed, but Ishmael, his son by his second wife, Hagar. Ishmael was not in the end killed, and went on, Muslims thought, to be the father of the Arab peoples.

My favorite spot at the Roma was a quiet balcony haven outside the pension's sitting room. An iron railing girdled the balcony, leaving barely enough space to squeeze a shellacked wooden table and two chairs. It served as a fine place to view the city. Mick's tanned fingers pointed out the panorama of rooftops. "To me, this is primo Cairo," he muttered. A landscape of TV antennas, windows held together by grungy tape, and balconies with laundry hanging like leaves from clothesline vines. The rooftops rambled forever in large and small quads, littered with the most colossal assortment of junk and rubble imaginable—rocks, plastic bottles, sheets, hunks of plaster, rubber tires. There was an unmistakable charm to it all. A charm enhanced by the chants from mosques that drifted across the evening air.

28

PYRAMIDS AND SPHINX
ON A TWO-SPEED HORSE:
FAST AND STOP

THE NEXT DAY, MICK SPLIT to Syria on vacation and I grabbed a crowded transport to Giza to visit the pyramids. The thought of seeing these ancient wonders sent chills up my spine. The only other whites on the bus were a couple who had boarded with me but gotten separated in the surging crowd. However, you certainly couldn't miss her—in skimpy clothes that barely covered her bulging bosom. Most of the males on the bus tried valiantly to keep their eyes away from her. Why would someone dress like that in a Muslim country, I wondered.

A mother grabbed the surprised Western woman's hand and led her to a seat she had vacated near two other ladies and a child. An old man handed the foreigner a cardboard box folded in half. Where he got it was a mystery. The foreigner thanked the old man and laid the box on her seat, to sit on. "No, no!" the old man cried. He yanked the box from under her and politely placed it over the front of her body. The women nodded heads in approval.

As the rickety bus lurched through the streets of Cairo, a man in a tan *jellaba* indicated his seat, saying: "Welcome!" I thanked him. The kindness of the locals impressed me. I stared out the window expectantly, wringing my hands in anticipation, almost giddy under the surface. I was on the way to the pyramids!

A childhood memory surfaced of a petrified, white-faced Egyptian priest in the 1930s movie *The Mummy*. He had coal-black eyebrows and his pupils blazed in horror as soldiers in short dresses slowly wrapped the last bits of gauze around his chin and mouth. He had attempted to resurrect his dead lover, the princess Ankh-es-en-amon, and for this infraction, the soldiers were busy burying the priest alive, deep in the pyramidal chambers. Ugh, what a way to go.

The bus dropped me off at an inverted "V" intersection in Giza, under a bright sun. In the dry desert warmth, I followed directions to turn right, and trudged up a steeply inclined, sand-splattered concrete road to a sign that read: "entrance to pyramids."

A skinny tout crossed the street and confronted me: "You like to ride camel through pyramids? Come! Come!" He shrugged his shoulder in the direction of a vast lot. Noncommittal, I crossed the street and looked into the lot. It was filled with standing horses and camels munching on their cuds like old folks chewing gum. Horses whinnied, hens plucked at grain, and black flies nested in the bodies of the animals. Stone stables and wooden shacks, the color of pigeon droppings, held hay and created a sort of fence on the downhill side of the arena. All around the lot attendants in long, dirty-white *jellabas* tended to the animals.

I was a traveler, right? Open to new experiences, right? But, I hated horses.

"How much for a camel?" I inquired of the child tout.

"You come, I get you good camel."

"How much?"

"Fifty pounds. Not much!" (It was about seven dollars.)

"Too much for me, I can walk."

"Fifty pounds good price. Include price of admission."

We settled on thirty and walked into the dust and smell of large animals. The tout took me to a midget of an old man in a sullied white robe. He had a sallow face, with cheeks so concave they looked like they had been sucked down his throat in a fit of coughing. He wore the signature Muslim mustache, and his eyes looked as ancient as the pyramids, but were vibrant and hard to read.

"He speak good English," said the tout, who then chatted with the old man in Arabic before leaving.

The old codger eyed me. "*Ali!*" he called out, followed by rapid-fire Arabic. Ali, of medium height with dark, bushy eyebrows melding together above his nose, brought over a juiced-up horse that took one look at me and laughed.

I pointed to the departing tout. "I told him I wanted a camel!"

"What difference? Horse okay!" the old guy replied, with no discernible emotion.

"I hate horses. I want *camel*!"

"Camel not good." Then waving his arms as if he was tracing dunes in the desert, he grumbled: "Camel go up, down. Bad for back. Horse better."

"I will not ride this horse!" I spoke in a low monotone, almost a whisper so as not to upset the horse.

Horses had big, inscrutable eyes. I didn't have a clue as to what they were thinking, and they intimidated the hell out of me. On a horse I was no longer in control of my fate. When I was a kid, my sister got a horse after we moved from the city to the country. Its name was Bluebell, the first and only *blue* horse I've ever seen. The whole family was proud of Bluebell's color—as if we scored a coup or got a great bargain on a talking dog.

My sister would invite me to climb on to the horse, then, when I was halfway up, she'd slap its rear and yell "*Heyeeah!*" Bluebell was off to the races. As if hanging from the stirrups halfway down the saddle wasn't challenging enough, the barn fit Bluebell with nary an inch to spare. Bluebell had sized me up as a coward from the beginning, and to the howling laughter of my sister, left me dangling from the barn's entrance door each time she gave it one of those slaps. The truly incredible aspect of this whole experience was that she talked me into repeating it so many times.

Neither Ali nor the old man made any effort to fetch a camel. It was becoming clear that he probably didn't even own one. We dickered about the merits of the two beasts until his unwavering commitment to the comfort of the horse made a dent. Before I knew it, these words flowed reluctantly out of my mouth: "All right, all right! I'll take the horse." I couldn't believe it. My sister, in this man's skin, had done it once again.

Ali saddled up my horse and mounted his own. We left the lot and cantered along a narrow brick-and-dirt road through a shantytown of huts, which served as home and bazaar for the have-nots of Giza. The garbage-strewn shantytown rimmed the golden desert that harbored one of the jewels of humanity.

As we bounced along, people shouted: "Welcome!" "Where you from?" "What is your name?" At the end of the settlement, the road became a path that opened up to the vast spaciousness of the desert. At this point, my horse stopped dead, probably because it saw what I saw: a steep, narrow uphill climb on loose rock and shale.

"Are we going up there?" I shouted to Ali in a tremulous voice, sitting straight in the saddle with clammy hands on the reins. "Deserts are supposed to be flat!"

"It okay, horse knows way. Kick him! Kick him!"

"*Are you kidding?* Kick him up this mountain?"

I knew I should have taken a camel.

"How far to the pyramids, Ali?"

"Don't worry, I explain later." He rode over and whipped my horse twice with a switch. The beast bolted up the treacherous highland terrain, galloping along a tight ridge with me holding on as if my life depended on it—which it did. Looking down, I consoled myself with the thought that this horse knew it would die along with me if we toppled off the cliffs on either side of the trail.

The ride was three or four miles, but fortunately, after the original shock of steep terrain, we descended on to the flatter hardpan of the desert sands. Ten pyramids lay ahead in silent grandeur, on sweeping, golden sand hills that undulated in the distance like waves in the ocean. The pyramids were arranged in order of size, and purportedly provided the pharaohs with "steps to the gods."

My horse, it emerged, had two speeds: as-fast-as-possible and stop. I felt like a city slicker as I groped for balance and bounced up and down like a yo-yo, while the stop-go horse flashed over dunes carrying me breathless between the most revered structures in the world. I dubbed him "Trigger," as in "hair trigger."

When Trigger was in *stop* mode, Ali impatiently wanted to take its reins to lead the way, but I refused. The wafer-thin Egyptian, with slightly sticky hair, sat on his snorting Arabian steed, his skin bronzed and leathered from the sun. As if suddenly remembering that rich tourists give baksheesh (a tip), he let go of my reins, wiped the disgust from his face, and commenced guide-talk. Pointing across the colossal line of structures, Ali described them in a high-pitched voice that sounded as if he'd made a grave mistake mounting his horse. "Three big pyramids and seven small ones. The big ones—Khufu, Khafre, and Menkaure. They here four, five thousand years. Take name of three pharaohs who build them." Then he named the smaller ones, using his fingers to keep track. "Last one ... no name. Come, make horse run like Clin-ton."

I just sat there on the horse glued to the power and majesty of it all. Here I was in a famous desert, under bulbous, white clouds, surrounded by the choking suburbs of Cairo, looking at the massive remnants of the *Old Kingdom*. Less than a stone's throw away, Khufu, the Great Pyramid, stood 140 meters high. More than two million limestone blocks sat silently in the sand. They each weighed about two and a half tons and were transported in floodwaters from the city of Aswan over four hundred kilometers away. The stones had to be placed in perfect symmetry to prevent a buildup of pressure that could collapse the structure like a deck of cards. Mathematicians, stonecutters, architects, administrators, and an army of workers toiled and died on its construction, over a period of ten to twenty years.

The pharaohs created a whole city for the workers who built these tombs. Theirs was a society preoccupied with immortality. Some believe that like those who built the great cathedrals of Europe, this society saw these structures as a tribute, not so much to the divine nature of the pharaohs, as to the divine nature of society itself. Some believe the pyramids decreased in size over time because the kingdom grew weary of the royal competition to become closer to God. Maybe it was a resource problem, like the decline in building great bridges in the US—a simple matter of economics.

I removed my sunglasses, wiped the sweat off my neck with a bandanna, and took pictures. When the wind began to pick up it became obvious why people in desert climates wear long clothes. On the return trip, Ali took me to see the Sphinx. During another of my horse's stop modes, he asserted that he liked Clinton better than Bush.

"Why?"

"He beat Saddam Hussein."

As Ali raised his whip to drive my horse, I noticed several scars on his face and arms. "How did you get those?" I asked suspiciously, pointing to two brutal zigzags.

He held back the whip and proudly fingered each scar, then opened his sun-faded, khaki shirt to display more, which had been out of sight. "I get this one when horse throw me into rocks and this one when horse fall...." Before he could finish, my horse went into *go* mode.

Smelling-distance from home, our horses stopped at a T in the trail. The left branch went back to the riding lot, and the right up another steep incline to the Sphinx. Ali's horse reared in protest while Ali fought for control. "Shit! I'm not going up there," I thought. But from out of nowhere a five-year-old kid grabbed the reins of my horse and led him up the narrow, rocky path to the Sphinx.

The Sphinx looked as if it was guarding the pyramids and was as impressive as Khufu. Carved out of a gigantic piece of limestone, it stood 22 meters high and 73.5 meters long. Nobody really knew how old the Sphinx was or how many times it had been restored and many stories and theories surrounded it. One was that Tuthmosis IV uncovered the Sphinx from the desert sands at the instigation of the sun god Ra. Another held that the pyramid maker Khafre (sometimes called Chephren) had the rock shaped into a lion's body with his face, wearing the royal headdress of Egypt. More recently, some scientists argued that they had found evidence of water erosion on the Sphinx and dated it two or three thousand years earlier than previously thought. The giant statue's construction would have been when the area had significant rainfall and was forested. Thousands of years ago, the rains stopped and forests gave way to the desert that occupies sixty percent of Africa—and is creeping through the rest.

Ali, playing guide, added some less plausible stories. He claimed archaeologists had discovered love poems written on the Sphinx, and that Turkish soldiers used it for target practice and shot off the nose during the First World War. He also said that the Sphinx's nose looked a lot like his uncle Hamadi's, so that Hamadi was probably related.

At the lot, Ali hit me for baksheesh. I anted up, thankful to return in one piece. Back on the ground, I felt brave and rugged. After all, how many people have ridden in and out of the pyramids on a crazy horse with two speeds?

29

EGYPTIAN WOMAN

N THE CAB BACK TO Cairo, the driver coerced me into visiting a papyrus shop. "You stop, have cup of mint tea. Buy something for wife or girlfriend maybe."

At the shop, a five-foot-three saleswoman, Omaima, flashed charming brown eyes at me and inquired into my background. She stood behind a glass counter, hair in a bun, wearing a long, red, cotton hijab and a beaded necklace, which she twisted to occupy her hand. "You a writer? Get papyrus that tells a story. It is expensive, but papyrus lasts for thousands of years. A person could easily rip a single leaf off the plant, but when cut in strips, dipped in water and pressed, it is as strong as iron."

"Writers starve, so we can't afford much," I answered, immediately liking her spunk. "Where did you learn your English?"

"American University in Cairo."

"The major?"

"Commerce."

"What did they teach you about selling?"

"If you have a pleasant discussion or quality art, people like you will buy." She turned around and grabbed several papyrus prints from bins in back of her. Then she unrolled them and translated the stories: "The goddess Nut swallowed the sun, which recedes into her body giving birth to the day." She unrolled another: "This is a very nice picture: Nefertiti's love affair with Pharaoh Akhenaten and their devotion to Aten, god of the rising sun. Their worship is thought to be the first monotheistic religion."

Negotiations for the papyrus of Nefertiti's love affair were brutal. After a back and forth bout, Omaima frowned petulantly: "Okay," she said, "we'll flip a coin for the difference. You are a sporting man!" She flipped and lost. "I'll flip again." Another loss. After the third toss, she demanded: "Throw this coin away!"

Before long I was running through pictures of my family, Omaima commenting on each picture: "I like your daughters' smiles. Your face looked fat then. Your wife is beautiful, like the hieroglyphics of her name. I like her dress! You know what they would do in Egypt if I wore a short dress like that?"

"Would you ever wear it?"

"Only at home!"

I spent a week in Cairo's hot, dry weather eating fruit, drinking fresh orange and guava juice from stands, and eating *kushari,* a combination of lentils, rice, macaroni, fried onions, and tomatoes. I wandered narrow alleyways through the poorer sections of the city, to the dusty Kahn el-Khalili bazaar, and to landmarks such as the Citadel, a stone fortress that once protected the city. People constantly interacted—the beggar with twisted legs who pointed to the tea he bought with the 25 piaster coin I gave him a half-hour before. People said hello first, welcomed me, and helped with directions when I looked lost. I responded with my best smiles, occasionally patted their shoulders. Their energy made me want to do good deeds. And always the questions and comments, the vast majority of which concerned family. "Where you from? I have a cousin who lives there. Are you married? Do you have children? How many? Why they not with you?" Family was important.

Occasionally, a veiled women comfortably locked eyes with me, knowing there was no chance of harm. These women looked mysterious and attractive. Did isolating the power of eyes bring its own attraction?

30

RAMSES II—
REAL MEN HAVE 100 WIVES

L EAVING CAIRO AT 6:45 P.M., my train was to follow the Nile
southeast for twelve hours to Aswan, a romantic city perched
on the river's banks. Aswan was the last outpost before the
sweltering Nubian Desert and Sudanese border. Heeding the advice of several travelers, I would spend a couple of days in Aswan,
before venturing into the heart of the desert to Abu Simbel to
visit the great temple of Ramses II. Then, I planned to sail north
on the Nile in a felucca to Edfu and on from there to the ancient
city of Luxor, and more temples. Everything in Egypt is ancient.
Not ancient like Roman ruins. I mean, *ancient*. In the Egyptian
Museum in Cairo, for instance, mummies were so numerous they
were left out in halls, like an overflow of sick people in a hospital.

As the train rattled south, I twisted, slouched, and curled up
in a ball, searching desperately for comfort in the straight-backed,
leather seats. To distract myself, I engaged in conversation with
my neighbor, a middle-aged man in baggy slacks and a blue shirt
that ballooned at the chest and narrowed at the hips. Occasionally
stroking his glistening mustache, Baghel explained in near perfect English that his name meant "ox."

We began to discuss Islam. He told me how Muhammad
worked as a shepherd and camel driver, married an older, rich
woman, and had four daughters. That while Islam recognized the
Torah, parts of the Old Testament, and the New Testament, its

main teaching consisted of the Koran, which in his words "more or less governs our daily life."

"I'm told the Koran hasn't changed since it was written. Is that true?" I asked.

"Not a word of the Koran can be changed. It is the law of Allah dictated to Prophet Muhammad."

"Fourteen hundred years is a long time to go without revising. How can you adjust to a modern society that is changing so fast?" I asked politely.

He thought for a moment, rubbed his mustache, and let out a belly laugh that turned all heads in our vicinity. Just as fast, his emotions shifted and his finger shook in front of my nose to the cadence of his solemn voice. "That is the issue, is it not? Many do not want to change. And some want your Western gadgets, but not your values."

"Can you have the gadgets without the values?" I persisted. "How long will Muslim women be content to be second-class citizens when they can watch TV and see Western women living in relative luxury, exercising rights that only men have here?"

"The women in our society do not consider themselves to be second class," Baghel countered. "They have an important function to serve by raising children and taking care of the home. There is no need to change that! For what? Is your society happier? Prophet Muhammad set up specific rules to protect women from abuse by men devoid of divine guidance. You have visited Cairo. Women are safe day or night. Can you say the same about the United States where there is so much violence against women?"

"Times change! In the United States, many women, like my daughters, would rather put up with the dangers of city violence to be free to have a discussion like we are having now." The words *integrated individuals* from our family charter suddenly had an expanded meaning.

"You live in a different society. The Prophet preached against excessive attachment to physical objects. That is why our mosques are so Spartan and why a Muslim takes off his shoes before entering. Materialism shifts the emphasis from family and children to possessions. Women in our society have six or seven children. If you want a good family, the emphasis must be on the children and someone must care for them. That is the function of a woman."

"In your country. Mine recognizes that each individual has equal rights."

"Where is your country going, if the individual is more important than the family?"

Wherever we were going, I had a feeling that the rest of the world would eventually follow.

We continued to get acquainted, while the train rolled ever onward through the fertile Nile valley. Outside the window, the scenery was spectacular in its contrasts. On one side of the Nile lay desert, craggy buttes and unending waves of blond sand, on the other side, irrigated emerald greenery—crops and palm trees bursting with life. The further south we traveled, the hotter it got and the more women I saw swathed in black, faces veiled against the sun. Men hung out in groups, or walked the parched streets in white and blue robes open at the neck and flowing to the feet. Camels, oxen, donkeys, and motorbikes with riders in turbaned heads and trailing white robes, which whipped in the wind, replaced cars and trucks as modes of transportation. Boys kicked soccer balls in fields of sand. The towns were severe. Their dwellings made of mud, stone, twigs, and cloth. Minarets, tall, thin towers with loudspeakers in them to call the faithful to prayer, rose from local mosques.

Legs crossed, Baghel lit a cigarette and blew smoke into the air, unconcerned about the direction it traveled. Slipping the Tevas from my feet and folding my legs in a semi-lotus position on the seat, I offered him water.

"What is the terrorism all about?" I asked.

He accepted the water, careful to pour the liquid into his mouth in such a way that his lips never touched the bottle. He slowly handed the water back, and then pointed to the window. "Look outside and tell me what you see."

I watched the land go by for a minute before answering. "Desert, the green of agriculture ... lots of kids ... mud houses."

"That is it. In Egypt, the Nile brings life to the desert, like a mother bird brings food to its young. But only a very small portion of my country is fit for agriculture. The rest—desert! Each year, more mouths to feed. The newspaper writes that one million people are born every nine months in Egypt. And the old? They do not die as early as in former times."

"So ... how does that translate into terrorism?"

"Simple my friend! The main concerns in life here are family values, friends, and food. Every year it is harder to maintain family values and put food on the table. Most Egyptians welcome tourists and Western ways, but Egypt cannot feed itself. Some react to difficult times by blaming TV and Western tourists for infiltrating Muslim life with a culture that seeps into our skin like a bacterial infection.

"Countries such as Iran send money to incite the more simple-minded people. It is not so much a problem as the newspapers say, but still we lose tourists and the economy worsens. I am a small businessman. Tourists mean to me a better economy, but to others ... eh, a change in the old life.

"Let us see reality! People here are simple farmers. They eat vegetables. They are unlike you Americans. They do not move fast. Do not work in air-conditioned offices. They live cheap. They need children to take care of them in old age. They fear change."

Baghel departed the train in Luxor, but before going he grabbed my arm. "You must be careful in Aswan. The further south you travel, the more suspicious the people are towards Westerners."

Shortly after Baghel left, I fell into discussion with a young American writer Randy, who also taught English in Cairo and studied Muslim culture. He said he wanted to soak up the flavor of the Middle East as a backdrop to mystery stories he wrote.

I still marveled at how easy it was to meet people traveling. Once in a while with the younger travelers I thought about my age, about graying sideburns and thinning dome. During these insecure moments I reminded myself that I had been around young people all my life, and they enjoyed me just as much as I enjoyed them.

Randy and I kicked around Aswan for a couple of days. He had a soft, boyish face, glasses, California-straight teeth, and lots of fluffy, brown hair, the kind that blew in the breeze but didn't lose its composure. His scruffy beard struggled to grow, like grass in the crevices of a country road. His body was lean and he wore jeans together with a pastel, short-sleeve shirt and hiking boots.

Randy was the type of guy you'd expect to find reading a novel under the shade of a maple tree on a warm summer day.

We shared a room at the Nubian Oasis for $4 each, and perused the outdoor markets and great bazaar, frying in the breezeless, hundred-degree heat. We swapped stories while sifting through thin fabrics, squeezing fruit for firmness, and sniffing deeply colored spices—indigo, saffron, and burnt umber. Outside shops that sold perfume oils and gold, elderly donkeys pulled carts and 1940s vintage cars, and horse-carriages crawled along cobblestone streets. Randy bought a necklace of hard brown nutshells, which he immediately put on. Like other parts of Africa, the blooming of nature was everywhere—in the jasmine, in humans, and in animals. I hadn't seen cats and dogs with bulging teats roaming the streets since I was a kid.

"Men are with men and women are with women," I said to Randy, as we passed a covered cafe with men smoking shisha pipes. "Only in Cairo do you see couples."

"I think it's good for men to have friends. My dad, for instance, he's isolated. One of the reasons I travel is because I don't want to wind up like him. The men here have friends they see every day. They talk all the time.

"Despite a comfortable life, my dad is cynical and bored at fifty-one. He's an engineering executive for an electronics firm in Silicon Valley. He works all the time, comes home late and is too tired to do anything but flip on the TV and bitch at the Democrats for giving away his hard-earned money. That's not for me. I'm not going to spend my old age on a sofa worrying about my assets."

"Don't be too hard on your dad, Randy. I worked like that for a quarter of a century."

"What did it buy you?"

"Well, it bought me a good lifestyle like your dad, an educated family, interesting people—and this trip around the world."

Even while saying this, my mind flashed back to the stream of tour groups filtering through the Egyptian Museum. Leading the way were bustling, chattering, gray-haired women, a generation freed from family responsibility. Invariably dragging behind the ladies were the sagging, burned-out carcasses of their husbands—mouths frozen open like dying patients in nursing homes, minds entombed and starved by apathy. The men finally had time in their lives to travel. Too late!

"Was it worth it?" Randy fixed me with curious gray-green eyes.

We stopped to watch a young man holding the reins of a horse and leaning out of his carriage to ogle and proposition a Western woman in a sleeveless shirt and tight shorts. "You take ride," he advocated. "Five kisses, half price!" She flushed with anger and walked faster beside her bristling boyfriend.

"I have no regrets. My work was exciting. When I got out of school, probably not long after your dad did, I was hungry with ambition. Got married in graduate school, had two kids by twenty-four. Worked my ass off. The work ethic was hardest on my wife. 'Your work mistress,' she used to say. Eventually I burned out though. More the sense of being stuck than the hours."

"My dad's stuck. Sometimes I wonder who he is. Just once I would like to see him do something uncharacteristic. Get a friend. If my mom dies, I don't know what he'd do."

Randy struck a chord. I was stuck before I decided to travel. Sometimes I felt like a package, stamped: *Denis Hickey, husband and father*. On the outside, family and job provided everything, but as the only male in the family, I watched games on TV alone, and thought about things the women would never suspect. Inside, I had a hidden personality.

In late afternoon, as the land cooled, we walked to the river to take a felucca to the Temple of Isis at Philae and its famous gardens. A twenty-year-old, bare-chested Nubian sailor with wiry muscles and a bright smile prepared the felucca for its half-mile journey. "I fuck ninety-four white women," he proudly announced to us while untying the ropes and tossing them into the crescent-shaped vessel.

"That's something to be proud of," I replied, feeling the red blush of anger run up my spine as I stepped down into the felucca from the dock. "How many Muslim women did you fuck?" The mate shrugged, and went about the business of preparing the boat for sailing.

"Get used to it," Randy advised me. "Some Muslim men can be crude to white women."

We sat cross-legged on the bare planks of the felucca's deck, the wind cautiously and occasionally thumping the canvas. The hot sun beat down and water sloshed lazily against the side of the boat. Ahead, the temple rested majestically on a palm-studded island in the middle of the Nile. Perfect, honey-colored desert dunes rested on one side of the river, and the brick bulkhead of Aswan on the other. I leaned and whispered to Randy, shooting a hostile glare at the young sailor who smiled when our eyes met, not comprehending the disdain. "Why do they have to be such jerks about women?"

"It's the culture. Islam tries to restrain desire."

"That doesn't seem to apply to Western females."

"That's because they are seen as loose women and whores." He laughed at my frown. "It's understandable, really! Muslims watch Hollywood stereotypes on TV. They compare clothes Western women wear. Some women just don't know how to keep their body from falling out of their clothes. They watch unmarried travelers sleep in the same room. Sometimes women go topless on beaches."

The Bold and the Beautiful on TV at the Pension Roma immediately came to mind. "I wonder if he's even had one Western woman."

"Think of it this way: A Muslim man barely gets to see a women's ankle until he's married! And they marry later these days, so an unnatural amount of desire builds. But don't make the mistake of thinking all Muslims are crude. They really are thoughtful and generous people."

At four the next morning, Randy and I boarded a cream-colored van bound for Abu Simbel. The early departure was necessary to make the seven-hour round trip to the temples of Ramses II before the full sting of the scorching desert heat. As the bright haze of daylight began to illuminate the desert, I studied my map.

South of Aswan the green of agriculture disappeared, leaving the blue of the Nile surrounded by the mustard color of sand. A single, needle-thin, red line ran parallel to the blue for almost three hundred kilometers, and then stopped at a large dot on the map, while the blue line meandered into the Nubian Desert and Sudan. The red line was the road, the dot, Abu Simbel.

Abu Simbel consisted of a pair of large hills overlooking the Nile into which the temples of Ramses II were built. There were three reasons these temples rival the pyramids in Cairo. First was the architecture and sculptures of the temples themselves. Second, the colossal task that a UNESCO team undertook to rescue this treasure from burial under Lake Nasser during the damming of the Nile in the Sixties. They literally cut up a mountain into two thousand huge blocks weighing between ten and forty tons each, transported the blocks hundreds of meters, and reconstructed them precisely. Third was the majesty of Ramses himself.

It wasn't yet nine o'clock and already the sun was baking the hard sand. Randy and I stood on a ridge high above the pristine blue of the Nile, surveying the temples from the front. "The books portray Ramses as a handsome dude," Randy said. "A giant, six feet four inches tall."

"The average height couldn't have been over five feet back then," I surmised. "He must have eaten a lot of zebra."

In front of us to the right stood the smaller of the 3,300-year-old temples. Ramses dedicated this one to the cow-headed goddess of love, Hathor, in honor of his favorite wife, Nefertari. The magnificence of that temple was dwarfed by the second, to the left, carved out of the face of a cliff. This temple was dedicated to Ramses himself. Guarding the entrance into Ramses' temple, four huge granite statues, twenty meters high, depicted the various stages of the pharaoh's life. All four Ramses sat on thrones. Perched under their knees and in front of the platform stood carvings of beautiful women. Crown on head, hands on thighs, he sat straight with square, muscular breasts and arms. His face and eyes were handsome and round. A long, rectangular goatee dropped from the chin. Ramses II, ultimate man, gazed upon the land as if summoning the desert to bow before him.

"Ramses ruled Egypt for sixty-six years and lived to be at least ninety," Randy said, acting the guide. "Even at that age he probably made Sylvester Stallone seem like Mother Teresa. There are more surviving temples dedicated to Ramses in this world than statues of Lenin. He tamed the Hyksos and Libyans almost thirteen hundred years before Christ. And had a hundred wives and two hundred and ten children, including one hundred and six daughters. Can you believe it—he married four of the daughters."

"The man definitely needed a domestic secretary."

We entered the temple under the guard of the four colossuses. In awe, we sauntered into the inner sanctum, through a limestone hallway adorned with huge statues and wall carvings of Ramses' many victories. He stood in chariots shooting arrows or throwing spears at the Hyksos. Further in, seated on thrones in the innermost chamber, were four gods—the falcon-headed sun god Ra-Harakhty, Amun, Ptah, and Ramses, who obviously fancied himself divine.

"On February and October 22nd of each year," Randy was saying, "the rays of the rising sun reach across the Nile into the inner sanctum, and illuminate one of the four gods. Guess who?" So that was where the movie *Raiders of the Lost Ark* got the idea.

I would love to have been able to go back in time and observe the living man whose masterpiece was intact over three thousand years later. Whatever kind of person he was, he must have been more refined than some of his present-day countrymen. As I was to discover within the next forty-eight hours on my felucca journey to Edfu.

31

NEAR DEATH ON NILE FELUCCA WITH HANDSOME CAPTAIN NIYA

E ARLY IN THE MORNING ON the second day of the felucca sail to Edfu, a cooling breeze blew across the Nile. It was a pleasant break from the hundred-plus temperatures of the past few days. The air smelled fresh and clean. Two Kiwi women, Kara and Frankie, and a good-looking South African, David, all in their late twenties, joined Captain Niya, his first mate Ashrif, and me in the felucca. To relax and do nothing but sleep, play dice, read, eat three meals a day, and listen to the smoky-blue water of the Nile lapping against the side of the boat was sheer luxury. There was absolutely no reason to suspect what the gods had cooked up.

Of ancient design, our felucca was about forty feet long with a twenty-five-foot mast near the bow. The distinguishing feature of the felucca was its single huge sail, more particularly the immense spar (technically called the yard) attached to the sail. It was as long as the boat and similar to a tree in design, thick at the bottom and narrow at the top. A chain connected the yard to an eye-link at the foot of the mast, allowing it to swing outward at a twenty-degree angle and cross the mast twenty feet up, such that the sail curved towards the stern.

On our boat, where the yard crossed the mast it was fastened by a single cable and lots of frayed, old rope. The cable didn't look like much, but it apparently stood the test of time. Just above the deck, a removable canvas canopy shielded passengers and crew from the fierce sun. The middle section of the deck was wide abeam and covered with mats and sheets for lounging and sleeping. Ashrif stored backpacks underneath the floorboards, along with plenty of bottled water and food for the journey.

Sometimes both sides of the Nile were so rich in crops and palm trees that it looked like an emerald fairyland. At other times, one bank bathed in green while the other burned the golden color of untamed desert. Children played, swam, and squealed in the Nile, while men worked the fields. The women pounded clothes against rocks at the riverbank and gathered water in jugs to transport back on their heads. Men and women in Egypt appeared to share manual labor more equally than in other areas of Africa I'd seen—an advancement in civilization according to Elizabeth Cady Stanton. By offering equal opportunity, the industrial West had gone a giant step further. I appreciated nature, always moving forward, always experimenting, always the curious traveler. Yet why had nature driven so fast for sexual equality in recent years?

Captain Niya and Ashrif were both Nubians. Nubia was once a separate region, between Egypt and Sudan, whose kings ruled Egypt in the eighth and seventh centuries BC. Ancient Egyptian paintings showed sensuous Nubian maidens, wearing long, brown wigs and see-through dresses. It was ironic that much of Egypt's history (or at least the depictions of it) was characterized by a scarcity of clothing, yet the current population covered up. Between AD 250 and 500, Nubia was ruled by a mysterious culture labeled the X-Group by archaeologists. Little is known of them but their royal mound-tombs were filled with horses and attendants, slaughtered to accompany wealthy corpses. Nubia then converted to Christianity until, under Arab domination, it became Muslim in the sixteenth century.

Today's Nubians are still a remarkably good-looking group of people. Captain Niya, for instance, had swarthy features, thick, curly hair, large, serious, honey-colored eyes that complemented the shade of his skin, and a handsome, narrow face punctuated with high cheekbones. A simple, baby blue, cotton tunic covered his tall body from neck to bare feet. He told me that he was forty, yet his forehead was wrinkle-free.

For two hours that morning, we sailed north in a dream, on the calm, celebrated river. Surprisingly, for such a famous route of commerce, the Nile was not more than a half-a-mile across at its widest. Along the river's edge the wind had sculptured individual miniature pyramids in the dunes, exact replicas of what I had seen in Giza. Should wind and not humans—or alien visitors— get the architectural plaudits for the pyramids?

Suddenly—literally within seconds—the wind's mood shifted to anger. It churned the water. Small ripples became three-foot waves. The sun shone brightly, but the smell of the air was electric. We struggled against the elements for forty minutes as the billowing sail strained and thumped before the now pounding wind. I became more and more conscious of the size and weight of the yard.

Finally, tired of fighting nature, Niya scurried barefoot up the mast to trim the sail, but left it slack and blowing in the wind, with the mighty yard pulling out and slamming inward against its meager shackles. Ashrif killed his cigarette and scampered up behind the captain. Together they gathered in and tied down the flapping sail, while David guided the boat towards the approaching shore.

The boat beached on the golden sands where the wind was less severe. On the desolate horizon, three young Arabs riding donkeys appeared. Out of the quivering heat haze, they headed our way. About a half mile up the shoreline, another troop was approaching. Where did they come from? I remembered Baghel's departing warning on the train, "You must be careful … The further south that you travel, the more suspicious the people are towards Westerners."

I had a premonition these guys would be trouble. Thinking that on land I could better assess any danger, I slipped on my Tevas and jumped to the shore. Before long, five men in their mid-twenties and three young teenagers surrounded me. They were barefoot and dressed in an assortment of tangerine and sky-blue, ankle-length garments, baggy pants, and palm-leaf hats. Two of the men carried curved knives.

The group was nice enough at first, with the usual assault of personal questions. Then the gang caught sight of the deck of the boat and began gawking. I shook my head in disbelief. Kara was stretching her shapely body in tight shorts and a black bikini top.

She quickly covered up, though, when one of the men pointed at the donkeys with a grin: "Come! You take ride! Come!"

Their exhortations didn't pass the smell test. Even the donkeys cannot have been that keen as the Kiwis mounted them for a short stroll. The girls scraped their feet on the ground, looking like adults on a merry-go-round. As I'd feared the rides warmed the titillation meters of the other men, and they dug in on the shore as we returned to the felucca to wait out the wind.

Sitting, arms-crossed on the sand, not more than four feet from the boat, they continued to stare at the women. The older voyeurs chattered in Arabic, flinging hand gestures and glaring sullenly at us, while we stretched out on the boat ignoring them. Hoping to get a feel for the mood, I occasionally looked up from my book. Each time my eyes leveled on a rather handsome, but rugged-looking guy, who seemed to be the leader. With a look of intimidation that could wilt the lovely jasmine, he slowly and methodically raised his clenched fists, thumbs pointed towards the solid blue sky. The hands then flipped, double thumbs down towards the sand. What was happening in his mind? I wanted to talk to him, find out his thoughts. Instead, I was thwarted by the barriers of culture and language. The mood was tense and ugly.

After a second thumbs down, David, for some inexplicable reason, felt the urge to playfully caress Kara's shoulders and face. Then he laid his body between her legs, using her abdomen as a pillow for his head. As if that wasn't enough, he began to tickle Frankie. People do the damnedest things in a crisis. It forced me to break my vow to abstain from giving advice for the second time on this journey. "David," I grumbled softly, "what the fuck are you doing?"

He looked up startled and holstered his hands. The gawking went on for the better part of an hour. They stared and taunted with their eyes, and removed their shirts and swam around the boat in an intimidating fashion. All the while, Captain Niya and Ashrif were cool. They slept under the bow waiting for the wind to die down. "If they're not worried, why should we be?" I thought. Then again, they were a Muslim crew!

In the end, the leader sauntered back along the beach in the direction he came from. The other men followed, but not before a shouting match erupted between our aloof captain and a rather mean-looking dude, who kicked the boat before departing. I got the sense that it wasn't the insult to the boat that the captain was angry about, but the accumulated degree to which the guys had been assholes. Niya decided it was time to leave while the getting was good, and to my complete surprise the teenagers stayed behind and cheerfully pushed the boat into the Nile as if nothing had happened—like you'd help a stranger change a tire.

Nothing was to go right this fateful day. Felucca adrift, the yard ripped furiously at its chain tether at the foot of the mast. In violent protest against the force of the wind, this huge wooden beast finally reached the limit of its patience, and with a savage thrust ripped free. The loose end swung upward and floated ominously above the felucca. The sole protection against that naked tree hurtling down and crushing the boat was the thin cable and tattered ropes at the joint of the mast. If the cable snapped, we'd all plunge to watery graves.

Niya yelled, pointing at the mast, "Ashrif!" Again the second mate ditched a cigarette and scrambled up, followed closely by Captain Niya. They desperately raced against time to reel in the yard. David and I hustled to secure the chain tether, marveling at the skill of the crew thirty feet up. They held on to the mast with their ankles and thighs while they worked. During the entire episode, the ladies from New Zealand moved not an inch from their choice spots in the sun.

When the yard was secured all was quiet once again. I applied a miracle cure called *muti*, which I discovered in Zimbabwe, and Band-Aids to Ashrif's hand, which had been gored in the excitement. After patching up the first mate, I shuffled to the stern to see the captain. He sat puffing a cigarette, legs crossed, one hand on a rope controlling the yard and the other on the rudder. "Captain Niya, what was that all about … back there on the shore?"

He shook his head leisurely and inhaled smoke until the ash flared red. Then he removed the cigarette and motioned at Kara with a tilt of his head. He spoke softly in a serious tone meant for just the two of us. "This not New Zealand. Girls need be more careful. Arabs feel insult at bare female skin!

"Some excited … but, also feel insult. When woman visit another country she must respect culture.

"For me ... okay. I take Western girls on my boat. But others ... they are not so much in contact with white women. They are not animals!"

He had a point. I remembered watching an Arab man walking ahead of his spouse along Pier 39 in San Francisco. She wore black silk from head to toe with a veiled face. I was furious that this couple ignored the customs and freedom we valued in America. They exercised their freedom, but violated our culture. Same same with Western women in Egypt.

Sex was such an overwhelming issue to the Egyptian male. I was reading *The Beggar* by Egyptian author Naguib Mahfouz. He portrayed the sexual inhibitions and frustrations of men. The Muslim sealed up his natural hungers for reasons considered advanced fourteen hundred years ago. In contrast, the Western world leveled a media-blitz of sexual fantasy at males, while simultaneously denigrating the powerful animal inside. Men struggled with a double message: restraint and stimulation.

Still waiting for a favorable wind, we chowed down on onions, rice, and vine leaves stuffed with cabbage. Food Ashrif had cooked using a small butane stove stored under the deck. It took two hours for the winds to die down. Then, up with the sail and off to the races, as we set a blistering pace in a contest with another felucca. Niya skillfully squeezed ahead of the competition, and we sailed fast and free for twenty minutes. All of us reveled in a challenge that, for the time being, changed the mood of the day.

Without warning, the keel clipped something in the water and the boat bucked. Whatever was under the surface bent the keel and crippled us. As our rivals raced past, we floundered, sail loose and flapping in the wind. Niya shook his head. "But river deep here," he muttered in disbelief.

The keel was designed to be retractable, so the felucca could be beached by the river's edge at night. It retracted by yanking up a handle inside the boat that pulled the keel's upper portion through a chute built into the stern. Our twisted keel wouldn't retract, so Niya headed for the east bank to search for a deep-water refuge to do the necessary repairs.

He spotted a wooden dock and began to steer the rapidly moving boat toward it. Ashrif frantically prepared to rope us to the fast approaching dock, but the boat was so heavy and traveling at such a speed that if there was a collision, it would surely smash the landing place to splinters.

At the last second, Niya veered away. "Not good," he yelled in explanation. "We must try to reach west bank. Hope for deep water."

The captain struggled with the damaged boat, as he turned it towards the other side of the Nile and steered to avoid a small island down river between us and the west bank. But before we knew it, our crisis turned into real danger.

One of the monstrous cruise ships that navigate the Nile appeared to have miscalculated the position of the island. It had changed course to avoid running aground. And we were directly in its path.

Technically we had the right of way, but you could feel that the captain of the behemoth had no intention of changing course again. Events happened fast, yet time slowed to a trance. Each second became a minute, each spray of water a wave, each sound an echo. I had time to think: *What the fuck is that guy doing?* I measured the speed of our wounded felucca and the speed of the unstoppable, oncoming monster. I saw the frightened eyes of my companions. Captain Niya's lips and forehead wrinkled in rage. I heard him screaming at the approaching ship.

The cruise ship captain stared impassively into space atop the lofty bridge. I looked into those stern eyes below his blue cap with gold seaweed on it. He wasn't going to change course. We were dead.

I calculated the risks of diving into the water. Who could survive under the block of steel and propellers that was heading straight for us? For what seemed like the hundredth time during this eternity, I measured the geometry and distance between the two vessels. Somehow the angle of escape had changed. We were going to make it—barely. The cruise ship nearly swamped us in its wake. As it edged past we were tossed and turned, while high on its upper deck three casually dressed, gray-haired tourists played shuffleboard. I don't believe they ever saw us.

We reached the west bank and deep water to attempt an *African Queen* style repair of the keel. Niya slowly peeled his blue tunic in preparation for diving. He was a modest and religious man. I felt his embarrassment as he stood in his underwear in view of the women. After numerous unsuccessful dives into the cold Nile attempting to straighten the steel keel, Niya decided to fix it on land. The keel was so large and bulky. How could it be removed and then fixed?

Within fifteen minutes of touching the sandy shore, the desert provided the answer. Several eager-to-help young men rustled down a ten-foot embankment, stripped off their clothes, and began to help Niya, who was diving to detach the awkward keel.

The unfastened keel looked as if a herd of rampaging elephants had trampled it. Magically, the men produced a mallet to pound the keel back to its original shape. The process took three hours. By this time, the captain was shivering. He stood staring at the Nile, his brown skin covered with goose bumps. He contemplated the task of reinserting the keel underwater and fixing it with a steel bolt. It was like trying to thread a needle in a brisk wind with gloves on. He did manage to reinsert the keel into its track, but his cold hands dropped the bolt. It sank irretrievably to the river's bottom.

Undaunted, our rescuers disappeared into the desert, then reappeared with several bolts. Close, but no banana. Just when it looked hopeless, a felucca returning to Aswan came to our rescue. Its captain, another handsome and muscular Nubian, flashed an engaging smile while suggesting that we tie the keel with a rope he held in his hand. Noticing Niya's condition, and without a moment's hesitation, he dove into the water with the rope to implement his own idea. It worked.

I suddenly felt very respectful of the resourcefulness and community spirit of Egyptians. Our problem was their problem. They seemed unconcerned with time.

Back in action, we sailed through an orange sunset into dusk, and farther into the star-studded darkness of night. Shooting stars and methodically moving satellites entertained us. Ashrif, using a pan for a drum, sang call-and-response songs that we all danced to, including Niya. People along the riverbanks called to us and sang along. Soon the wind died down and night matured. Captain Niya set the rudder. We drifted as we slept, no other boats, no other sounds to compromise the soothing gurgling of water. I woke throughout the night to the gentle light of a honeysuckle moon and dark images passing silently on the riverbank. Were they goblins in a fairytale forest surrounding Aladdin's cave?

Dawn brought clarity. Palm and lemon trees in stepped, grassy layers merged with dense papyrus beds from which a heron rose to the beat of its heavy wings. Like slides in a noiseless projector, the topography changed to desert, then to brown hills, then finally to sand hills folding into green reeds.

The familiar sounds of roosters, nightingales, and donkeys mingled with the deep, authoritative melody of Islamic chants. A single white minaret, like a rocket at launch, heralded a small town of mud-brick homes built into the riverbank. A whisper of wind brushed my features as I lay under thin covers watching the glassy-clear water mirror the sky and shoreline. They were like painted shadows on canvas. I couldn't believe my good fortune. Imagine, sailing down the Nile.

32

SLEEPING WITH SWEET SUE BY
VALLEY OF THE KINGS

LATER THAT MORNING, WE DEBARKED at the dusty town of
Edfu. Paki, a smooth-talking, nineteen-year-old tout, immediately attached himself to our group. Playing middleman,
he negotiated a rate of five dollars each to drive eighty miles to
the four-thousand-year-old city of Luxor in a green hunk of junk
passing as a taxi. A hook-nosed driver with a thin mustache,
hairy wrists, and the expression of a wolf, turned the car towards
Luxor and rammed his foot on the accelerator. I fingered the
Trust card in my pocket, as the needle on the aged speedometer climbed and the wolf played chicken with oncoming drivers.
After miraculously reaching Luxor in one piece, Paki directed the
taxi to a hostel acceptable to all but me. It was clean and centrally
located, but after another life-threatening experience I was ready
for pampering at Club Med.

"Paki, would you ask the driver to take me to Club Med? But
tell him I'm *not* in a hurry."

Paki and the wolf conferred at length. "The driver say will
cost ten dollars."

"How far is it? It only cost five to drive from Edfu!"

"It is long drive to Club Med, and driver must return here for
passengers to Edfu."

"Tell him eight." Done! I said farewell to my mates and reen-
tered the cab, feeling disappointed that the resort was so far from
the heart of Luxor.

Sans Paki, the driver negotiated no more than four corners in this ageless city of three hundred thousand people, honking his horn at cantering horse-and-buggies, donkey-carts, and cars looking like old Packards. He gassed the cab on a straightway for about five hundred yards and stopped in front of a curb sign that read Club Med.

"This is it?" I snapped. "I thought it was outside of town?"

He shrugged. "No Ingileezee!"

Paki was a little prick, but I paid the driver the agreed amount. After settling in the swanky Club Med, I wandered over to the hostel where the group from the felucca were staying, hoping to bump into them. Loneliness aside, I felt an inexplicable urge to be there. Inside the hostel, I walked past two people arguing noisily. As if guided by an invisible force, I turned and hesitated. A woman, dressed in hiking boots, floppy African dress, and a soft bush hat, caught sight of me and stopped in mid-sentence. Puzzled, mouth open, and hands on hips, she stared at me. "Ssese?" she finally asked.

"Sue? Is that you?" The last time I had seen her she was headed to see gorillas in Uganda.

She pointed at the young man in front of her and ranted: "I rented a bike at my hostel from this sleazy guy. He delivered a broken down hunk of tin. Then I found him here, and now he says he wants more money for another bike.

"What are you doing here?" She tilted her head sideways as if seeing me for the first time.

There was something familiar about the guy. "Paki," I purred. "Didn't you say Club Med was a long taxi ride? How much was your take?"

He squirmed, and tried to fast-talk himself out of one predicament before facing the other by offering Sue a bargain price on another bike. Then he bolted for the door promising immediate delivery. We had to laugh.

"Sue, I can't believe you're here! I just entered your name in my diary. And here you are! Incredible. What a coincidence."

We agreed to meet early the next morning and take the ferry to the west bank to bicycle around the Valley of the Kings and the Valley of the Queens. Sue said she'd track down Paki and order a second bike.

"Make the weasel give you a big discount. He talked me into an eight-dollar, one-mile taxi ride."

Sipping Grand Marnier in the lounge at Club Med that night, I met a polished, middle-aged Egyptian with deep eyes and shiny black hair parted to the left. He seemed friendly, and explained he was waiting for a "lady in red." I figured coincidence or fate had served up a guy who could shed some light on my growing curiosity about the Arab male. After a few pleasantries, I related the story about the rude gawkers we met along the Nile, and asked him what he thought.

He laughed good-naturedly and stroked his chin with a finger that flashed a gold ring topped by a large, sparkling ruby. His slacks were meticulously pressed and he wore freshly shined, black penny loafers. Leaning back into his soft leather chair, this Muslim gentleman quietly sipped scotch and soda.

"They were immature and confused. Men and women in my culture do not go out together. Most men are virgins at twenty-five. Married couples often do not see each other naked."

This was fertile ground. "You're kidding? How do they … you know … during intercourse? Don't they get a glimpse then?"

He smiled a charming, maybe even provocative, smile. "My family, for instance, are of the old school. Not me, you understand. Old school people often have sex using a sheet to cover and preserve their modesty."

"You're kidding. Really?" I sniffed the pungent, sweet aroma of the Grand Marnier. I was certainly curious about the intimate details of people's lives, but I was always surprised at how easily they divulged those details. Although he could have been putting me on, I proceeded as if he was telling the truth.

"Does the Muslim religion seek to eliminate all desire?"

"Perhaps! We are ruled by passions that God has bestowed to test our will. The logic of the Muslim towards sex is simple. He thinks, 'I must have her, but it is sinful. The devil makes me sin by placing temptation in my path.'"

These words had barely escaped his lips, when his femme fatale, wearing a red, strapless, tight-fitting cocktail dress, swept into the lounge and snatched away my instructor of Muslim mores.

"Midnight belly-dancing," he whispered on the way out.

Early the next morning, the faint barks of mangy dogs competed with the sounds of a city waking up. Luxor was famous in ancient times as Thebes—a major religious center and capital of Mentuhotep II, who reunified Upper and Lower Egypt. In modern times, Sue and I were cycling through its baked-brown streets towards the ferry to the west bank of the Nile and the Valley of the Kings.

Carved into limestone cliffs, this valley was the burial site of the pharaohs, starting with Tuthmosis I, father of Hatshepsut, one of the few female rulers. The most famous tombs were those of Tutankhamen, who ruled for nine years and died in adolescence, and Akhenaten, the romantic whose love affair with Nefertiti had been described to me in Cairo.

We parked our bikes and entered the limestone caves, stepping carefully down fresh-smelling wooden stairways into the dank underground. We filed past mummies and frescos of angular, pencil-thin gods and goddesses with heads of cobras and jackals. The clarity and vibrancy of the colors—ocher, indigo, amber, turquoise, black—were striking after all these years. A one-eyed caretaker added an unexpected detail: the excavated mummies had dental work—bridges, gold crowns, and fillings in their teeth.

Leaving the Valley of the Kings, we out-peddled touts who yelled "Welcome to Alaska" to visit the splendidly preserved gravesites in the Valley of the Queens, stopping briefly at the relatively modest Valley of the Nobles. We crawled into tombs to view more frescos. Scrabbling ahead with a flashlight, the caretaker told us that the shy-looking Nubians with strings tied around their elbows, depicted in some of the pictures, were criminals. The string was the equivalent of police handcuffs. Although he could have told me anything and I'd have believed it.

Back on our bikes, we fought wind and scorching temperatures. We passed donkey carts dripping water and peddled to the Temple of Hatshepsut. Her tomb had been chiseled into the base of ginger-colored granite cliffs that towered high above in the background. The temple rose three stories high and had an entrance supported by impressive white columns.

Sue enjoyed reading guidebooks and educating me about the history of people long dead and buried. Seems there was always someone with a guidebook to educate me. And such a pretty guide.

On the move again, we passed a bottle of water back and forth trying to wash away the dryness from our throats, until the bottle emptied. We stopped at a shack for bottled Cokes, and endured the stares of barefoot kids and adults with missing teeth.

Sometimes I lagged behind, watching the strong flex of Sue's calf muscles and feeling the sweat funnel down my back. Occasionally I showed off and raced ahead. Sue projected a no-nonsense exterior. It was in her walk and talk, even in the way she rode a bike with the determination of a pioneer. Her ruggedly baggy clothes, slightly large nose, and brown hair bundled in a swirl under the African bush cap enhanced the image. However, as time peeled away the shyness of a new friendship, I discovered a tentative softness in Sue's gray-green eyes. A sweetness shining through the insecurity of a woman traveling alone. I dubbed her "Sweet Sue."

As the day wore on and we turned our bikes for home, Sweet Sue's mind began to churn. "Club Med, huh?" she mused. "You say it's got a pool!"

"Yup, beautiful pool."

"I've been traveling low-budget so long it's hard to imagine what a pool looks like. Does it cost much?

"I deserve a break! It's not as if I don't have money. The Peace Corps paid me two years of service at the end. I've got money.

"Denis, would you mind if I stay with you? I could pay the added cost."

"No problem," said I, cupping my hand unobtrusively to check my breath. "I have a spare bed."

Back at Club Med, Sweet Sue tossed her backpack on the bed, grabbed her bathing suit and makeup bag, and disappeared into the bathroom. She returned with contacts rather than glasses, long, lush, brown hair draped over delicate shoulders, and gold earrings. Her trim, voluptuous body was slipped into a pale-blue bikini. A tattoo of an angel peeked out of the bikini on her right cheek. Removing her travel clothes was like peeling the prickly exterior of a pineapple to expose the sweet fruit within. I was thunderstruck!

We loafed in chaise-lounges at the poolside. In the pool, we pounded a volleyball back and forth. At night, we dined in the club restaurant and then attended a late-night cabaret wearing colorful African clothes. I kept wishing I had the power of clairvoyance to tune in to her thoughts. My thoughts were about one thing: I was going to be sleeping in the same room as a young woman I hardly knew, but did she want to *sleep with* me?

I wanted to look attractive for Sue, but I had little sense of who I was as a sexual being, having spent half my life as a family man. Before marriage, I was too young to come to any conclusions. Was I handsome? I didn't know. Kathi thought I was attractive. What did that mean? This woman was not much older than my daughters.

My cerebral board of advisers, the same august committee that debated the Alice situation in Nairobi, concluded that I faced a formidable risk of rejection should I decide to take myself seriously as a Don Juan. The dissenting hormonal voices argued vehemently against that view. "Sue's attracted to you! Why else would she be here?" My "head" responded sharply: "Because she trusts you—you're married, and besides, look at yourself, you've got silver sideburns. Look at it from her point of view, she gets a nice place to stay at a low price."

By societal standards, my married status should have been a major consideration, but I was free of responsibility and loving it. The board agreed that individuals have rights.

Funny, my hormones had been dormant during the excitement of travel, but now my animal instincts prevailed. Was my growing lust for her physical, a question of intimacy, or both? Were physical and intimate inextricably linked in the male physiologically? Was there any difference between me and the Muslim sailor who claimed to keep a scorecard in Aswan? On the outside, I wasn't as hungry as these guys, maybe because female companionship had always been available to me. On the inside, the desire was without question instinctive. Something important to do. Women always seemed to be on the moral high ground regarding sex, but weren't we born into our respective roles?

Rationalization ended and the enjoyment began. At the cabaret, I felt the rhythm of my body beneath those African clothes. I high-stepped and low-stepped, stepped in and stepped out. Oh, I felt suave, cool. And Sweet Sue? She swirled as in a dream. Her lipstick glowed, her skin smelled of honeysuckle, and her hair, beaded earrings, and necklace twirled in rhythm with the music. The French patrons sipped their drinks and watched. I knew something would happen that night. And it did.

Six or so dances into dreamland, I stretched to pull a nifty move from my repertoire, but pulled instead a muscle in my derriere. Talk about an abrupt change of mood. I went from thirty-year-old stud to washed-up journeyman, feeling every one of my forty-eight years. I staggered from the dance floor to the tender embrace of a chair, hopeful that it was just a hitch. Sweet Sue hardly noticed. She swirled to the music with the grace of an impala, eyes partially closed, lips slightly parted. A few of the French faces smirked my way. I felt like a schmuck. Writhing in pain, I waved at Sue to rescue me. Fate had dealt a blow more serious than a hitch.

"I've got to get the hell out of here," I whispered.

"Why? Is something wrong?"

"Yeah! I think I pulled a muscle—in my bum, as the Aussies say."

She lent a shoulder and helped me out the door, upstairs to our room on the second floor, and on to my bed. With agonizing precision, I shed my long pants exposing my briefs, took a few muscle relaxants, and applied the African *muti*. Despite my discomfort, we stretched out on our respective beds and talked late into the night.

I discovered that men discussed sex in an attempt to gauge where a woman was coming from. A "risk of rejection" gauge perhaps. I also learned that this "gauge" was almost completely useless. In any case, I came clean on my fling with Alice, and Sue justified her African boyfriend. The mutual honesty was a refreshing antidote to my pain and humiliation.

"Lots of Western women have sex with Africans. Traveling is about experiencing. And besides, who's to know?"

"What did you like about him?"

"Oh, he was cute and sensitive. And he cared about what I thought ... treated me special."

"How about men in general?"

"You mean, what do I like about them?"

"Yeah."

Sue had stripped to her panties and, with her back turned towards me, put on a thin nightshirt. The sight of her nipples pressed against the shirt eased my pain somewhat. She slipped under the bed sheet, one leg exposed.

"I like their looks and ways of doing things. Like how they play. Men are adventuresome and they take risks. They really know how to stir up bloody hell, you know.

"They surprise me ... I like to talk to men. I think men are more honest than women. And I like the way they feel, you know. Solid, um ... tall and enveloping when they hug."

Silence prevailed. Did I fit into any of those categories? As if to get the attention off her, Sue stifled a grin and pointed to my butt. "How's your—?"

"The *pain* ... is excruciating."

"Seriously?"

"As long as I don't move I'm all right. My body heals quickly, but to be honest the thought of traveling like this scares me." I wanted to switch subjects.

"What's it like traveling as a women in Egypt, with guys gawking at you?" I really desired her.

"The guys are obnoxious. If I'm buying something, they press their lips against my ear and whisper, 'Seven pounds, but if you're nice you can have for free.' They treat Western women like prostitutes, always looking, always taunting. They think we're easy to go to bed with."

"How does that make you feel?"

She stroked her hair, withdrew her eyes from mine, then folded the pillow beneath her head and hugged it.

"I hate it. I guess it challenges my sense of self-worth. That's always been a problem for me. I have to be careful of how I dress, how I look at people. Sometimes I'd like to wear skimpy bathing suits, dress the way I want. To flaunt the rules. But here it's not *in* for women to show their bodies. I respect that—it's their culture."

Her eyes connected with mine for a brief moment. Romance had not fled my thoughts, even in this wounded state. Intimacy and desire were so interrelated. What was she thinking? Should I invite her into my bed? Here we were, lieing no more than four feet apart, talking to each other and talking to ourselves.

"It's much easier for guys," I said. "The touts hit on me all the time to buy. They just want my money, sometimes to talk. I can still use my eyes."

"You're lucky. A woman learns to avoid eyes early in life. How can I use my eyes and convey to men that I'd like to be friendly, but I'm not available?"

I laughed at the irony of it all. I couldn't even figure out what it meant for her to be on the bed next to me, much less figure out what her eyes said. Was she available? Why not just ask her? I chickened out.

"Short of outright telling them, Sue, I don't know. You're talking to the wrong person."

The conversation waned; Sue flipped off the light and stared into space. Her hands were now neatly folded on her chest and both legs under the sheet. I lay there listening to the buzzing silence, as if I had passed a test I wanted to fail. Katharine Hepburn's voice as Rosie in *The African Queen* chimed caustically: "Nature, Mr. Allnut, is what we are put in this world to *rise above*."

The muscle responded well to the *muti* and lots of rest by the pool. After three days, during which time we had gotten to know each other well without furthering the romance, Sweet Sue purchased a wooden cane with the handle carved in the shape of Anubis, jackal-headed god of the dead. "Take this. We're going to visit the Temple of Karnak."

The Karnak temple complex was one of the biggest religious sites in the ancient world and a symbol of the Egyptian empire's power. For two thousand years, successive pharaohs added rooms to the temple, inscribing hieroglyphics on the walls, which told stories of Egyptian life. A sprawling granite edifice—it easily encompassed three city blocks—it was located at the edge of the city and commanded a majestic view of the Nile. The complex was open to the stars and guarded by twenty-six ram-sphinxes. Mysterious, it languished in various stages of dusty decay, from perfectly hewn rooms, obelisks, and spiraling columns, to huge broken chunks of granite that had slammed against the earthen floor countless centuries ago.

Sue must have searched every nook and cranny of the hodge-podge of chambers and vestibules, which contained over eighteen thousand stone statues and columns ten feet in diameter and forty feet high. I explored what I could without aggravating my injury.

Once boredom enveloped me and I called to her from a musty room. I was waiting diabolically in the dark and as she stepped tentatively into my lair, I yelled: "aahhh!" Her feet left the ground at least six inches, and then she charged forward pounding my shoulder until I yelled: "help! this woman is beating an invalid!"

Outside the gates of Karnak, Sue dickered for a horse and buggy to return us to Club Med. Frustrated with the negotiations, she yelled at the surprised driver, "No way! You're just trying to rip us off."

"Let's take the ride, Sue," I whispered in her ear, "the difference is only fifteen cents."

"You pay the difference then. He's trying to scam us."

"So what? Travelers are always complaining about being ripped off. What's fifteen cents to you? To him it's a lot. Yesterday, you were willing to pay the hotel ten dollars for a lunch you didn't order to avoid a fuss. What's the point? Squeeze the poor, but don't look bad in front of the rich."

As the buggy jounced along the dry streets past kiosks selling everything from soup to watches, Sue sat in thoughtful silence. She wiped a film of sweat from under her eyes, dropped her hand to her mouth, and, feeling the pain of discovering something about herself she didn't like, exclaimed: "Oh my God, you're right! And I came to Africa to help the poor. I swear to God, Denis, I'll never do that again."

My admiration for her went up immensely. The nice thing about a young person is that their mind is not made up.

That afternoon, Sweet Sue escorted me to a curbside bus station, next to a gyros shop. I was off to Hurghada where I would spend the night. Then I planned to cross the Red Sea, unlike Moses, by the morning ferry to the Sinai Peninsula, eventually winding up in Dahab, a former hippie hangout to the north. Sue was off to Aswan the next day. Standing at the door of the bus, flanked by Egyptians, I summoned up the courage to take her aside out of earshot.

"Sue, I have to tell you something," I stammered. "These last few days with you have been more *pure* fun than I've had in a very long time. I've admired you from the moment you headed across Uganda to see gorillas. Also ... I wanted to sleep with you, but was afraid to ask."

I then extended my hand goodbye.

"No way!" she said, and slipped her arms around my waist for a long, tender hug, her eyelashes and lips touching my cheek with a warm farewell kiss.

"Maybe we'll meet in Dahab," she said. Then, as I boarded the bus, Sweet Sue yelled out, "You should have asked!"

MIDDLE EAST

WHERE FAST MEETS SLOW

33

STONED IN RED SEA HEAVEN

N THE CROWDED, SWEATY BUS, I massaged my aching bum while watching Sue standing inside the gyros shop. Her eyes followed the bus's departure. My cheek still pulsed from her kiss, as if warmed by a cozy fire. I recognized what her eyes said to me: Another goodbye. I'll miss the intimacy, and maybe we'll meet again?

The doddering clunker of a bus rattled towards Hurghada on a narrow two-lane road through a land engulfed by sand. Tasseled curtains hung from window-rods to block the fierce sun and brown faces peered out from kaffiyehs, pale-blue turbans, and black shawls.

People yelling up and down the aisle competed against the trilling Middle Eastern music pouring from overhead speakers. A shouting match broke out. Two men screaming, their faces red and arms flailing. Male passengers on the bus acted as peacemakers—holding back the combatants and arguing their cases for them. When a consensus was reached all was forgiven. Dangling a cigarette from his purple lips, one of the flushed antagonists plopped next to me, a jade and gold plate in his lap. Before long, he gave up his seat to an old man with gray skin who handed me a chicklet and a lemon slice to chew on. Then a wrinkled, heavily veined hand, owned by a crone in a faded black dress and veil, reached forward past my left shoulder to adjust the shade. The hand softly touched my bare arm and lingered for a moment.

I spent the night in Hurghada enjoying chicken roasted on a spit. In the morning, I boarded a slim two-decker ship that rolled for six hours across the Red Sea to Sharm el-Sheikh. I expected the water to be at least a shade of red, but it was a spectacular crystalline blue. Its whitecaps sparkled like sunlight off sapphire. Soon the rugged peaks of a hazy Sinai appeared in the distance, then golden cliffs that dropped straight down. It must have taken Moses weeks to escape across the Red Sea.

The Sinai Peninsula was taken from Egypt by Israel during the 1967 Six Day War. The Israelis controlled it for a generation, then handed it back. What did the residents of Sinai think about being won and lost like a poker chip? The area was reputed to have the most spectacular scuba diving in the world. Wedged between Israel and Egypt, the peninsula was surrounded by the Gulf of Suez, the Red Sea, and the Gulf of Aqaba. My destination was Dahab, a lazy Bedouin town on the Gulf of Aqaba noted for relaxation and soft drugs. It was fifty miles northeast of Sharm el-Sheikh.

In the van to Dahab, I struck up a conversation with a lanky Australian with curly, red hair, who my grandfather would have dubbed a "long drink of water." The driver tuned the radio to some atonal local singing, triggering three Americans in the back of the van to complain. Their irritation graduated to whining barbs about the volume of the music and also the dangerous speed. What was the big deal? The speedometer never exceeded a hundred-and-ten kilometers an hour, and the one-lane road was straight with nothing in sight but honey-colored dunes, a few wild camels, and isolated white tents of roving Arabs. The van couldn't have been more than ten years old, and I checked the tires: good tread and no missing lugs. This was a walk in the park compared with what I had experienced.

In early afternoon, the driver left us on a desolate dirt road outside Dahab. Open desert and orange mountains on one side, the sea and civilization on the other. The Australian dropped his pack on the sand and asked where I was going. He was slightly stooped, like many tall people. Watching the Americans pour from the van, I spoke quietly into a cuffed hand: "I'm going to stand right here and get a bead on those guys. Then I'm heading in the opposite direction."

"I'm with you, mate," he said. "The name's Mark."

We wandered on a dirt road through a maze of residential stucco huts until we reached the sea. At that point, we discovered paradise. A sandy road ran along the Gulf for at least a mile. Traffic was sparse, but diverse—meaning no cars, a few camels, locals in long clothes topped by turbans or scarves, and bold ten-year-old boys flashing white teeth while racing bareback on powerful Arabian horses. It smelled of animals, the sea, and food. Restaurants with vibrantly colored murals of fish and scorpions cooked various scrumptious dishes on the desert side of the road, and then, on the sea side, served the food to tables of travelers lounging on weathered couches underneath canvas covers. And traipsing among the travelers, on carpeted floors, little Arab girls peddled string bracelets. Dahab reminded me of a sultan's oasis in a Bob Hope *Road to ...* movie. The lone inconvenience was the flies, the kind that dig in when you attempt to brush them off.

"Woo-hoo, mate, this is my kind of town!" Mark hollered.

"My boy," I said, reaching up to grab his shoulder, still afflicted with a swollen ass, "This place is tailor-made to rest a bum bum!"

Turning and following an alleyway away from the water, we came across the Fighting Kangaroo camp, a circle of concrete huts with palm mats over dirt floors and three-inch pads for beds. Ten seconds after unhooking our backpacks and flinging them on the beds, a skinny guy with a mustache, dull eyes, and secretive demeanor stood at the doorway. "You wish to buy drugs?" he inquired in a hushed voice. "Ganja, hash, something stronger?"

Mark and I gave each other one of those "it's okay with me if it's okay with you" looks. He squinted at the tout, "Is it safe here?"

The tout shrugged and stepped closer, lowered his gruff voice. "Safe, yes! But you must be careful. Do not advertise."

"How much?" Mark queried, his bright blue eyes narrowed for business.

"Fifteen dollars for this." The tout dipped a hand into his pocket producing a plastic bag with a half-ounce of ganja.

"How do we know it's good?"

"Dahab not very big. I am easy to find."

We paid ten dollars and the little guy moved on to the next hut. Mark rolled a joint and sealed it. We sampled the goods while discussing the bare essentials of each other's lives. He hid the plastic pouch under the floor mat just before blasting a loud fart that rendered the hut uninhabitable.

"It's nice to know from the get-go what kind of a guy you are," I said.

Dahab's shoreline seemed an endless series of pillowed and carpeted hangouts serenaded by early Seventies Western music. Further south the dirt road forked through a quaint town with lots of shops and merchants who actually waited for customers to speak before beginning their sales pitch.

Mark and I chose a hangout, flopped on a couch, and ordered mango and coconut shakes. A sniff away, the Gulf sparkled peacefully in the afternoon sun. And next to us, in a space the size of a football field, a herd of mature camels and their babies lay on their stomachs in the warm desert sand, their long necks extended upwards, mouths yawning and chewing cud in the desert winds. They were content with life.

The real character of Dahab came out in its squads of throaty little girls. They wore kerchiefs and flashy sash dresses, carried cloth satchels filled with colorful strings, and had spunky personalities and throaty voices in the style of Mae West. One sashayed up to Mark. "You buy bracelets?" she demanded. "We make very good bracelets for you hair, you ankle, you wrist—"

"No, that's okay, maybe tomorrow," Mark sputtered defensively.

They surrounded and separated us. The eight-year-old looked Mark dead in the eyes. "Why not now? I make best bracelets. Ask anyone!"

"I'm not buying today!"

"Okay, okay. I make you best deal. One hair bracelet for you nice hair—three pounds."

"No!"

"Okay, okay. We play backgammon. You win, I make bracelet for you. I win, you pay me one pound." Mark hunched closer to the table and began to play.

The girls and travelers were made for each other in this haven by the sea. Sitting cross-legged, stringing bracelets and braiding hair, the girls quietly passed the time of day or talked a-mile-a-minute. My buddy was Anita, a saucy ten-year-old with light brown skin and lush brown hair wrapped in a purple kerchief. Her face was just emerging from the rosiness of childhood to the trimness of pre-pubescence, unblemished except for an old gash under the left eye. She wore long turquoise pants under a ruffled, navy-blue dress that sparkled with silver bobbles. Anita communicated with the skill of a snake charmer, utilizing her most endearing features: sultry brown eyes swimming in a milk-white sea and empowered by thick eyebrows and long eyelashes, and a deep, throaty, commanding voice. "You buy only from me," she decreed, sitting between her calves that angled outward. "My bracelets are best. Tell me your price!"

I bought a wrist bracelet and tested her skill at backgammon. "I win, five pounds," she asserted. "You win, two pounds." We played. She cheated! With any brief distraction such as a sparkle off the water, turning my head to make an observation or receive a drink, anything, and she'd rearrange the chips. "Wait a minute! Were the chips laid out like that?"

"Yes, yes, you move!" Then, because she couldn't stand stupidity. "*No!* This better move."

(Another distraction.)

"Wait! You threw twice!" I'd squeal indignantly.

"I throw six and three!"

"Before that! Before that!"

Across the way a nine-year-old had just gammoned a Swiss guy, and a German woman sat peacefully talking with a friend as another girl wove string into her long, brown hair. My tally that day: *Purchased*: one hair braid. *Won*: one safety string for sunglasses. *Lost*: one mango shake in a double or nothing game, and ten Egyptian pounds (three dollars).

After dinner and a long exploratory walk, Mark and I sat under a blushing sunset. He puffed on a cigarette telling me he was traveling for a year to decide his future.

"My uncle did the same when he was young. He saw me struggling to decide whether I wanted to marry and be a cotton farmer like my old man, or strike out on my own. One day, my uncle pulled me aside and said, 'Mate, you'll be thirty next month. Get your arse out for a while. Go see the world.'"

"Do you like farming?"

"Hard to say. Farmers are tied to the land. My dad's dream was to own his own farm. His dream of land is an Irish narcotic that controls him."

"Dreams have a way of being controlling. Has the trip helped?"

"Got a bloody Dear John letter from my girl a month after I left." He chuckled sardonically. "Took care of one decision."

"What happened?"

"Another bloke. She needed me close to the hearth."

"What does striking out on your own mean?"

"That's a tricky question. Cotton farming is what I know. I like farming, but I don't want to be tied to a gum tree and flogged with it."

We chewed on this comment for a while, listening to the water and occasional groans of camels. He rubbed sweat from the rim of his Yankees baseball cap. Soft melodies from slow songs drifted past.

"Except for my mid-thirties," I said, "I always knew where I was going. Getting there became a matter of how to deal with things coming up along the way. You know what I mean? It's like crossing a rocky stream. You can see the other side, in that sense you have control, but you don't know which stones to step on until you reach them."

"How did you know what you wanted?"

"A kid's zeal synthesized into a few words for portability, I guess." I told him about my vision. "Then it was a matter of seeing the stepping stones."

"And you can make it happen?"

How did my *controller* personality develop? Maybe it was being the control-freak child of an alcoholic or the process of deciding whether to forgive my dad after a fight? It could even have been my summer job during college years working as a beach patrolman.

I looked over at Mark, who was in his own reverie, and spoke in a mellow pace that comes with all the time in the world.

"Your dad did. It's a matter of control really. In college, I worked summers as a beach patrolman at a town beach in New York. They gave me a badge that I pinned on my bathing suit. On weekends it was residents only because of the crowd. Sometimes you'd get a non-resident car loaded with screaming kids, and mom and dad in dire need of several shots of vodka. I'd let them in. Sometimes a non-resident cop flashed a badge. I'd say sorry. Control needs to be exercised.

"By the end of my third year in college, I got bored with the job and worked as a bookkeeper for a hotel and dining theater in the Hamptons. It didn't take long to figure out that the waitresses were steeling. Information on the dinner checks was erased, written over, or scratched out. When the owner asked what could be done I said, 'Make me general manager at night and I'll fix it.'

"Meanwhile, I used to eat at my own table in the dining room and get seconds if I wanted. Then we got a new chef. He told me no seconds, and, by the way, you have to eat in the back room with everyone else. Actually, I had fun eating with the waiters and waitresses and kitchen help, but the effrontery stung. So when the chef came to get his check from the bookkeeper, that would be me, on Friday, I just couldn't find it. After a day or two, the chef said I could eat at my old table. 'Seconds?' I asked. 'Sure!' What I took from it? Money controls! Check out the IMF in Africa.

"Later on, I even worked as a controller in Silicon Valley. Controllers control. From there I became a CFO and so on, before starting my own firm fixing companies in trouble. That's the ultimate in control. There are no rules except the ones we set. It has to be that way. The company can't afford any more big mistakes.

"That's my story. I used the control narcotic. But now I have no control, and I'm loving it!"

Mark and I were building a friendship in Dahab. We grabbed bed mats from the room and slept under the twinkling stars, bundling up in our *khangas* to avoid mosquitoes. The next day, we snorkeled at one of the world's most notorious diving sites, the Blue Hole.

Though Mark fell in love with a young Dutch woman, we both were captivated by the gorgeous Israelis sunning themselves and showing lots of skin. The Israeli men looked a world apart from the funky travelers and the thin, much smaller Egyptians. Dark-haired with strong eyes and jaws, and bodies bulging in muscle shirts, their haircuts and sunglasses conveyed self-confidence. Achmed, the owner of our preferred hangout, said the locals got along with Israelis, that they had gotten to know each other during the occupation.

Mark tried to get me to join him in Syria, but I needed to be in Siberia by the third week in July to catch my boat to the Arctic Circle during the very limited period of ice thaw. I would miss him, but by now I knew that someone else and some other experience would take his place.

The day he left, I got into a conversation with Achmed about dress codes. He complained about occasional Israeli women and some female travelers and tourists that wore clothes inappropriate to his country.

"I know what you mean," I said. "In San Francisco, where I live, once in a while I see a Muslim woman wear full-length garments and a veil over her eyes. Same same."

"What wrong with her clothes?"

"In our culture the veil is degrading to women. It is a sign of lack of freedom."

"I no see how that is same as Western women with little clothes in Egypt."

I tried to explain but got nowhere. It reminded me of the same discussions I had with occasional Westerners that saw no harm in wearing bikinis on beaches and shorts and low-cut blouses in Muslim countries. Same same.

After a week in paradise, Anita wove an ankle bracelet for a going-away present, saying: "No charge you." I felt honored. What happened to these dynamos when they grew up? There was little evidence of young women in the village.

I challenged Anita to a single game of backgammon—ten pounds to her five. The wager exceeded her house limit, so she organized a consortium of bracelet makers to fund her. Before the game, I treated the girls to my favorite breakfast: crepes with bananas and a scoop of vanilla ice cream covered with creamy chocolate and fresh fruit. They attacked like starving piranhas. The backgammon was nip and tuck—my traveler's luck against the pooled cheating talents of Anita and friends. Anita won, of course, and blew the money on ice cream and soda in less than ten minutes. Anita said she got forty percent of what she made, her mother the rest. Windfalls must have been an exception to that rule.

34

LOST IN THE LOST CITY OF PETRA

NUWEIBA WAS A DINKY EGYPTIAN town surrounded on three sides by brown shale mountains. The Gulf of Aqaba lay on the fourth side. At nine in the morning, a daily ferry left Nuweiba for the city of Aqaba in Jordan. Inside the huge ferry terminal, thousands of Arabs waited in colossal passport control lines to catch the ferry to the city that Lawrence of Arabia snatched from the Turks during World War I. The long lines existed because neighboring Israel was off limits to most Arabs, and Saudi Arabia was as difficult to get into as childproof packaging. Thus, Nuweiba was the major crossing point for the Arab lands.

Westerners were ushered to the front of the line for red-carpet treatment. The only snag was that the border guard didn't recognize my passport picture. Who could blame him? Staring behind plastic was a staid businessman with short hair combed left to right—quite a contrast to the tanned person in a blue bandanna with a string-braid dangling among long tresses. Did anyone miss that businessman back home in the fast-paced world?

Officials escorted a group of about twenty whites up the gangplank and into a huge room with benches and a big blue carpet. I struck up a conversation and shared sardines, cheese, bread, and butter cookies with tall Leo from Amsterdam and fragile-looking Inez from Argentina. They happened to toss their backpacks on the floor next to me and the process of traveling, which naturally brought people together, did the rest. One merely had to say, "Where are you coming from?" If the personalities meshed, one had companions. We were all after the same things: adventure and the intimacy of camaraderie. Leo, the son of two college professors, told me he had traveled extensively in Asia and the Middle East. Currently, he attended the American University in Cairo hoping for a political science degree, which had eluded him for ten years. Slightly gaunt, he had that fastidious look of a loner. Inez often stroked the bangs of her coal black hair. Her green eyes hinted at a mischievousness under layers of shyness and upper-class formality. They had met on a train in China the year before.

Early the next morning, our threesome caught a van that drove deep into the Jordanian desert. Our destination: the lost city of Petra. The heat during the three-hour ride gradually rose to around a hundred degrees with little humidity. The terrain belched up a few patches of greenery and mountains in the distance. Lizards scampered across the asphalt road. Halfway to the Jordanian capital Amman, in an area known for its huge canyons, Petra was the location of the Holy Grail in *Indiana Jones and the Last Crusade*.

In the film, they rode horses through a long gorge, exiting into the courtyard of a magnificent, salmon-colored temple carved out of sandstone. After a twenty-mile drive from our guesthouse and a short hike, we entered the same narrow gorge as Indiana Jones. We joined the scattering of tourists, most of whom were walking like us with a few cantering on horseback, and flowed like an incoming tide through a concave space barely wide enough to fit a horse and buggy. After several kilometers in the gorge, a bright spray of sunshine illuminated a stunning sight before us: the two-tiered temple with columns shown in the movie. The Treasury, as it was popularly known, rose a hundred feet high and was carved out of the sheer face of the rosy cliff. Bas-relief gargoyles and deities were framed by the columns and surrounded by a variety of striking geometric designs. But unlike the temple in the movie, this magnificent structure was just a chiseled façade on the outside, without quarters inside. The structure is basically a tomb and the façade just for looks.

Breaking the spell of the Treasury, we turned right and faced a vast canyon enveloped by jagged buttes, cliffs, and rugged peaks rising up from the blond desert floor. Etched out of the cliffs were caves, ornate cathedrals, and burial sites. On closer inspection, the cathedrals, like the Treasury, were also facades. "What happened to the inhabitants?" I asked Leo, who had been to Petra once before.

"From what I understand, a half million people once lived in the vicinity. They serviced caravans for two thousand years. Then sea routes opened and overland trade dried up, along with Petra's water supply. Afterwards, only a handful of Bedouins knew of its existence until the nineteenth century when a Swiss, masquerading as an Arab, discovered the secret."

Eagles and ravens circled above as we climbed a huge butte above one of the central valleys. Color definitely fine-tuned Petra. Its overall salmon hue was embellished by streaks within the rocks: burgundy, pearl-white, baby blue, and peach. As the light of day shifted, so did the colors.

My injured derriere started to complain around four in the afternoon.

"Instead of the gorge, shall we take a shortcut back?" asked Leo in his Dutch lilt. "This trail I know parallels the gorge, and then cuts across a rocky ridge intersecting the gorge at the three kilometer point."

A fair idea, but I felt a strange uneasiness. Twenty years ago, my old college buddy, Pete, and I took a couple of Yamaha bikes to California's Mojave Desert. Surveying the barren wasteland and mountains in the distance, he'd handed me a rag and a book of matches. "Here, take these," he said.

"Why?"

"Because if we separate, everything will look the same to you. Mountains that seem five miles away could be fifty. You might never find your way out. Put that rag in your tank and light it with a match. I'll find you." He made an impression. Deserts were dangerous.

We walked on sand and gravel for three kilometers, under the still scorching sun. Lizards got bigger and ants fewer. The wind picked up. Leo guided us sharply to the right, up and into a tunnel of solid rock. The tunnel opened at the top so the sunlight exposed shiny marble walls of polished peach. Once through the tunnel, we zigzagged single file into a lonely canyon, climbing over and wiggling between huge boulders. We jumped sandy pools of slimy water and squeezed (Inez easily) through pink rock forests. I razzed Leo about whether he'd passed his Boy

Scout wilderness exam. Once in a while, Inez timidly inquired: "Leo, are you sure you know where you are going?"

He simply nodded and continued forward, the essence of smug confidence.

We dodged and squirmed, jumped and climbed. At six o'clock, I began to carefully monitor our water supplies. Several times Leo trudged on ahead to scout the route.

He seemed so sure of himself. However, our confidence in him started to disappear, at about the same rate as the water. His assured answer to the question "Are you sure you know where you are going?" began to erode. "I am sure!" became "I am sure I recognize the route," then "I am almost certain." On the last of his scouting trips, he returned ashen-faced, shaking his head in confusion. "I cannot understand. We must have taken a wrong turn."

The sun continued to drop.

Inez and I scrambled past him to the jagged edges of a cliff that hung high above the desert floor. In every direction, a lonely, rain-starved, rocky wilderness stared at us. We were lost in the lost city of Petra, with two empty water bottles and another two-thirds gone. Leo sat down and dangled his legs over the edge of the cliff, massaging his chin. Inez adjusted the white cloth turban she wore, looked at me, and shrugged nervously.

"Let's go back the way we came, and then go through the gorge," I suggested, taking off my Lawrence of Arabia tourist hat and tying on the more comfortable bandanna. "If we hurry, we can get to the Treasury building before dark. There's probably two hours of light." I turned to Leo. "How far to the gorge and out?"

"Maybe ten or eleven kilometers, but I am sure I can manage to find the shortcut."

"Leo, the sun's fading. Our water's mostly gone, and I have no desire to be wandering among boulders in a dark desert. I'm wondering whether you know the way back!"

"I can get us back!"

What kind of wild animals lurked about? Would we be likely to meet Arabs in the dark gorge, waiting to pounce on stragglers? I decided to think positively, but covering all bets, pulled a hundred-dollar bill from my money-belt and stuffed it deep inside my sock. Next I transferred the Swiss Army knife from daypack to jeans.

I'd learned over the years that there were those who persisted in a losing situation because their ego found it intolerable to admit they'd made a mistake. I had a hunch Leo was one of those people, and had no wish to test myself out here. "Let's start back," I ordered and marched off in the direction we had come from. No sense coddling Leo's ego anymore.

Adrenaline surged through my veins, washing over the pain in my bum and rendering it mute. As for Leo, he badly sprained his ankle shimmying down a nine-foot embankment. We moved on regardless, hoping to reach the gorge entrance by nightfall. While sympathizing with Leo, I pushed the pace to build leeway. An unspoken tension arose between us, intensifying after he discovered the junction where he went wrong. Still in the rocks, he got nothing but frowns for the suggestion that we try the "shortcut" one last time.

On that long march back, I thought how naturally control came to me and how easily I gave it up. But I couldn't hold back when confronted with a crisis. My travel personality appeared mellow, but as soon as conflict appeared, out popped Mr. Powerful. The same guy who wore the title "controller" on the way up the business ladder. A controller assured that every dollar was spent ethically and legally and was in line with a plan or forecast. He made sure everyone was playing by the rules. There was conflict in this job, clashes of willpower, diplomacy. You needed to be willing to quit if your integrity was compromised. Unfortunately, I could never quite integrate the hard-driving businessman and fun-loving father personalities. It was almost as if they had separate missions. What should you do with a personality that got you home, but didn't belong when you got there?

I kept an eye on Leo limping and lagging. Inez walked between us in the fading twilight. She took events calmly, and although her body looked fragile she proved to be resilient and fit.

We trudged through the darkening desert for two hours, listening to the dragging of our boots on dirt and the occasional screech of an eagle. The land cooled and the vastness of raw nature turned from the trust of day to the potential treachery of night. Mouth dry and dusty, I turned to check Leo. He kept pace about a hundred yards behind in the dusk, a pathetic and heroic figure. Inez looked wide-eyed, determination energizing her walk.

My first controller position was at Fairchild Camera, the mother company of the semiconductor industry. Riding the often traumatic ups and downs of the semiconductor industry in Silicon Valley, I sat through monthly divisional staff meetings watching the interaction of top executives. I was always learning about the use of control, the inner workings of growth, products, organizations, and people. Six years later, at thirty-five and on the executive staff of a leading-edge computer startup, I had become a sophisticated manipulator of events. Meaning I figured out where I wanted to go, and how to use resources to get there.

We reached the Treasury just after dark, searching its confines unsuccessfully for water. Except for ghosts, Petra was deserted. The silver light of a half-moon barely penetrated the eerie walls of the gorge, which once again swallowed us whole. We shuffled along cautiously, weary, parched, and anxiously listening for any unusual sound. We pictured all sorts of intrigues in the silhouettes created by the shadowy light. Would some violent Arab slash at us from a dark corner? Or was that just our Western imagination?

Exiting the gorge like commandos, we peered through faint moonlight, scanning horse stables that catered to tourists. We breathed a collective sigh of relief—nobody stirred in the stables. Hardly disturbing the dust with our boots, we stumbled quietly past them. A quarter of a mile later, we reached the safety of a paved road. Only then did I metaphorically take the rag out of the gas tank and pocket the matches. I smiled cordially at Leo, and thanked him for the thrill.

The tension between us receded, but its taste lingered. We were two people who liked to exercise control, without any clear agreement on how to hand it over to the other. I chided myself for not finding the right words to achieve harmony on that rocky cliff in the desert, so that Leo could save face. The old "won the battle, lost the war" feeling.

Inez flagged down a black Toyota driven by a local who deposited us at our guesthouse. We arrived just in time to catch *Indiana Jones and Last Crusade* on video. They probably played it every night.

35

ENGLISHMEN VS. ARABS—
A QUESTION OF POINT OF VIEW

T HE NEXT MORNING I TRAVELED alone to Amman in order to
obtain entry to the Israeli-occupied West Bank. Inez gave
parting instructions: "Never mention to Jordanian officials
that you want a visa to Israel. The West Bank is—how do you
say?—occupied territory belonging to Jordan. They require a *visitor's permit.*"

Amman struck me as a clean city, whose crisscrossing highways linked symbols of Western infiltration—McDonald's, Pizza Hut, even a Safeway grocery—to the old way of life with its full-length clothing, exotic sounds, and the smell of meat sizzling on skewers at street corners.

I took a cab straight to the Ministry of Interior for a permit. Before long, I was fishing for extra passport photos and joking with two Brits on holiday, who introduced themselves as Phil and Paul. They said they ran the service department for a large British auto manufacturer in Saudi Arabia, slipping in that the deposed Ugandan dictator Idi Amin was one of their customers. During the form filling, they realized that I was without accommodations. "Stay at our hotel," said the older of the two, in a thick Cockney accent. "It's a bit on the boring side, but I fancy it'll do until you get your permit sorted out."

"Why not?" I thought. Fate sent these blokes my way, might as well ride in their rented car.

After checking in at the Middle East Hotel, I joined the guys in their room. A half-finished bottle of Jack Daniels sat on the bedside table along with a phone and six vanquished large bottles of beer. Phil, the younger of the two in his early thirties, grinned at the mess: "In Saudi, squire, alcohol is as hard to come by as loose women."

We were an odd threesome. Dressed in slacks and plaid, short-sleeve shirts, with short, cropped hair, they smoked each cigarette like it was their last. I didn't smoke, except for the occasional joint, and sat there in whipcord pants, T-shirt, and an ankle bracelet compliments of Anita in Dahab.

Paul was, as the expression goes, a real work of art. He looked as if he had been preparing for a mid-life crisis since his early teens. Now that it had arrived, it suited him well. His pug nose sneered disdain for the world, and a smile could not possibly have wormed its way into his sullen eyes or across his smoldering, red face. Paul managed the service business and Phil was his right-hand man.

"The only reason me and Phil are in Saudi Arabia," Paul complained, pointing his cigarette at Phil and wrinkling his nose for emphasis, "is for the bloody money. God knows, a bloke needs extra dosh with the prices these days. Tell him, Phil. A bloke earns every penny putting up with Saudis. Three years in that desert is a jail sentence. Am I right, Phil?"

Paul splashed Jack Daniels into his glass and raised it. "Cheers, gents!"

Phil hated the Saudis, too, but had been trained to be more "user-friendly." "It's a cruel dictatorship, as far as I'm concerned, run by a bunch of rich religious fanatics who look down their bloody noses at us. Westerners live in fenced-in compounds so we don't contaminate them. The wankers import workers from Egypt and Asia to do the dirty work. They whip them with bamboo canes if they—"

"Fucking right! Tell him about the women!" snorted Paul. "Tell him how the bastards stare at our birds for hours. But their women can't get into a car without their brother or father. Tell him."

"Saudis have these old men who walk around with sticks. They cane a bloke on the legs or backside if his clothes don't conform to code. Your American servicewomen caused all sorts of shit during the war with Iraq. If one of those old geezers used the stick on a Yank, he'd get an automatic jammed under his cheek bone and a pissed-off lady threatening to blow his fucking head off."

Paul grinned for the first time, and handed me the sloshing bottle. "Take a swig. I reckon his throat's parched, ain't it, Phil?"

That afternoon, we shopped at Safeway for beer. The huge store sold everything from food to furniture in an atmosphere of cleanliness that stopped just short of white gloves. Air conditioning, shining floors, the purity of quiet shuffling. They bandaged food in plastic and styrofoam, then wrapped it again in plastic at the register. This didn't fit the old-world image.

In contrast, we visited a section of Amman in the evening that was unmarked by the advances of modern civilization. Crowded shops with dust on the floors lined busy sidewalks. Chicken rotated on outdoor rotisseries. The air filled with the hum of human chatter. Watching Phil and Paul stiffly peek into a butcher shop, where two fully dressed chickens, dangling in rigor mortis, were being handed over to a patron, I wondered what the guys thought of Jordanian Arabs. Just then, something on the second floor of a corner building caught Phil's attention. "Spot of tea, gents?"

Watched over by portraits of a smiling King Hussein and his beautiful American spouse, men sat comfortably sipping tea, smoking long-stemmed hookahs, and playing games. It felt like an English working men's club, only the tables were weary, the pipes had long handles, and dominoes was the game of choice instead of snooker or cards. Several mustached faces in turbans looked up to welcome us with toothy smiles. I reciprocated. Paul and Phil walked stiffly to a table, noses uplifted. They lit up a nanosecond after we touched down. Cradling the cigarette between his thumb and index finger, Paul leaned towards me and whispered suspiciously, "Do you feel it?"

"Feel what?"

"They hate us in here!" he said, looking like he had just smelled dog shit.

After surveying the room of copper faces, I looked into Paul's eyes and said: "Paul, try smiling! People return what you send their way. I've had nothing but good vibes from these people."

Paul epitomized the lonely ones who see only frustration and drudgery in life. Think negatively, attract negative experiences! It was as clear as a baby's smile: positive energy made life so much easier. Nevertheless, I liked hanging out with Paul and Phil. They seemed to need company like mine and treated me like a visiting cousin.

The next morning, we traveled through blistering heat down a straight, jet-black road with a sparkling white line down the middle, heading towards Israel and the Dead Sea. Maneuvering the Toyota with his index finger, Phil occasionally nodded agreement to Paul as he smoked and recited how Saudis used religion to mold and control thought. How much did Phil and Paul's outlook color what they saw? My impression of the people in Egypt and Jordan was that they were worlds apart from the picture of Muslims I had formed in the US. The culture valued women as mothers and undervalued them as individuals. But the picture of the men as cruel seemed inconsistent with the texture of the soft faces and slow pace of life.

Still, the Brits were talking about Saudi Arabia and I hadn't been there. "What makes the Saudis so arrogant," I asked, shortly after we accelerated past an armed checkpoint in the middle of nowhere.

"Oil. They don't need to cater to tourists, so they can tell foreigners to bugger off. They teach you to hate them."

"If it wasn't for oil, they'd be like the rest of them, marketing their sand hills to tourists to pay bills."

"If oil prices keep going up, we might all end up working for the bastards."

No way did you dive into the iron-colored waters of the Dead Sea, unless you liked your eyes pricked with needles. So Phil, Paul, and I eased ourselves in. The water had the consistency of light pancake batter and was so laden with salt that only a boulder could drown. People floated on its surface like astronauts in outer space, reading newspapers or playing catch with a rubber ball. A rifle shot away from the gray mountains of Israel, two middle-aged Western women stripped to bikinis, which certainly grabbed the sparse male audience's attention.

Near the Western women, an Arab family of ten enjoyed their holiday. Two men frolicked in the water while teaching a little boy and girl to swim. On land, grandma smiled a gap-toothed grin, pouring instructions at a pair of giggling young ladies entering the water dressed in full-length, black, two-layer gowns. A five-year-old cried from the sting of salt.

Except for the clothes, that could be a family anywhere in the world. What did the Brits see? Were they staring through a negative filter at evil Muslims, or could they refocus to see people enjoying themselves?

36

ISRAEL: FITTING WESTERN VALUES INTO AN OLD CULTURE

P HIL AND PAUL DROPPED ME off at the Hilton at seven in the morning to catch the bus to Jerusalem. The bus crossed over the rickety King Hussein Bridge into Israel. This bridge was so small it could have been built from an Erector Set. I asked Israeli immigration not to stamp my passport to avoid future hassles entering Islamic countries, and by eleven signed under dorm room number two in the guestbook of the California Hostel in modern Jerusalem.

Blue-lace panties, bare breasts, and the scent of sleep greeted me. Another first—mixed dorms. Most of my roomies were women working in Jerusalem bars. Slightly embarrassed, I said hello to those struggling with the light of day, tossed my backpack on the dusty floor, and hit the sack.

Jerusalem was a tale of two cities: a walled-in treasure of antiquity whose look and feel reached back to biblical times, and an ultra-modern metropolis housing attractive town squares designed for foot traffic and surrounded by typical urban infrastructure. The Old City was not tourist hype. It was ancient, completely encircled by a thirty-foot, gray, stone wall with tall towers guarding arched entry gates. Outside the walls though, except for the Mount of Olives to the east, a desert metropolis grew like an invasion of locusts. It was an invasion of Western culture: shopping malls, banks, pizza, Carvel ice-cream, beefy bodies, and businesses buzzing with computers, faxes, and the bleeps of watches and phones.

Walking around the metropolis buying necessities, phoning home for an update, and getting cash, I soon found a quaint redbrick city square and a table with a pink umbrella. The sign overhead read: New York Pizza. A good place to read and watch the scads of locals and tourists floating by. The IMF did not appear in the local papers, but there were lots of stories of Holocaust victims. Israel stole the spotlight in the international news. *USA Today* featured articles surrounding a large picture of a sixteen-year-old Palestinian's funeral. The caption read: *Peace within reach—not in hand.* They failed to comment on a smaller picture showing a hundred thousand peace demonstrators in Tel Aviv. Made you wonder how the media could affect the outcome if they focused on the positive.

Chewing pizza with fresh tomato sauce and good cheese, I saw all sorts of young people between eighteen and twenty-five in uniforms and civvies, strolling by or congregating in groups, laughing and talking as if they were planning a party. Except that machine guns were slung over many of their shoulders like pocketbooks.

By chance, I ran into an American I'd met in Dahab, Jane, outside the Jaffa Gate. She recommended staying at the Lutheran Guest House in the Old City. She stayed at this hostel when she arrived in Israel three years ago. "It's a perfect place for you," she said "Clean, flowers, birds chirping in the garden, sweet little tables to write on. You'll love it!"

Jane was meeting a friend at the Arizona, a bar in the metropolis, and invited me to join them. The friend turned out to be a good-looking, dark-featured Israeli by the name of Alone. He had very white teeth and a quiet, confident demeanor. Sitting at the bar with Jane to my right and Alone next to her, we randomly chatted as Bob Dylan sang soulfully in the background—until we stumbled into a deeply charged topic. It started when I made the innocent comment that if the Israelis and Palestinians could make peace, Israel, with its product know-how, would soon have trucks filled with everything from Pampers to cell phones rumbling over a drastically restructured King Hussein Bridge.

"That's not likely," Jane said sullenly, flipping her brown hair out of her eyes. "The oppressed have become the oppressors.

Every day, newspapers run articles about the Holocaust to keep guilt in the public eye and take attention off what they are doing to Palestinians."

She had already filled me in on her background in Dahab: Jewish family; graduated five years before with a psychology masters in art therapy; came to Israel to find herself; and lived in a kibbutz before locating a permanent job working with physically handicapped Palestinian children. "The little Palestinian kids are afraid." she said. "The fear is in their paintings."

"What do you mean?" I asked. A faint look of disapproval clouded Alone's face.

"Sometimes the paintings have short arms, indicating powerlessness, or gloomy, brown and black, pencil-thin figures. Sometimes the Israelis drive huge machines and are painted as giants compared to Arabs. Or the Israelis have full facial details, but Palestinians are missing a mouth or nose. So much fear. I grew up believing that Jews helped the less fortunate."

"This is a war, Jane," Alone said when it was almost clear that she had finished. "These people are terrorists. They blow up buses with children in them!" His emotions were fluid but controlled.

"Those are the extremists, Alone, and you know it. How come ten Palestinians are killed for every Israeli? All extremists? There is nothing democratic about treatment of Palestinians in Israel. Let's be clear, this is apartheid.

"Palestinians need identity cards like in South Africa. You gobble up the land and tax them without effective representation in government. You discriminate in pay, limit exports, control the news and education, ban political parties, and control water.

"This is a fucking desert, and you decide water rationing!" She stopped almost screaming at Alone and sighed heavily. "We've been through all this before. Why can't you get that you, Israel, sets the stage for violence?"

Alone took a break to look around the room. I was sure he believed Ben-Gurion, Israel's founding father and first prime minister, who said. "If I was an Arab leader, I would never make terms with Israel. It is natural; we have taken their country. Sure God promised it to us, but what does that matter to them? Our God is not theirs. ... They only see one thing: we have come here and stolen their country."

"An American talks to me about apartheid," Alone fired back calmly. He plucked a cigarette from a pack of Marlboros he had placed next to his glass. "I've seen your cities. The blacks live in ghettoes surrounded by an army of police to protect against spill-over into white neighborhoods."

"You have a good point, Alone," I said, treading softly. "What's your justification for what she calls apartheid?"

"This may seem foolish to you, Denis. God gave us this land three thousand years ago. And God does not care about time. Now we need to defend ourselves, because we were almost annihilated.

"I don't deny it's hard on Palestinians. But we are surrounded and don't have many options. And how can Americans complain? You finance us in return for a strategic position to monitor your oil.

"And look what you did to your native population. A hundred years ago, you talked about Native Americans as being less than human, to justify your own land grab and ideas of destiny. I visited America. I heard the way you talk about Arabs and Muslims. You support Israel because we are alike. So the justification is that we need the land to survive."

"Why does one people's dream have to be another's disaster?" Jane shook her head and squeezed her eyes shut in exasperation at Alone's beliefs. "I can never get past this point. To create a home for Jews, your country is imposing your values on poor people with strong family ties who are desperate enough to blow themselves up? You will never, *never* win.

"I agree that nobody invades nicely, but I thought we Jews were above that. What good is the dream if we trample other peoples' rights? It doesn't lead to peace, because the adult will do to someone else whatever was done to him as a child."

"You know I don't believe in trampling other's rights, Jane. You know that.

"Okay, let me repeat my old refrain. There are three issues: partitioning Jerusalem; the welfare of refugees in Lebanon; and the settlements. Those are difficult issues, and you don't mention how difficult these people are to negotiate with."

"Well, what would have happened if the billions that go into fighting Palestinians went into their education and welfare?"

"You simplify the situation," retorted Alone.

Before Jane had a chance to respond, I asked her why she stayed in Israel.

"Because most Israelis want peace. Alone does, too. He takes the hard line because it makes him feel powerful. I say fuck the power! Take men out of the equation. A couple of grandmothers from each side could negotiate better than their sons. At least they wouldn't be fighting for fifty years."

Having had the last word, Jane jabbed Alone good-naturedly with her elbow, jolting the ash from his cigarette into his beer. He removed the ash with his middle finger, which he then pointed at Jane, also good-naturedly. Jane and Alone were obviously good friends because the difference in their opinions had not resulted in an almighty slugfest.

Jane and I tentatively arranged to meet the next morning at the Jaffa Gate. She promised to show me Old Jerusalem if she could break a previous commitment. Having already checked into the Lutheran on the other side of the gate, glorious as advertised, I waited in vain for her. Rather than let negative thoughts fester, as I would have in the past, I shrugged off the disappointment. I'd discovered traveling that disappointment often leads to opportunity.

I threaded my arms into the straps of the daypack, took a slug of water, arranged my hair in a small ponytail, and walked between the towers and curved stone doorway of the Jaffa Gate. In hot sunlight, I followed a bright stone road into the interior, passing a scattering of parked cars and driftwood-white brick tenements. Gradually the road narrowed and only foot traffic could maneuver in the cramped passageways through the maze of bazaars filled with tourists buying leather goods, pottery, jewelry, baubles, and all kinds of food.

The tourists were white and tan, and dressed casually expensive. They had glistening hair, occasionally smiled, and generally acted like people on vacation. At major intersections, young Israeli soldiers with machine guns walked around watching. Most of the vendors were male and Palestinian, while most of the food stand customers were female and Palestinian. Palestinian bodies were smaller, thinner, and suppler than the whites and tans. The women's faces were mostly visible, sometimes veiled. I didn't judge Muslims anymore, although I wondered of course about the undiscovered talents of half the population. To me it seemed a waste, but then other talents went into their families' welfare.

Western women looked more confident, wore considerably less clothes, and showed they had power. But when I looked more deeply into the two cultures of women—Western and Arab—I saw great similarities. All appeared gentle, caring, and talkative. Both wore jewelry and dressed to fit their personalities and bodies. They were all buyers and mingled easily among themselves. Women were a sisterhood, no doubt about it. When I looked at the Palestinian men in the shops, I saw people suppressed. Those I dickered with had the aggressiveness in business of other Arabs I'd seen, but their eyes looked into mine without the same humor.

The difference in the role and look of women must have been another root cause of the problems between the Israeli and Arab cultures. To me, the Israelis were the elite landing corps, leading a cultural invasion armed with electronic communication, money, a liberated female mind and body, a superior attitude, and a dream. You would think the Arabs couldn't win. They lived in an old society opposed to change and were up against women contributing their brains to large-scale progress. The combination of women's brains and talent for organization and the aggressive creativity of men were unbeatable. And here on this beachhead, birth control and freedom for women had run smack up against a slow pace of life and large close families. Was the underlying issue the change in family values? One group was busting into the future, and the other tenaciously holding on to the past.

Working my way to the Wailing Wall, four reasonably dressed Palestinian juveniles accosted me, squealing for handouts. "Give me one shekel." "Give me you sunglasses." "Give me—" Their persistence required Beggar Response Number Four. Yanking a shirt and exposing the bronze belly of its surprised owner, I hollered: "Give me your shirt! Give me two shekels! Give me your watch!" A hand grabbed my shoulder and a familiar voice cried: "You're always around a crowd of cheeky kids, mate."

I turned, looked up, and grinned. "Well, if it isn't the Dahab sheik!" Standing before me, with a bigness that matched the open space of Australia, clothes riddled with travel-dust, was the Aussie cotton farmer himself. Mark wore a green bandanna around his forehead, dark sunglasses, a smirk, and a top-loaded backpack that looked welded to his body.

"G'day, Yank! Know where a guy can get a room?"

"Something bad happens, and look who shows up!"

"What?"

"I was just thinking about the odds of meeting you among thousands of people. How the hell are you? What are you doing here?"

"It's fate, mate. Hey, nice rhyme, don't you think?"

On the way back to the Lutheran, where we were going to share my room, Mark and I drained a glass of fresh, cold, sweet orange juice at a gyros stand. "Tell me Long Drink of Water, have you run into other people like this?"

"You mean by chance? Sure. At first I thought it was coincidence, people traveling in the same circles. But I've run into people in different countries a lot!"

"I feel like I've got this force field around me that radiates out for miles."

"Amen to that, mate. I've talked to heaps of travelers about this very subject."

After checking in at the Lutheran, Mark joined me to explore the Old City: the Wailing Wall and the cobblestone neighborhoods around the bazaar that were partitioned into the Jewish, Muslim, Christian, and Armenian Quarters. Not far from Herod's Gate, we stood in a stone square the size of a tennis court. It was surrounded by a bewildering number of curved doorways and white stone buildings. Spotting the towering gray domes of the Church of the Holy Sepulcher, Mark turned sharply and disappeared into an alleyway. "This way!" he commanded.

Entering the church, we slipped a shekel into the crinkled palm of a grumpy old cleric in a black cassock, and crowded into a velvety room dedicated to the Blessed Virgin. Then we climbed slate steps to the second floor. Mark crouched to inspect glass cabinets filled with gold and silver jewelry, sparkling stones, and a bejeweled statue of Mary. He forked out more money to crouch and sink his hand down into a dingy, black hole to touch Calvary—reputedly the very ground on which the Romans crucified Christ. The contrast between Christ's poverty and this church was stark.

Outside again, we came to stone stairs leading down to a large square in front of the Wailing Wall, out of which green weeds peeked, and occasionally flowed, through the crevices in the hewn rock. A large indoor prayer room and two-thirds of the wall space was reserved for males. Inside the room, Orthodox Jews with long beards and black outfits, not unlike those worn by the more conservative Palestinian women, prayed to the old Temple wall, bowing their heads fast and continuously like woodpeckers. Mark took my picture with one of the guys, paying four shekels for the privilege.

On the way home, we bought vegetables at the market and cooked a stir-fry in the hostel kitchen, next to an American archeologist who was fretting about the safety of the bazaars in light of the bombing of Baghdad the day before. Cooking together on another burner was a handsome, conservatively dressed couple from Pretoria, South Africa. Dominico and Sheila were Messianic Jews in their late twenties. As such they observed Jewish customs, but believed Christ was the messiah. Dominico stood eyeball level to me, had thinning, blond hair and a clear tan complexion. Sheila possessed a humble beauty—black hair, full lips, and penetrating, green eyes. She worked for a non-governmental organization helping black women in South Africa develop small businesses. By coincidence, again, they had an intimate knowledge of the only family I knew in South Africa, the Josses, who I stayed with in Chicago at the start of my journey.

After dinner, the South Africans joined Mark and me in a jasmine-scented alcove outside the dining room as we talked about "coincidence." Mark, sitting on the concrete ground, hugging his long legs and resting his chin on his knees, spoke with a shy twinkle in his eyes. "Maybe the slow speed of travelers allows us an opportunity to see our surroundings clearly. What those living life on *fast-forward* see as 'coincidence,' others see as being in the present. Being in the present allows us to see doorways to many destinies."

"A divine plan of sorts that works like interactive video," Dominico interjected.

"Kind of reminds me of when I was a kid in Catholic school," I said. "The nuns drummed into us that we had free will, yet God has a divine plan for each of us. They said it was a mystery! You're saying there are lots of plans to choose from depending on the speed we move. The nuns just didn't have interactive video to explain divine providence.

"Maybe dreams or visions that focus on positive outcomes create an energy that opens the right doors regardless of speed. In my youth, I envisioned how my girls would turn out, and generally the right doors opened—and I was moving *fast*."

"Dominico and I want children," Sheila added, putting her hand on my arm, "but we are afraid of bringing them into the world and not being able to measure up."

"Maybe if people focused on positive images, we wouldn't have to worry about messing up?" Mark said softly and took a swig of water. It had passed midnight, the hostel was peaceful, and our voices low enough to be speaking in church.

"Perhaps that is how visions work," Sheila mused. "One simply knows what one wants and lives it. We Jews got the homeland. But where I come from, unless we share the wealth fairly, we will never be at peace. If a mass of people envision a peaceful settlement, maybe that is how it is created."

THE WEST

SEPARATION

37

LONG-TERM RELATIONSHIPS

THE TRAIN SILENTLY CRUISED AT 180 miles per hour through compact, gray towns with spiraling steeples, spotless roads, and red-roofed, white houses with geraniums bursting from planters below windows. We slid through the geometrically precise German countryside of holly-green pastures and impeccable black forests, which looked as if they were swept clean every morning. Raindrops blasted the train's windows leaving a film of miniature bubbles. I was a half an hour from Hamburg where Christian was waiting.

On my lap were five letters in a care package from Kathi, delivered by friends in Munich. She said she'd sent a message on the wind, so when I felt a breeze it would be the touch of her love. Sweet. I looked out the window, my eyes moist.

Memories of our first separation four years before and my current emotional distance from Kathi began to cut into this tenderness. I always thought I'd be married forever. I used words such as "the greatest that ever was," as in "I've got the greatest family that ever was," or "I'm living the greatest love affair that ever was," better than Romeo and Juliet, better than all those "happily ever after" movie romances.

But then all sorts of differences wedged between us. Some related to our generation, and the changes in roles of men and women during the Seventies. Some were differences we brought into marriage, such as our self-esteem levels and family habits. Early on we trusted. My controlling nature and drive for money had a lot to do with the deterioration of that trust.

In my defense, I wanted to talk things out, but never seemed to be able to bury a major issue with Kathi. Most people I've talked to complain about communication difficulties. Despite our success communicating at family meetings, we both complained about a need to be heard and haggled about whether a marriage was a partnership to be negotiated or a union with unconditional acceptance of the other.

When the girls left for college fifty percent of the family dynamics walked out the door. There was a liberating quiet about it—the phone mostly stopped ringing. There was also a loss of excitement. A loss of innocence, too—Shannon and Chimene were each becoming their own woman.

The girls didn't appear to notice any turmoil between Kathi and me, or avoided involvement if they did. Several couples I knew had separated for a few months. As far as I could see it didn't help matters: either they weren't apart long enough to re-member what they once had, or it was long enough to know that what they once had was finished. Nevertheless, after twenty-one years—with the girls in college—and unable to compromise, we separated.

I never wanted to fight like my mother and father in my marriage. And rehashing with a counselor frustrated the hell out of me. So Kathi and I took a twelve-month sabbatical from each other to concentrate on what attracted us in the beginning. Kathi hated the thought of separation. To me, we were married for twenty-one years with a year off for bad behavior. But I knew I wasn't "the greatest" anymore.

We rented a second residence, a cozy one-bedroom apart-ment with a fireplace in San Francisco's Twin Peaks area. Close to where Kathi attended classes for her Ph.D. She lived in the apartment the first six months and I got the house, then we switched.

It was during my six months in the house that I came to know Christian. He first came into our lives when he attended Prospect High as an exchange student, often coming over to our home for the girls' parties. Later, we sponsored him for entry into the US as a student majoring in Russian Politics at Berkeley, which is when he stayed with us.

Tall, good looking, and charming, he had the muscular body of a swimmer. He kept his little boy playfulness as he aged—a contrast to his intensity as an ambitious student trying to live up to a scholarly family tradition. He would speak excitedly, causing his big brown eyes to sparkle and a slight German accent to sneak through. He drank coffee and smoked to give his hands something to do while he conversed, which he did with an intellectual brilliance that, combined with his warmth, made him immediately likable.

Together in the house, we often talked late into the eye-rubbing hours of the morning. He had a curiosity that would have killed the proverbial cat long ago. We helped each other improve aspects of our personalities. I had to avoid being Mr. Know-It-All, while Christian's challenge was listening. He taped his version of psychologist Abraham Maslow's words to the wall:

LISTEN! ... without presupposing, classifying, improving, controverting, evaluating, approving or disapproving, without dueling ... without rehearsing the rebuttal in advance, without free-associating to portions of what is being said so that succeeding portions are not heard at all.

We set house ground rules in a democratic fashion. "Christian," I explained, "I *do not* want to be your father. Let's divide duties equally. Since I am the breadwinner, how about if you cook and clean? A deal?" Of course, a deal! It took three months to resolve that "cook" meant five nights a week, and that cleaning was to the standard of the neighborhood we lived in, not some college flat off Telegraph Avenue. Christian's first meal was spaghetti—the heaps of pasta smothered in a pink sauce and garnished with parsley. He explained that yogurt and cream cheese provided the pink lumpy look. I handed him a cookbook, and before long our home became a Mecca of culinary delight, with Christian the maestro of spice.

When it was my turn to live in the Twin Peaks apartment, Christian visited once a week, bringing gossip, food, and philosophical treats. We walked down Ashbury to Haight Street visiting coffee shops and bars, handing out dollar bills and chatting with the homeless. He told me one night he couldn't communicate very well with his dad, and appreciated that I was both role model and friend. I felt honored.

However, recalling life alone in the apartment conjured up images of an answering machine blinking in the dusk of night, eating alone, moldy bread, glasses that accumulated on the kitchen's Formica counter until the cupboard was bare, and brief, temporary romances.

I had never lived by myself. I always had family or college roommates until Kathi and I married in graduate school. We agreed that there were no rules for living apart. I learned about quiet and independence, about appreciating many of the little chores that devoured Kathi's day such as sewing buttons on shirts, taking clothes to the cleaners, or fixing a drip in the bathroom sink. Socially, I found that singles got lumped together at group events, while married female friends often shied away like sheep from a hungry wolf. Also I discovered that most of my friends' advice reflected their situation, not necessarily mine.

My body showed the vulnerability that my mind denied. For a week, I couldn't lift my head because of a serious neck problem that flared up. It was so bad that at one point, in an LA meeting with bankers of an ailing Silicon Valley company, I lay on the floor discussing strategy because it minimized pressure on my neck. Now, that was devotion to duty.

I was a work-related adrenaline addict, yet I dreamed a lot about when I was a little boy in my blue boat catching snappers with a bamboo pole. I decided to drop my average workweek from sixty-five hours to fifty-five. I even downsized the golden *number*. It now read: *enough money for Kathi's education, retirement for life, emergency funds for grandchildren, and leaving a healthy inheritance.* I fantasized about downsizing, like the companies I rescued, of living simply, and following Christ's philosophy of renouncing worldly property.

I wanted to purge our marital problems once and for all. I studied our families like I tore apart a troubled company, trying to discover the origin and extent of our differences. In the meantime, we dated each other, and I relearned how to romance my wife.

When the sabbatical ended, we wrote a partnership agreement starting with what we liked about each other and goals for living happily. We defined partnership as an equal sharing and contribution to some defined purpose, surrounded by respect, commitment, trust, honesty, lack of dominance, and interdependence. Kathi's goals were a career as a Ph.D. in psychology and good communication between us, while mine were appreciation for her and a romantic marriage without ownership.

Kathi was confused by my goal of marriage without owner-ship. I wasn't really sure what it meant either, but subconsciously, if not consciously, the need for the "nobody pulling my strings" part of my vision became compelling. This might sound like re-lationship heresy, but the freedom from guilt and responsibility I felt as a single person was a wonder drug.

These were the issues I looked forward to discussing with Christian.

38

CHRISTIAN'S DILEMMA IN HAMBURG

ROM ONE OF THE CONCRETE platforms of the Hamburg
Hauptbahnhof, Christian inspected each car of the recently
arrived Munich train. A wide grin settled on his face as I
stepped down from car 502. "Denis, over here," he screamed, buried my face in his bear hug, then ripped the backpack off my
shoulders to carry it.

From his small flat, we set out to explore Hamburg. Shafts of
sunlight shimmied through muscular rainclouds, lending the city
a sheen of elegant tranquility. Cobbled sidewalks and gray-stone
gothic buildings sparkled in the late afternoon rays. A clean smell
from the Elba River, like a forest after rain, filled the air as we
sipped beer, munched bratwurst, and listened to bouncy German
songs at a downtown street fair.

The citizenry of Hamburg were bulky and very tall compared
with those of Africa and the Middle East. And there weren't
many children on the loose—in fact, there weren't many children
at all. People avoided eye contact. It was ironic that Third World
people hold eye contact and hide the body, while First World
people hide the eyes and uncover the body.

After the snack, we walked along the Reeperbahn, an avenue
of amusement centers, fast-food outlets, and bars, and down a
street whose entrance was shielded by a zigzagging network
of red wooden fences about Christian's height. "Follow me!"
Yanking my shoulder, Christian crossed the wooden barricade.

On the other side, we entered a world of blinking red street lamps that leaned like sunflowers either side of a block of pink and burgundy houses. Picture windows, open halfway like Dutch doors, spilled colorful lighting on to the avenue. Displayed like mannequins inside the windows were some very much alive "dolls."

Christian and I kidded each other, like boys behind closed doors flipping through a Playboy plucked from under the mattress. "Let's talk to the ladies," I said.

"Where are you from?" one of the women asked. In her rose-colored little girl's dress she could have been Mary, Mary, Quite Contrary, except for the teasing eyes and rose-painted lips.

"America! My friend here is from Germany."

"Oh, I always wanted to go to America. I am from Bulgaria. Come to my room. I will show you good time, and you will help me go to America. It is small price to pay. Satisfaction is, how you say in America, guaranteed."

Christian told her that we would like nothing better, but that we had to move on. We had a lot of sightseeing left on this street.

Back on the other side of the scarlet fence, away from the saucy playground, we walked along the Reeperbahn towards the food fair. Gradually Christian's demeanor changed as the newness of my arrival wore off. Hands dug into the bottom of his pockets, he talked fast, half-listened to replies, and chewed his fingernails. His upper body formed a concave slouch oozing insecurity. The dimples in his cheeks and those big brown eyes were flat, discouraged. He freed his hands only to smoke, his breath coming and going like a turbulent sea. He complained about problems with money, no real direction, lack of romance, his longing for the US, inadequacies in German higher education, and on and on. Life was a maze and he was lost in it.

Back at the fair, polka music and laughter filled the air as night fell. We ordered coffee, red cabbage, and Wiener schnitzel and sequestered the end of a picnic table. Christian pointed to the mix of blacks, whites, and Asians milling about. "At least Hamburg treats race relations with intelligence," he said with anguish in his voice. He sipped the coffee, sniffled like he was on the verge of a cold, and avoided eye contact. "I suppose you've read about the skinheads and neo-Nazis beating up on foreigners in Rostock and Mölln?"

"In *Newsweek*. A featured article."

"We have this law called Article 16. Basically it gives asylum to foreigners. Now the rightwing Bavarian Christian Social Union wants Article 16 changed to prohibit foreigners who are not truly political prisoners. Which is total bullshit! We will never ever be able to stop the flow of illegal immigrants because there will always be more and more poor people trying to escape the conditions in their countries. They want their piece of the commonwealth.

"All those aspirations that Germany has had about projecting its picture into the international world, they've gone up in flames. If two years ago someone asked me where I was from, I'd say Germany. Ask me today and I feel ashamed."

"Aren't the troublemakers mostly young East Germans?"

"The East Germans I can understand. They grew up with communism as a national ideology, and now—bam!—it's gone." His words spilled out in a haunted swirl. "It's the silent, and thus very horrible majority that may actually think the foreigners are scum.

"As a nation we have never been able to deal with our past, to ask ourselves if there is something deep down in our psyche that paves the way for our anti-foreign sentiment. We talked about Hitler and the Third Reich all the time in high school, but I don't think we critically discussed the factors that led to fascism."

"But Christian, I'm impressed with Germany. Its low crime rate, few street people, and especially the dual university and trade school systems for white-collar and blue-collar workers. Maybe if we had a dual system of education in the States there would be smaller ghettoes. Also people seem very concerned about the environment here. I noticed that stores have site disposal for packaging. Hey, and last month weren't there hundreds of thousands of people demonstrating against the beatings you're talking about, by lighting candles for peace?"

"Maybe I'm full of shit. For example, Germany has hosted five to six times more political refugees than any other European country, given them benefits, too. What do you think?"

"You know I always thought you were full of shit!"

He laughed nervously, opening a seam to his former self. "You know what I mean!"

"Getting back to East Germans, I always thought Germany paid a tremendous sum of money to bring them into the fold. I've heard a trillion dollars."

"The government underestimated. No one is particularly happy about it. During unification we exchanged two of their Deutschmarks for one of ours when the market rate was about fifteen to one.

"Turns out the higher mark immediately priced East Germany's products out of the Eastern bloc marketplace. Their customers couldn't afford to buy from them, and twenty thousand companies went broke."

"When Chimene went to school here during her junior year abroad," I said, "she rode her bike to East Germany. It was immediately after the Wall came down. She said their goods placed side-by-side with Western products came off hopelessly inferior. The price was Western, but the quality Eastern—a double whammy."

Christian and I originally planned to cross Siberia together and take a boat to the Arctic Circle. But Christian ran out of money, so he tentatively arranged a single berth on the boat, but hadn't yet gotten confirmation from the trip's organizer. In fact, he hadn't heard from him in three months. I was concerned. The direction and timing of my trip had been determined by that boat ride, and despite the loss of his company and fluency in Russian, I felt compelled to go to Siberia.

The morning before leaving for Russia, I was waiting for Christian at a sidewalk café on a busy street. To kill time, I watched people pass, looking directly into their eyes. With one exception, when they did notice me their eyes instantly recoiled. The exception was a couple I had followed with my eyes for about a block. When they reached where I was sitting and drinking coffee, the guy suddenly turned towards me and asked, "What do you think of me?" Before I could answer, he turned his gaze back to his girlfriend. I doubted he knew I had been observing him, just got stuck in the eye contact and was showing off.

When Christian arrived, we strolled down a grassy knoll beside a bridge on the Elba. Daisies swayed gently under sunny skies and a pair of swans floated towards us. A lazy day atmosphere.

Under the shade of a maple, Christian confessed he'd spent the money he had earmarked for Russia flying to California to look unsuccessfully for a job. He spoke in staccato phrases, constantly flicking ash off his cigarette and looking sad.

Pissed that he blew the money, nervous about crossing Russia alone, and tired of his complaining, I ripped a handful of grass and threw it at him. "What the hell is the matter with you, Christian?" I yelled. "All I hear is me, me, me! You haven't asked shit about my trip! You're talking about yourself like you're the only one in the universe. What ever happened to Maslow's listening skills?"

"That's not true, you've told me a lot about your trip."

"Not because you asked!"

"You bring it on yourself with your questions," he said as if he had been kicked and was lashing out. "Maybe if you gave people space, they'd ask you the questions!"

That was a shocking comment. Questions were the tools of my trade—that was how I learned. However, questions drove a wedge between Kathi and me. She said my questions made her feel manipulated, as if she was on the witness stand.

"This is not a good time in my life, Denis," Christian cried out suddenly, as if on the edge of tears. "I want to be back in the United States with my friends. You're the know-it-all, tell me how can I be happy?"

Now I felt guilty. Would I ever escape guilt? "You're right about the questions. I feel comfortable directing conversations. Maybe free association is something for me to think about and work on."

The rustling wind scattered maple leaves, while the swans bobbed and preened. Christian snatched a leaf, examined it, peeled the skin from its vein, and dropped pieces on his pants. I did the same. He relaxed. We talked about his dreams.

After a few questions, it turned out surprisingly that living in the United States was only number three on his priority list. Getting a master's at Oxford was number one and a master's at Cambridge number two. His real wish was hidden under the blanket of desire to be in the US. Money was the issue, but once isolated, this problem had a solution. We talked, and together figured out a plan of action.

276

The immediate crisis was settled. Silence ensued. The swans paddled in the silhouette of the city. A nearby church bell chimed twelve and a jackdaw stood proud on a branch in the maple tree.

39

CUTTING STRINGS, AND WHATEVER HAPPENS, HAPPENS!

CHRISTIAN TOOK OFF HIS EMBROIDERED cowboy boots, twirled his toes, and proudly flexed his arm muscles in the early summer breeze. "Look, I'm still buffed," he said.

"That's a better word than the one you first used a while back showing off your muscles. As I recall you said, 'I'm stuffed.'" He laughed.

"How is Kathi taking your absence?" With priorities set and his life in order, Christian's curious personality returned. I was still a little deflated at his "questioning too much" comment.

"It's hard to say, our voices on the phone have too much about the business of life and none of the gooey stuff."

"She probably wanted you out. She probably planted the seeds of this trip using subliminal messages when you were asleep. She knows what a pain in the ass you are!"

"Very funny!"

"Doesn't it feel strange to be away so long from someone you've lived with for twenty-five years?"

"I'm not lonely the way I thought. Other travelers say the same. There's so much going on all the time. Time changes people. In my mid-twenties I was reviewing foreign subsidiaries for Fairchild Semiconductor and found a sinkhole of losses in the Munich business that no one anticipated. A swarm of big-wigs flew in from California and decided that I should stay in Germany another four weeks. I had a desperate sinking feeling missing Kathi and the kids. So much that I calculated the percentage of my life I would be gone, because every day a part of me died."

"You don't separate for a year after separating for a year unless the problem didn't go away. And no one leaves for that long without severely wanting change. What's the root problem?"

"The root?" Once again that question. "The root, I think, is trust."

"How do you mean?"

"Well, I think a relationship is like a savings account whose currency is trust."

"That's an interesting analogy."

"Think about it. You open the account with a large deposit, early love, for instance, which sizzles through every part of your body. Kathi and I made a ton of deposits the first ten years from giving emotional support, pride in each other's accomplishments, romance—"

"And withdrawals?" Christian probed.

"Withdrawals would be arguments, lack of communication, not appreciating what the other is doing, those kinds of things. After a while, we began to withdraw more than we deposited until we were overdrawn."

"Do you think your first separation in San Francisco got you back in the black?"

"I couldn't recapture the feeling of falling in love that I intended, but we recaptured a nice flame. It revitalized our marriage. We healed a few old wounds and became more tolerant. But the underlying habits that caused our issues were still there. I don't know if we are in the black."

"And you left home to find out. Guys leave, right?"

"I think they can't bear the frustration of not being able to solve the problem. Yeah, I left, but it took a while. When I was living alone at the San Francisco apartment, I'd drive to work over the Bay Bridge thinking about how I wasn't appreciated. I'd think: 'Okay, store the frustration for now. When I'm traveling, I can flush it down the drain because I'll be free to spend time and money on myself, without guilt. Live simply, like a rolling stone.' That was my mantra."

"What triggered you to make this break *now*, anything in particular?"

I told him about the presentation in San Francisco when the wires in my brain short-circuited and the graphs lost all meaning, and about the churning fear that my life was too busy and going in the wrong direction.

"So, Denis, what's next?" Christian asked in a now easygoing and intimate manner.

What *was* next? Every day traveling there was something new and unexpected.

"I guess I don't have expectations, Christian, except to change a few habits and create balance in my life by the time I get back. I'm free, dude. There's no old environment to lock me into patterns of behavior I don't want. I would never change my past—never, ever! But by myself I'm happy every single day now. It's intoxicating. So I am going to wipe the slate clean of the past for a while and be someone new. Trust fate. And whatever happens, happens!"

RUSSIA

TRANSFORMATION

40

FIVE-FOOT-NINE ABE LINCOLN: "IT'S TIME WE SAW OUR NEIGHBORS"

ONVENTIONAL WISDOM SAID NOT TO go to Russia. The de-
frocked comrades were nastier than a pack of rabid roosters
and you'd never make it across the airport lobby with your
money-belt intact. If somehow you did make it, the taxi drivers
would slit your throat and toss the empty skin and sagging bones
into a Moscow alley reeking of vodka and urine. Also, the food
tasted like maggot loin, and the parasites in the water would eat
so much of your innards that your carcass could be sent home for
half the price of the letter describing your demise. Even if you
did survive the airport, taxi, food, and water, the Russian mafia
would finish the job.

As the Aeroflot jet approached Moscow from Prague, I had
reasons to be nervous. First, the plane was old and dimly lit.
Second, I was going to take a train four thousand miles across
Siberia, turn left, and boat up the sixth-longest river in the world
to the Arctic Circle—all without an interpreter. Third, there was
no confirmation that a boat was available. I hadn't heard from
the voyage coordinator, Andrei Pavlovich, so I faced the prospect
of traveling through a potentially hostile land without knowing
the language, then being stranded in Siberia. Christian suggested
the alternative of visiting St. Petersburg and Finland, but those
pesky voices inside my head goaded me: *Chickenshit! The Arctic is*

the cornerstone of your journey. You navigated the Ssese jungles using sign language, how rough can Siberia be?

On a bleak Moscow afternoon, I cleared immigration, cashed a hundred dollar traveler's check for a hundred thousand rubles (inflation was rampant), traversed the drab and surprisingly small airport lobby with money-belt intact, and survived the taxi ride down broad, leafy boulevards to the three-star Petrivina Hotel. From there, I called Christian's friend Sasha.

"Do not stay at hotel," he said in heavily accented English that placed vigorous stress on Rs and vowels. "Stay with us. I meet you. I am average height, wear blue sweater, um, black beard, and hair, um, maybe little gray."

To pass the time, I ordered a Pilsner in the bar. How did the proud Russians feel about the hotel decreeing that purchases be in dollars or deutschmarks? Before long, I spotted a man my age in faded jeans, black sneakers, and a smoky-blue sweater, which needed a vacation. With brown eyes, beard, and worries scribed on his face, Sasha looked like a smaller version of Abraham Lincoln. He stretched out a hand of friendship and I grabbed it.

After a brief chitchat, he guided me through gray drizzle to a murky underground escalator down to the metro. Pointing to a colored chart in the train, Sasha explained the subway layout in his husky voice. The metro looked easy to navigate, except for one detail—the names of the stops looked like they'd been written by a printer suffering a nervous breakdown. How in hell would I ever get to the Arctic unable to decipher Cyrillic?

During the ride, Sasha explained that he and his wife, Irina, were professors at Moscow University. She taught socio-economics and he mechanical engineering. At Mayakovskaya station, we exited the train on to a gleaming honey-colored, stone-tiled platform. Sasha swept his arm in a wide arc encompassing the high, vaulted ceilings, pale blue walls with gold leaf detailing, and huge marble columns decorated with neoclassical figures. "Example for tourists," he said, a smile briefly brushing his face. Above the metro, we crossed a small concrete plaza displaying a bearded statue of Mayakovsky. Pointing at a street sign bearing Mayakovsky's name, Sasha remarked: "In Russia, many streets, writers' names."

A sullen mist blotted the sky, rubbing pinpricks of moisture on to pewter-colored concrete buildings. It smelled of old bricks and summer in the city. Shortly, we entered a courtyard with a gazebo, two swings, a basketball court, and a few very drunk teenagers swilling vodka. We walked across the courtyard to a grimy apartment building, and ascended to the eighth floor in the caged elevator. Sasha apologized for the boys. There was widespread unemployment and a premium placed on city housing due to an influx from the countryside. His apartment was large compared with the five square meters per person allotted under the old régime.

"Our flat humble, but we own," he said. "Perestroika! Government must distribute assets. We receive flat."

I barely had time to process that incredible statement in my conscious before Irina welcomed me in chopped English. The flat was much more comfortable than the building's exterior suggested. Smiling shyly she led me down a hallway to her son's room, one of three smallish bedrooms with high ceilings. He was staying with family she explained. The extra room was rented to students.

Irina stood about five-two, with a kind face, rosy cheeks, and plump body. Soft, curly, brown hair, obviously treasured, graced her shoulders. For twenty dollars, including meals and conversation, I would stay in her house for five days.

By the time I unpacked and freshened up, dinner was on the table. First I presented Sasha with a quart of Smirnoff vodka, and Irina with three sets of embroidered stockings that elicited an appreciative blush. This blush, plus the grin on Sasha's face, dissipated the uneasiness inherent in first encounters. Sasha opened a polished wooden cabinet with glass doors, and carefully placed the Smirnoff among the bottles of domestic vodka. He filled three simple glasses with one of the local liquors and placed his arm around Irina's waist. "American vodka to impress friends. For drink—Russian!"

The sun shone bright with summer warmth the next morning as Sasha guided me through the broad boulevards of Moscow. Rectangular, look-alike apartment complexes gave way to the palatial, rust-red inner city buildings that led to Red Square. Lenin's Tomb—complete with a line of admirers and the curious seeking admittance—stood at the entrance to the square, a vast plaza of polished black brick. To the right, a fifteenth-century turreted wall protected the Kremlin. And to the far end of the plaza, St. Basil's dreamy architecture dominated the landscape. Four of its five red steeples, arrayed at different heights, were capped by emerald and gold pear-shaped cupolas. The fifth, twice as large as the others, could have stood in for the palace in *The Wizard of Oz*. The richness of the cathedral and its icons testified to the wealth and splendor of Tsarist times, and must have awed the masses with the mystical sovereignty of the Church. Now it stood as a relic, tourists quietly filing up and down its narrow spiral stairways to the cupolas.

On the left, across the expanse of attractive brick, a three-story, cream-colored building, looking like an army barracks, housed a gallery of shops selling every type of Western product imaginable. The mall's shoppers were rich Russians or Westerners enjoying Russia's transition to a market economy. The middle classes stood behind white ropes, stretching like ostriches to glimpse the merchandise. Craning my neck behind the ropes along with Sasha, I asked: "Hey, does it bother you to be on the outside in your own country?"

Sasha pushed his hands deep into his jeans and backed away from the goodies. "What choice? Yeltsin risk materialism, um, satisfy desire of masses before …" He breathed deeply, for it clearly took energy to form words.

"Backlash?" I said as he searched for the right word. "It means violent opposite reaction."

"*Da! Da!* Understand. Backlash against capitalism."

"Did you feel repressed under communism?"

"*Nyet!* In ways we live better. Other ways, not so better."

"What ways better?"

"Olden days, time for family. Better medical. Not much homeless or crime. And always, job!"

"And in what ways not good?"

"Under old system, no freedom. Citizen must to belong to Party to receive best job. Citizen not move his home easily. But system good in beginning. No one knew what was best system in beginning. We knew what did not want. Communist Party make plan for better life for all citizens.

"Today, young with talent, they win! People too young to retire and too old to learn, they lose. Also, old lose—inflation!"

The "losers" supported Communism, he explained, since it represented security for them.

"Also," he said, as we gazed once more at the silhouette of St. Basil's, "now free to travel. But, of course, no money!"

The fourth night, Irina prepared dinner in the small, wallpapered kitchen with pots hanging from wall hooks and an ancient stove with three burners crusted like briquettes. Before long, sausage sizzled and slimy, black mushrooms, pickled the summer before, bubbled. Grabbing cucumbers and tomatoes off the kitchen windowsill, and cheese from a worn fridge the size of a house safe, she began slicing on a card table.

Mixing gestures with halting English, Irina asked about America. "You own house? What you house like? How we compare? All Americans rich? Women work?" I sat leaning on the kitchen table, watching and answering her questions. Suddenly she stopped slicing and turned her cat-green eyes on me: "American men cook, clean?"

I knew a controversial question when I heard it! "I believe that men do little cooking or cleaning if there is a woman." I spoke slowly, simply and also with hand movements. "But that is changing. Divorce—you know divorce?"

"*Da!*"

"Divorce high. Men must cook and clean. Also, more young men push baby carriages and share cooking and cleaning with working women. But it will be many years before average married man cooks and cleans and changes diapers, and average married woman shares financial responsibility with man."

"*Da!* Must learn young." She pointed to the sizzling frying pan that looked like the outside of a charred potato. "You cook?"

"I like to cook. For most of married life my wife cook. She is wonderful cook. I cook on weekends, and when she work and went to school I cook more. I am a good cook." Inspired, I offered to make spaghetti for her and Sasha the next night. She smiled, and without hesitation accepted, saying she'd help shop for ingredients. Turned out neither she nor Sasha had ever tasted spaghetti.

41

RUSSIA'S TRANSFORMATION AS TOLD BY RUSSIANS

WHILE IRINA SHOPPED FOR INGREDIENTS, Sasha went to stand in a daylong line purchasing a round-trip train ticket for me to Krasnoyarsk, Siberia, and a one-way ticket out of Russia to Odessa on the Black Sea—both at Russian prices. There was a two-tier pricing system. Foreigners paid ten times more than locals but received express service. For a distance of 13,000 kilometers, a third of the circumference of the earth, Sasha would pay fifteen dollars for my ticket and I'd give him thirty dollars. Given that he and Irina earned seventy dollars a month each as professors, it was, as the Dahab bracelet girls would say, "good *for* him, good *for* me."

I spent the day bopping around Moscow with Elise McBride, the daughter of a friend I met in the Bahamas. She was living in Moscow to broaden her horizons. Elise collected me at noon, and from that moment we talked nonstop.

The fresh air smelled of roasting walnuts as we made our way to the metro. Everywhere there were the signs of a society in transition. We passed a line of people waiting for medical vouchers, while, below street level, I spotted a robust young Muscovite with the American flag imprinted on the rear pocket of his skintight Levi's. People dressed in jogging pants, feet migrated in Reeboks, and Western music blared from ghetto blasters. At the same time, guitarists sang for donations and vendors hawked vouchers. Elise explained the vouchers were shares in former government assets, such as Aeroflot, now owned by citizens, but that nobody understood their value or how they worked. I figured that those who did understand would be buying up the vouchers for practically nothing.

Everything seemed to be going too fast for an orderly economic transition that would spread the wealth. Karl Marx was worried that capitalism didn't know how to slow down and the growth would eventually become unrestrained and explosive—the theory of dissipative structures. I could see what he meant. Still, Sasha and Irina now owned an apartment they used to rent.

We emerged from the metro into a conglomeration of shops and apartment buildings that could have been Brooklyn in the early 1950s except for the width of streets. Clothing stores, hair salons, taxis, newsstands, butcher shops, travel agencies, produce stands, street galleries, pharmacies, auto repair shops, bars for Western business professionals—all bustled with activity.

Newspaper headlines screamed of rampant inflation, paralysis of federal power, and threats to halt Aeroflot flights unless employees got 51% ownership. They talked of rich Western evangelists acing Russian religions out of TV airtime, the IMF negotiating "market economy" guidelines in exchange for Western loans, and Yeltsin talking of a climactic battle with the speaker of the parliament, Ruslan Khasbulatov. Communists protested along government buildings, hoisting red banners embroidered with the hammer and sickle. The homeless begged outside buildings of new millionaires. This new ideology said: We are all still equal, only some have more purchasing power than others.

"How do you know my father?" Elise asked, her high Irish cheekbones supporting intense blue eyes.

I told her about my first separation with Kathi and how we celebrated our reunion on a Lilliputian island in the Bahamas. "That's where we ran into this tall, thin adventurer who had sailed solo from Florida. He was challenging the locals to a race around the island."

"That's my dad!"

"He adopted us, and took us sailing to remote islands. He said he learned to fly by seven, had flown jets in Vietnam, and that his great-uncle was Wilbur Wright. He told of meeting the Hopi Indians and of a mission to the Amazon he assumed for them. There were stories of magic and famous people. I asked him how he got to do these things. He said, 'Events are happening all over the world. Traveling increases the odds that I'll be there when they do.'"

Meandering along the city streets, Elise told me she came to Russia to escape the influence of a conservative mom and wild, unreliable dad. When she first arrived in Moscow she cleaned guns for the Mafia, which as far as she could tell was integrated into the government like ivy on a trellis. Recently she interviewed prostitutes as a journalist. As she said, "Intrigue runs in my blood."

Elsie guided me round the capital. At the largest McDonald's in the world, she said most Russians could only afford to go there once a year. Inflation had been 2,300 percent the prior year. She showed me how to avoid a line forming at a deli by stealing in the back door just before it opened. Inside, we received a ticket at the bread and cheese counter, stood in a separate line to pay, and received a second ticket entitling us to pick up the goods at the original counter. "Full-employment held over from the old system!" Elise remarked.

At one of the many street markets I purchased a melon, bottle of champagne, two roses—one for Elise and one for Irina—and a bunch of bananas. We rounded out the shopping with pasta, Italian herbs, and a small canned ham from a Western mini-mart near Red Square.

Back at the flat, Irina smiled and sniffed the rose, carefully placing it into a vase. I relished how travel had given me the opportunity to admire gentleness in women. Elise spoke Russian with my hosts and helped Irina place a humble assortment of silverware and plates on the table. Sasha poured Russian vodka into converted jelly jars for pre-dinner drinks. Meanwhile, I grabbed a blackened pan for sauce and the biggest pot I could find to boil water.

The ingredients for spaghetti left much to be desired. Okay, the pasta, olive oil, garlic, herbs, and meaty black mushrooms were fine. The strange pigmy-sized black onions and pans that looked like campfire veterans presented a challenge. But the main ingredient, a half can of refrigerator-aged tomato sauce, struck fear into my culinary ego. Irina, who had misinterpreted my request for cans of whole tomatoes, pointed to eight tiny fresh ones ripening on the windowsill. Whatever! I struck a match, lit the front burner, and went to work.

The meal commenced with a vodka toast "to friends," then the melon and champagne. By pasta time we sat warmly around their wooden kitchen table. Irina, translated by Elise, was explaining how the Communists gained control of the country.

"The seeds began in 1857 when we lost the Crimean War to the English and French, who objected to the Russian encroachment into the Ottoman Empire. Russians could not compete militarily with a society that could efficiently transport people and military equipment."

"You must remember," interjected Sasha, tapping his glass of vodka and leaning forward to make his point. "Russia was land of serfs, owned by nobility. Railroads new. England free serfs three hundred years already. Western world have modern government and benefit of Industrial Revolution. We no have chance."

Elise said she never considered the effect of the Industrial Revolution on the ability to wage war, and asked Irina, the socio-economics professor, how that precipitated a Communist takeover.

"In the late 1800s, the Tsar tried to catch the industrialized West. He emancipated serfs, but forced them into brutal land rent servitude. From a pool of farmers emerged a working class—the proletariat—and an entrepreneurial class—the bourgeoisie. Near the end of the nineteenth century, we borrowed much money from the English and French, and began to import machinery and experts from Germany to help build industry and railroads.

"We had limitless natural resources, but needed money and expertise to extract them from the ground. And always there was the problem of food. Russia's farmers had little incentive to produce enough to feed a growing population.

"Then in 1905, we lost the war to Japan over Korea's minerals and seaports. How humiliating it must have been for the Tsar, and the people, to lose to tiny industrial Japan."

Having polished off seconds of the surprisingly good pasta, Sasha cleared his throat, sat back in the chair and summarized. "Russia was giant standing on feet of clay. No could produce military equipment. No could move supplies and people ten thousand kilometers across Siberia to Pacific."

Irina spoke Russian slowly to Elise who continued to translate it for me.

"Our first revolution in 1905 ended when the Tsar consented to limited freedom for his people, allowing a Duma, like your House of Representatives, to be formed. But the vote of a single noble was equivalent to 540 workers. Nevertheless, industry surged at tremendous speed, drawing farmers from the fields to increase ranks of workers. Output doubled and re-doubled from 1906 to 1915, while loans from the West increased to massive proportions.

"This is very important. We sold grain to pay loans. Russia lives and dies on grain output. The drain of workers and poor farming habits further strained the food supply. Society was very complex for the Tsar."

Elise stopped interpreting and slowly counted on her fingers. "Complex!" she said, "Let's see, you had the Tsarist administration, the proletariat, the nobles, the peasants, the industrialists or bourgeois—"

"Must not forget," Sasha added, "was church! Losing power, *da!* But strong. Revolution also add much problem. Ah, Irina, help!"

"Western bankers, German suppliers, monopolies, new laws, Duma, new building, streets. You can imagine Tsar Nicholas ripping his hair out trying to keep up with paperwork!"

"Maybe that's why his wife summoned Rasputin," I quipped. The Tsar's form of government was technologically obsolete. The whole thing reminded me of Silicon Valley super growth. To survive, companies like Microsoft needed vision, good management, money, and time. The faster they grew, the more of these things they needed. I couldn't think of anyone who could have managed this transition from agrarian to industrial.

"What part did the First World War play in the collapse?" I asked.

"War took away *time*," Irina said via Elise. "Russia owed Germany a lot of money, and England and France were in a trade war against the Germans and Turks. The Germans figured we would be on the side of England and France, and would not pay our debt when the shooting started, so the Axis powers blockaded the Baltic and Black Seas. Impossible situation! Without imports industry crashed, the workers revolted against harsh working conditions and greed, and there was famine."

"Worst," screamed Sasha, grinning from ear to ear, "under Tsar, was tax on vodka!"

We all laughed.

"So how did the Communists gain control?" I asked, when calm returned.

"She says Communism was a socio-economic inevitability," Elise continued, despite suffering from interpreter burnout. "The desperate Tsar, no hero like his father, abdicated. Then the provisional government ordered an offensive against Germany just as Russia was collapsing. The crafty Germans arranged for Lenin to return from exile. He convinced workers and peasants that war was folly, that it benefits only a few. He promised equality. Afterwards, the proletariat struck factories and refused to transport troops."

Irina then traced her thumb across her throat, a gesture foreign to her gentle character: "Finish!"

As an afterthought, she added that Western bankers hated her country because Lenin refused to honor Russia's debts. His reasoning was that the West supported the royalist White army against the will of people. She concluded the Whites and Western countries were business partners.

I mentioned that Western bankers paid for the industrial infrastructure. Irina replied, while gathering spent dishes, "*Da!* That other side of argument!"

After dinner, Elise and I went for a long walk and wound up sitting under Mayakovsky's illuminated statue until taxis were the only vehicles on the road. She told me that being the daughter of a Vietnam hero and adventurer screwed-up her life. Russia offered an opportunity to distance herself from her father and make a fresh start.

"I don't blame my dad, but he influenced my troubles," she said, recalling a time when she and a girlfriend were flying with him. "The engines failed and I watched my dad methodically go through every possible cause. Just when it looked like we were going to crash, he pulled out."

She paused to wipe away silent tears.

"To this day, I don't know whether my dad stalled on purpose."

Under Mayakovsky's gaze, I held her hand as her emotions settled. Composed again, she said shifting her environment gave her space to trust destiny.

We sat silently watching the glow of the Kremlin in the distance. I told her of my indecision about traveling to Siberia. I was nervous about traveling all that way without knowing English, only to find out that there was no boat to the Arctic Circle and no place to stay. I asked her what she would do.

"Your choice is to go to the Arctic or St. Petersburg! What do you think I'd do? You traveled all through Africa without speaking any of the languages, how tough can Siberia be? Trust the future, Denis."

42

THREE DAYS IN A TRAIN ACROSS SIBERIA

I CARRIED THREE ESSENTIAL ITEMS FOR my train journey to Siberia. Irina had given me a brown paper bag full of supplies, and Sasha had written two notes in Russian the night before.

Note One: Please take this man to the boat, *Chkalov*, at the river station.

Note Two: I am Sasha Petrov. I live in Moscow. The bearer of letter is a friend and traveler. Please extend to him your lowest traveler rates to Dudinka.

The third essential was a phonetic cheat sheet written during breakfast to the amusement of my hosts. It covered important areas such as:

Help	*Pama-gi*
I am American.	*Ya American-itz.*
I do not speak Russian.	*Ya ni gave-ryu pa-Ruski.*
My name is Denis.	*Minya-za-voot Denis.*
Where can I change money?	*Gdye mozh-na abmi-nyat dyen-ge?*
I am going to Krasnoyarsk.	*Ya yea-do Krasnoyarsk.*
I want to go to the river station.	*Ya-hat-chu itsi na retchnoy vox-al.*

The railroad station was a huge open building with a ceiling so high I imagined a bullet fired from a pistol would lose velocity and die before reaching the rafters. Sasha inspected a train schedule the size of a baseball scoreboard, then whisked me off to platform twenty-five for the twelve o'clock to Siberia. He warned that trains across the country are listed in Moscow time, but my destination, Krasnoyarsk, was seven time zones ahead. Then he disappeared into the dusty rust-colored train to find someone who spoke English. Passengers hung from windows kibitzing with friends and family on the crowded platform. Before long Sasha reappeared leading a six-footer in his early thirties wearing sneakers, a red-flannel shirt, and gleaming blue sweatpants with red stripes down the sides.

"Meet Andrei," Sasha said. "Andrei captain in Air Force. Only person speak English." He pinched his fingers as if examining a small pea: "Very little!"

Andrei shook hands firmly. "*Privyet*," I said, happy to make an acquaintance. Pointing to me, he grunted: "You see on train," then disappeared.

"You see on train"? If he was my "translator," I was in deep shit.

Sasha grabbed the backpack, and with me close on his heels, we boarded wagon number ten. Inside the compartment, Sasha introduced me to my travel mates: tall, heavily built Alexi with a shock of brown hair and muscular face; his mother, Anna, with her maternal smile; and friendly, Asian-looking Pauline in her mid-twenties. Alexi and his mom would exit before me, while Pauline was going to Lake Baikal, a day after Krasnoyarsk and four days out altogether. Introductions completed Sasha prepared to leave. "Safe journey, friend," he said, grabbing my hand in both of his. "Be careful!"

The sleeper looked cozy. Three feet of floor space separated dark-red vinyl bunks laden with towels, linen, and blankets folded neatly on top. The upper bunks hung down on chains for sleeping, but were raised during the day to allow freedom to socialize. Luggage was stored under the bottom bunks and in an alcove over the train's narrow corridor. A collapsible table jutted from the base of the window, while a glass door with white flannel curtains provided privacy. Alexi and Anna occupied the upper bunks. Pauline's bunk was across from mine on the bottom covered with her personal red-checkered woolen blanket. It *was* cozy.

Through backyards of the sprawling city, the train blew its whistle. Initially, I smiled a lot and used the cheat sheet and world map to communicate my home and itinerary. Andrei reappeared brandishing a pint of vodka in his right hand and a hunk of marinated pork fat the size of Pauline's forearm in his left. Dangling the vodka, he pointed at me and exclaimed *"Americanietz!"* He placed the liquor and meat on the table and whipped out a pocketknife big enough to hack down a pine tree.

"Vodka?" he asked, noticing my water bottle.

"Vada," I said. He winced, shrugged, and looked at the others in a way that reminded me of a W.C. Fields line: "Once, on a trek through Afghanistan, we lost our corkscrew ... and were forced to live on food and water for several days!" But then he erupted into a boyish grin and he and Alexi scrounged around for glasses. He proposed hearty toasts to *Ruski* and *Americanietz*. We all drained the glasses with a single gulp, whereupon Pauline and Anna rifled through satchels under the bed producing cucumbers, tomatoes, cheese, bread, meat pies, beer, and apple juice. From Irina's brown bag, I added a hunk of salami, bananas, hard-boiled eggs, bread, and a vial of vodka—saving the canned ham for a special occasion. The feast had begun.

Andrei knew a hundred words of English, give or take a few. With his vocabulary combined with my cheat sheet, Russian dictionary, and assorted flailing of the hands, we all managed to communicate. When you don't speak a language, every gesture and word takes on meaning. Alexi's intelligent eyes watched while Andrei translated. "Den-y, how much ... plane ticket to America?" We chewed while tossing the dictionary back and forth like a football. "Den-y, I want see America. I want travel." We chugged vodka and chased it with beer and juice. "Andrei, ask what *Ruski* think of West from TV?" We relaxed barefoot on the bunks. "Den-y, why *Americanietz* spend much dollar fight *Ruski*, but give smaller dollar when *Ruski* want change? What American do if *Ruski* not beat Germans in big war?" They asked and answered many questions among themselves. "*Ruski* fix own problems! They no *Americanietz* problems!"

Alexi said he wanted democracy now, but Anna, quietly speaking through Andrei, expressed a desire for the security she received under the old system. Mention of Gorbachev and Yeltsin brought raised voices and animated hand gestures. Andrei summarized: "No agreement! Gorbachev smart, introduce perestroika ... is new thinking. Glasnost is open book ... to past." With verbal effort and pantomime, he went on to say that Gorbachev walked a high wire between the Party, military, cynics, and reformers. But that people wanted benefits now. He also blamed Gorbachev for loss of pride.

We guys kept slugging down the vodka, chasing it with apple juice. The women had switched to chai. Everyone listened to Andrei as though the words were Russian. "Yeltsin hero. But ruble worth nothing!"

"What do you want, Andrei?" I inquired.

"Air Force pay eighty dollars month," he said, his blue eyes watered by vodka and sparkling with character. "Want three hundred!" He hammered his empty glass on the table and stood up. "Must go ... wife."

The train rumbled past Perm, fifteen hours out, seven hundred miles and two time zones into the three-day journey to Krasnoyarsk. It was six in the morning. Sitting on the bottom bunk with legs tucked meditation style, I watched the first of the sun's blazing rays melt into a pale-blue sky. We were deep in the steppes of mother Russia, her heart. The wind swept the feathered grasslands creating ripples that resembled waves at sea.

One could describe the Trans-Siberian Railroad as an extended picnic. As if satchels of food that people brought weren't enough, the train stopped six to eight times a day. Platform kiosks sold cigarettes, vodka, juices, ice cream, and cotton candy. Old ladies in babushkas and long, gray dresses peddled warm boiled-and-buttered potatoes, and mushroom and onion or cabbage piroshky, which were wrapped in newspapers shaped like inverted party hats. Others sold roasted chicken quartered on wooden skewers, tomatoes, sausage, boiled pigs' feet, dill pickles, and fresh raspberries, their red juice dripping from paper containers. At first I felt nervous stepping off the train, not knowing the duration of the stops. But others on the train saw the *Americanietz* wandering, and took it upon themselves to make sure I boarded the train on time.

With the thump-thump of wheels and Seventies light rock music flowing from train speakers, I taught Anna, Pauline, and Alexi to play Hearts and Minefield, the dice game I'd learned on Lake Kariba. Andrei visited the cabin every few hours, leaving his wife, Katherine, and son at the other end of the car. Then we played Russian card games. The gentle competition of the games brought out facets of each personality and allowed humor to flow. As the grasslands turned to forests of birch, aspen, and fir, and golden light gave way to gloomy rain and slashing lightning, these people made me feel at home.

During alone times, I drank water and reflected on my traveler's life. How neatly my twenty-six years in business had prepared me to understand some of the essence of history. Russia, for instance, was about transformation, a subject as close to me as my money-belt. Earning my spurs in Silicon Valley building companies, and later rescuing troubled ones, I knew about fast growth and decline, and about the two levels of reversing decline. The first is getting the patient out of the emergency ward, and the second is a commitment to healthy habits—in this case, perestroika. Companies in trouble rarely managed the second level. They couldn't change habits.

Cultures and countries operated in a similar fashion to business, probably because they had *people* in common. Some countries became absorbed into another, some faded, and some, such as Russia, had critical mass to buy time to transform. I empathized, both professionally and personally, with Russia's struggle to change habits. In just a hundred years, it had shifted from a royal-religious complex, which lacked the talent for the new world order, to a Communist regime that educated the illiterate agrarian population and within fifty years had put the first human in space. Now transformation was again required. Communism could not compete with the hi-tech, highly motivated, and better funded capitalistic democracies. The switch to capitalism meant three strong ideologies had governed the Russian people in one century.

Russia's critical mass was the strength of its people's character and its size—it crossed thirteen time zones and comprised twenty percent of the earth's landmass. The place was so immense that in three days my train would traverse only half its girth. Siberia alone was as large as Australia and Brazil combined. It was once the largest penal colony in the world, wild and untamed.

As the train droned east, I joined others exercising in the corridor, played cards, and read *The Marie Antoinette Tapestry* by Alexei Tolstoy. Russian writers had so much material they could fall out of bed and write a vibrant story. Out the window, white-washed houses with thatched roofs dotted a land of Eurasian forests, gray-blue rivers, and small towns. Sometimes I'd play with a four-year-old next door, tickle him or let him run his toy car across my foot. Periodically Andrei would give me the finger-hook and I'd join him in the dining car. He brought his own food and we purchased beer or wine, splitting the bill seventy percent *Americanietz* and thirty percent *Ruski*, owing to the disparity in wealth.

As for personal needs, the cramped bathroom required a masterful engineering effort to balance a toiletry kit on the tiny ledge below the mirror. Gazing at my reflection, I wondered: *Who am I?* I saw bright blue, youthful irises at the center of eyes that were—thanks to the mellow pace of traveling life—no longer bloodshot. Here was a man in his late forties with silver side-burns, soft, blond hair, and a creased forehead. The body was fit and trim, but the skin didn't fit as tightly around the muscles anymore.

There was no doubt I was an older person, but with trust and a 'beginner's mind,' I was building friendships with younger ones. My traveling companions allowed me to see that age was indeed a state of mind. Stripped of desire to compete for words and build ego, it was possible to combine vintage champagne with a shot of young vodka. The qualities I learned to perfect as a trav-eler—a healthy, easygoing curiosity and non-conflict-oriented attitude—were attainable to anyone. I thanked my grandmother for showing me how to be with young people, and my kids for the practice. Let the moment take me, I said to the mirror, and let fate reset my habits.

The evening before arriving in Krasnoyarsk, Pauline and I helped Anna and Alexi carry their parcels off the train. Nearby, a burly woman wearing a thick flannel shirt ripped the cap off a bottle of beer with her teeth and spit it on to the concrete. While the train idled, I shook hands with Alexi and kissed Anna's cheek. She handed me her address in Russian. Back on the train I watched as the two disappeared into the small country town. Would I ever need to refer to that piece of paper again?

Back in the compartment, Andrei lay sprawled on Pauline's wool blanket, dressed in his trademark blue sweats. He winked at Pauline and motioned towards me as if to say, "Ah-ha, alone with *Americanietz*." She turned crimson, swatted him, and broke out the cards for a game of *Chérie* (Hearts).

Two stops later, a weathered, slightly emaciated middle-aged man claimed Alexi's upper bunk. He stowed three of his four bags, and then, without stopping to catch his breath, politely rearranged the window table. While removing five packages from the remaining bulging gym bag, he introduced himself as Yuri and obtained our details from Andrei. Both laughed and gestured as if they were soul buddies.

The man carefully placed on the table cooked, gray, linked sausages, piroshkies, bread freshly baked by his mom, cucumbers, and a brown bottle that looked like sixteen ounces of beer. The train music had switched to vibrant Cossack. Spotting the bottle, Andrei cried, "Vodka!" and pulled me towards the dining car to purchase wine. Having accomplished our mission, he charged through the narrow corridor and shaky couplings waving the wine and yelling, "For girls!"

Andrei placed the wine next to Yuri's vodka and disappeared. He returned shortly with Katherine and her friend Elana, a husky electrical engineering student in transit from St. Petersburg to Lake Baikal. The women had painted their eyes, fine-tuned their hair, pinched their cheeks, and smeared lipstick heavily on their lips in preparation for a party. The party turned out to be my going-away bash.

They brought veggies, a large can of chopped beef, and cooked potatoes garnered at the last stop. I contributed chocolate candy, a large bottle of Welch's grape juice, and the canned ham saved for a special occasion.

We sat on the bottom bunks, hunched forward shoulder to shoulder. Andrei raised a tin cup: "Denis, drink like this!" Straining the muscles of his neck, he drained the vodka and chased it with grape juice. The ladies shook their heads and smirked. Warmed by vodka and camaraderie, my eyes caught Andrei's. "Thanks, you are a hell of an interpreter."

At five the next morning, as daybreak brushed the night, Andrei, Pauline, and members of the train crew hugged me goodbye on a deserted platform in Krasnoyarsk. I climbed a metal bridge and stopped midway to look down at the departing train. Familiar arms waved at me through its windows into a warm breeze, as the train tooted into the distance. I never felt so utterly alone.

43

MEETING THE MAFIA

M Y FEAR OF THE UNKNOWN partly abated after familiar negotiations with the taxi driver. With pained expressions,
a few *nyets*, and finger talk, the driver and I worked out a
decent price. Now, would the *Chkalov* be at the river station, and
could I book a passage?

The taxi skirted Krasnoyarsk, a fair-sized city punctuated by
a Byzantine church steeple, and we soon pulled into an asphalt
lot along the docks on the Yenisei. Nearby, a suspension bridge
crossed the river bringing a few cars into the city. "*Chkalov*," the
driver said, pointing.

Moored to the wharf sat a sleek triple-deck ship with
Cyrillic along the side. Instead of the tramp steamer I expected,
this cream-colored ship measured over a hundred and fifty feet
from bow to stern. Above the bow's hawsehole a red star the size
of a beach ball was proudly displayed.

Sudden exhaustion from the late-night party on the train
hit me like a dart from a tranquilizer gun, and I set off to find
the cruise director Christian had mentioned. "Andrei Pavlovich?"
I asked two sailors loitering at the edge of the gangplank. They
shrugged. Next, I attempted to pantomime a person (me) in desperate need of sleep by snoring loudly while leaning my head
against prayer position hands. They laughed and fetched a ship's
officer, who took me deep into the hull, to a stale-smelling room
with steel bunks stripped of bedding. The room's furniture—a
wooden chair, battered table, and austere clothes cabinet—contrasted sharply with the boat's flashy exterior. Light shone through

two portholes just above the waterline. I immediately collapsed into a deep sleep.

Five hours later, there was a knock at the door. A short, forty-five-year-old, impeccably dressed man with close-cropped hair introduced himself in Russian as Andrei Pavlovich. The cruise director! He read Sasha's letter introducing me and requesting a traveler's fare. He motioned for and flipped through my dictionary, like a man comfortable with authority. He indicated I should stay where I was and he would speak to me later. No mention of price.

That evening, I set out to find Andrei and was directed to a third-deck cabin. A woman in her mid-sixties answered the door. She stood barely five feet tall with stringy hair and intense gray eyes bulging behind coke-bottle glasses. Graciously inviting me into the two-room suite for tea, she introduced herself as Ninnell Andreievna Catashova Pavlovich. Ninnell spotted my dictionary and quickly found the words "retired teacher" to describe herself, and even before our tea was ready, had offered to teach me Russian until Andrei returned from "Polish problem." For three hours, she searched about the room finding objects to give the Russian word for: glass, fork, eyeglasses, ruler, book, comb. Finally she used the dictionary to explain: "Polish plane late. Russian pilot want more money." I was not much the wiser.

Sometime around midnight, Andrei returned. The cost of the fifteen-day cruise to the Arctic Circle would be $150. The traveler in me was ecstatic. I would have gladly paid the thousand dollars he quoted Christian.

The next morning, Ruslan, a pudgy, six-foot Russian with a cigarette dangling from his lip, tossed a duffel bag on the top bunk and moved in. His English was severely limited, but functional. After I shared what little fruit and bread was left from the train, eighteen-year-old Ruslan crooked his finger: "You come. I show you city."

Krasnoyarsk had about nine hundred thousand people, and was named after beautiful red rocks found in the gullies of the River Kacha. The confluence of the Kacha and the Yenisei was where the Cossacks built the first fort in the area to protect Russia from invasions from the east. In the late nineteenth century, gold was discovered and about the same time Russian royalty decided it was a good place to exile revolutionary leaders, including Lenin and Stalin. This strategy backfired, however, and Krasnoyarsk served instead as an incubator for revolution.

We entered the town through a small wooded park with its stone statue of Lenin in an ankle-length overcoat. Gypsies entertained a modest crowd in the concrete promenade, enticing a black bear on a leash to do tricks. Beyond the park, box-shaped four- and five-story buildings ran along sidewalks boasting the occasional fruit stand. On every other street, wooden kiosks with barred windows sold a standard fare of alcohol, juice, candy, and cigarettes at thirty cents a pack. Tiny cars dribbled by. We passed another statue of two muscular farmers hoeing, and another of a burly female raising a hammer and sickle to the sky.

Pedestrians wore heavy clothes with depressing colors, or sweats and T-shirts stenciled with the name of US basketball teams. Ruslan pointed out beautiful young women, of whom there were many, and I nodded silently. They walked with long, graceful strides, wore heavy lipstick, and chewed gum. People over thirty were not so pretty—all pudgy bodies and yellow or blackened teeth, or occasionally front teeth capped with gold and silver. I didn't see any hotels, except for a ten-story shell that had been abandoned long ago. Lucky the boat was there.

As we returned, Ruslan explained the "Polish problem." Half of the *Chkalov's* passengers were Russian and the other half Polish, but the Poles' jet plane had been delayed a day by a moon-lighting Russian pilot renegotiating the deal at the last minute.

Ruslan himself lived in Dudinka, the ship's destination in the Arctic. While he liked the trees of Krasnoyarsk, he was not so keen on its warm summer weather. It was about seventy-five degrees. Then he pointed to the burned-out ribs of a kiosk. "Mafia," he said.

Before re-boarding, I invited Ruslan to join me at the only restaurant in sight, near the port. Who could afford to eat in a restaurant, even one so dreary? The menu was limited to meat soup and grape juice, and the only other patrons were three hard-faced, dark-haired men in their late twenties. After they finished slurping soup, these guys carried over their wooden chairs, placed them back side first around our table, and plunked down two

pint-sized bottles of vodka. *"Americanietz?"* one of them demanded, pointing a finger at me as he sat. I nodded.

Sandy-haired Ruslan interpreted. He pointed to each of the
wiry bodies in turn: "He say his name Volodya. This one also
Volodya. And he Anton."

We toasted *Ruski* and *Americanietz* until we drained both
bottles. By now I was vodka hardened. Then the younger of the
Volodyas disappeared to return with a third bottle.

"Ask them, Ruslan, what they do for a living."

"Anton say, they in business."

"Ask them what business."

Guffaws from Ruslan! The older, more aggressive of the
Volodyas, sitting hawk-faced with his chin resting on the back of
the chair, smirked while he spoke. Ruslan interpreted, "Volodya
say business: buy low, sell high!"

A sullen waitress showed up occasionally to demonstrate
that service was not a priority. Ruslan concentrated on his job,
as if negotiating the sale of the *Chkalov*. As we talked his skill at
translating increased. The conversation wandered into whether
Communism would revive in Russia. "Anton say young are future
and young want Hollywood."

"Ask them if they know mafia?"

Ruslan's dimples swirled as he opened his mouth in surprise
at the question's audacity. "You want ask that?'

"Yes, it's okay, ask!"

He slugged down a huge gulp of vodka and mooched a
Lucky Strike from the junior Volodya, who lit two cigarettes in
his mouth and handed one to Ruslan. Then Ruslan conveyed the
message to the puffing Russians. The senior Volodya laughed and
slapped Ruslan's back.

"Volodya say mafia sell to people what people want buy."

"Ask him what mafia sells?"

"Volodya say, Hollywood."

When the spirits dried up, the senior Volodya invited me
to his comfortable boat, which was moored not far from the
Chkalov. Onboard we all drank more vodka and ate smoked fish.
As I left, Volodya wrote his name and address on an anemic napkin, inviting me to stay with him if I ever got stranded.

In my normal life, I don't drink much. A few beers here and there, a few glasses of wine. Water mostly. In Russia, vodka was water. Later that night, as the Polish and Russian passengers took residence in the various cabins, Alexander, the radio engineer, pounded on the door of my pauper's stateroom. A pleasant-looking, paunchy fellow with coal-black hair and a scar across the bridge of his nose, he had decided to spearhead the *Americanietz* adoption committee, armed with two skewers of roast beef and onions. He was drunk. We sat on the lower bunk polishing off the skewers while he spoke non-stop Russian. Then he grabbed my shoulder and herded me to the third deck near the stern, to his comfortable, one-bedroom, stained-wood cabin.

Ruslan sat on the floor beside the bed. This kid got around. At the far side of the cramped room, Magadoon strummed a guitar. He had a square face and the tightly muscled body of a prizefighter. Using Ruslan to interpret, he told a story of how, when he was in the navy, his submarine often surfaced next to US Navy vessels and the sailors waved to each other. Magadoon took an immediate liking to me.

Sitting on Alexander's desk and staring solemnly in my direction was Vitali, the boatswain. With his puffy, olive features and curly, black hair, Vitali looked Italian. His sober countenance reserved judgment on the *Americanietz*. Lanky Alexi, the third mate, sat next to me on the bed. During the night, other members of the crew wandered in to say hello to a real live American, dressed in loose and light African garb and Tevas. I was reminded of the parting words of a friend, who would be meeting me in Greece: "There will be a place where you are one of a kind, the single alien accent. People will want to meet you."

Despite not knowing what anyone was saying, I was glad to be here. The party broke up at four in the morning, long after the orange crescent moon called it a night. How in hell, I wondered, could we set sail given the condition of the crew? Yet before long tugboats were guiding the *Chkalov* under the suspension bridge, as faint sounds of train whistles mixed with gurgling water and Ruslan's breathing.

Later in the morning, the sun blazed while the ship's beefy-faced captain spoke on deck to a mixed audience of Russians and Poles. He spoke Russian and Andrei Pavlovich translated into Polish. Except for four beautiful young Russians sitting on the railing sunning, the crowd was heavily weighted towards people in their twilight.

There are days that rumble through the pages of time just waiting to be lived. Days fantasies are made of. This was to be one of those days.

44

One of a Kind—
The Single Alien Accent

THAT AFTERNOON, WE MADE THE first of our daily stops along
the two thousand-kilometer route. Walking down the gangplank, a strong impulse to turn found me staring directly
into the effervescent, almond-shaped eyes of one of the young
Russian women sunning on deck. She was smiling intently at
me. The hot sun intensified the luster of her auburn hair, full, red
lips, perfect white teeth, and stunning smile. Spellbound, I pulled
the dictionary from my back pocket and patiently translated into
Russian: "you ... have ... beautiful ... smile!" Smiling myself, I
turned and continued down the gangplank, wondering what the
hell that was all about.

Yeniseysk was a town of log houses with tin roofs and wooden-
shuttered windows. The homes sat on permafrost, which in
summer softened and sagged under its own weight, while in
winter the freezing soil pushed and bent the construction upwards into odd forms, but never to its previous height. The town
included a prison with castle towers (kremlins) favored by the
Romanov dynasty for exiling political dissidents. Its most famous
inmate was Petrashevsky, in whose radical circle Dostoevsky was
active.

Back on board, I received a second Russian lesson from
Ninnell while touring the ship. Above the bargain basement

where Ruslan and I slept, the ship had three shiny mahogany decks. Two were dedicated to indoor and outdoor recreation, while on the third was a quaint dining room. Meals were served at two sittings where one ate overlooking the Yenisei through graceful, lace-curtained windows. Ninnell said I belonged at the second sitting, and she taught me how to say: "Where is Denis Hickey's seat?"

After the lesson, I stopped at a cubbyhole liquor store to buy fine Russian bubbly for my table. Reaching for the bottle, I felt someone blowing sensuously into my ear and down my neck. Time crawled. I turned slowly, thinking that I didn't know anyone within ten thousand miles who would blow in my ear. Standing before me was the smiling young woman from the gangplank, her face lit up like the Northern Lights. Her smile could have powered the *Chkalov* or melted ice caps. Next to her, pushing to be introduced, as if to a celebrity, were three other young and extremely attractive women. I was "one of a kind, the single alien accent."

"My name Oxanna," she said in a throaty voice that did not seem to belong with the smile, but was strangely fitting. She raked her hand through hair that barely touched her shoulders, then introduced the other women. Ula, a dark-haired beauty with delicate, soft features, the grace of a Spanish contessa, and lush lips that glistened with scarlet lipstick. Tall Natasha, her curly, brown hair short, her face pleasant but unsure. Perhaps the most riveting of the four was Svieta, whose dazzling, long, kinky, red hair exploded from her head. Her eyes hinted of Asia and her smile vibrated a fresh, energetic character. All but Oxanna spoke rudimentary English. Between them, they conjured up limited conversation, welcoming me to Russia. Oxanna's aggressive body language talked for her.

Svieta expressed a desire for us all to meet after dinner. They had questions. I sat between Ruslan and Oxanna, and directly across from Ula and Ludmilla, a hard-faced woman with rakish hair and a silver-toothed smile who could have made a stereotypical KGB agent. At an adjoining table, Svieta and Natasha strained their ears to hear snatches of our conversation. The waitress delivered a decanter of delicious blackcurrant juice, and served bowls of fish soup, meat croquettes, potatoes, tomatoes, and cucumbers, while Ruslan translated my Russian gibberish into a proper question asking what each did for a living. Ludmilla worked as an engineer in a factory, mysteriously refusing to divulge the product. Ula studied electrical engineering, and Oxanna physical education at the university in Krasnoyarsk. Flashing amber eyes, Oxanna added through Ruslan that she ran the one hundred and two hundred meters in track.

After dinner, in sunset's blush, my new friends formed a semicircle around me on the second deck walkway. Svieta took charge beginning the interrogation in a high-pitched purr: "Denis, what you do?"

"*Ya pi-sat.*" I am a writer, I said, comfortable with the change of profession.

They quizzed me about Russian authors and found me lacking, then asked my age. The ladies inched closer, a soft competitiveness filling the air.

"Forty," I lied, chopping eight years off.

"Do you have wife?"

"Ex-wife," I lied again, but it was consistent with what I told Ninnell the night before when I decided to try a blank slate and follow fate.

"Do you have children?"

"Two daughters."

Svieta conferred with Natasha and Ula. "What their names?"

Uncomfortable being the center of attention while lying through my teeth, I nevertheless immensely enjoyed the thrill of becoming someone else for the first time, someone unconstrained by a prior life.

"Shannon and Chimene."

"Names pretty," said Svieta. "How old children?"

"Seventeen and sixteen," I calculated on the fly. Not bad, almost seven years knocked off their lives. That made me twenty-three when I had Shannon. That part was right.

Was this how women felt when guys were in the hunt, waiting to see who takes the prize? Whatever it was, it was sublime. Suddenly Oxanna, perhaps feeling left out, walked behind me and put her arms around my stomach, interlocking her fingers. She had staked her claim, but the other women didn't back off. Was it possible to be caught by them all?

I took my turn to ask questions. Svieta studied psychology and Natasha accounting in Krasnoyarsk. Oxanna hugged my back close to her. Her bangs hung tantalizingly down her forehead and she burrowed her eyes deeply into mine when I turned to look. The message was possession is nine-tenths of the law.

Preliminaries over, Ula suggested we join festivities in the cozy piano room on the third deck. Painted a soft cream, the room had a parquet floor and see-through silk curtains draped over curved windows shaped to fit the bow. A teenage boy played an ivory-colored piano, which sat elegantly on a red print rug in the middle of the room. The semicircle of classical columns, lounge couches, and supple loveseats completed the ambience.

Exhibiting enormous talent, the young pianist played folk songs while his ten-year-old sister sang, danced, and made us all laugh. I had no idea what she was saying but at one point I was doubled up. A local poet took over, crooning as he strummed a guitar. The crowd clapped and sang along. I felt the charms of an older time when people of all ages congregated together.

Svieta sat to my right, Ula delicately to the left. I felt, rather than saw, Oxanna. Standing behind and leaning over the armchair the ladies procured for me, her tranquil arms rested on top of mine as she softly stroked my skin, occasionally playing with the hairs. All I had to do was answer her hands and I would be sleeping with a beautiful woman and breaking a long spell of celibacy. A small gesture, really. A squeeze of the hand, stroke of the arm, the faintest pressure and the claim would be registered. Svieta, not more than two feet away, looked so exotic. Ula so engaging and Natasha....

I tried to concentrate on the entertainment, but my blood was rising in concert with the feel of Oxanna's warmth. Her soft breath was igniting my ears. I smiled, neither moving in a way that would discourage her—if that was possible—or encourage her. Keep your options open, my mind said, this moment is not going to happen again in your next four lifetimes. But a pragmatic "bird in the hand" voice began to make itself heard. It whispered: Enjoy her.

I stroked her arm in surrender. Thereafter, the events of the night moved swiftly. During the poet's second song, I gently squeezed Oxanna's hand, sign-languaging that I would be back, and headed straight for my cramped quarters to spruce up. On the way to the public bathroom, I was caught toothpaste-handed by the women scurrying to do some sprucing up of their own.

We reconvened at the disco. Dressed in black, the women looked smashing. Ula's form-fitting cocktail dress plunged below the shoulders, revealing porcelain-white skin. Where Ula exhibited class, Svieta's mid-thigh dress was pure animal. Oxanna kept pace in a loose-fitting, gold-laced blouse and matching pants that left her slim belly bare. Natasha dressed modestly. "She lives a lonely life ... She's gone tomorrow, boy. All that she wants is another baby," blared from the speakers.

We danced, like I hadn't done since Egypt. That is until a glassy-eyed Alexander—his cheeks swollen, and listing left from alcohol—invited the women and me to join his birthday party in the captain's lounge. He introduced me to the captain, three journalists—Israeli, South African, and Australian—and a person described by the Israeli in a whisper to my ear as a mafia chieftain who owned Krasnoyarsk. I flashed the latter a traveler smile, but immediately took a dislike to the hard eyes and dominating demeanor of the small, chunky, sixty-year-old gangster.

The journalists, whose stay on the boat consisted of one night, were to be ferried to a private plane the next day. That one night would give them material they needed to describe Siberia. I convinced them, or rather the fetching smiles of the women convinced them, to join us at the disco, so that they could catch— I glanced at the gangster—what real people did. In conversation, the Australian confessed that journalists captured what they experienced, and did not have the time, or maybe inclination, to research the wider truth of an issue.

Early morning found the women and I sitting in a booth drinking champagne in a quaint late-night bar and dance floor on the first deck. Clinking glasses with the others, I toasted to "four beautiful women and a lucky guy."

"To handsome man," responded Ula pointing her glass.

I nodded, delighted.

"A man is like good wine," Svieta added, "he ripens with age."

What exactly attracted younger women (or women of all ages, for that matter) to older men? Was it the adventure, a maturity that younger men lacked, or a feeling of security? On the other hand, for me, the attractions of youth were irresistibly simple and obvious. Jack Nicholson once said: "There's a very good reason why a man goes to someone of breeding age for a sexual situation. It's the way we're set up. By nature. Nature doesn't care what you think about marriage, it cares about reproduction." Right now I was irresistibly in nature's grasp.

Oxanna tired of the competition, grabbed my hand, and led me to the parquet dance floor. Her smile was in tune with the movements of her body—alluring, sexual, powerful. Once the bonding dance ended, I took her hand, said goodnight to the others, and, in a trance, ushered her straight to my room.

I savored the evening. It was wild and alive. The rush of taking a woman's clothes off—button by button, piece by piece. The splendor of having mine ripped off. I observed her with dual pleasures of lust and absence. Our hungry bodies clung so close our heartbeats mingled. The touch of flesh. The thrilling animal ecstasy of thrust and release. The sweet experience peeled away the layers I had plastered over my passions. It was a guy's fantasy.

Oxanna's gestures at breakfast announced to all that this fish had been hooked, cleaned, and fried. She poured heavy plum juice into our glasses—hers and mine—dished out corned-beef hash burgers, cucumbers, and tomatoes, and even doused my cream of rice with milk.

After breakfast, Ninnell and Andrei Pavlovich waylaid me, led me to their room, and bawled me out—in Russian. It was an unaccustomed feeling. People didn't yell at me! Ninnell's eyes burned behind her glasses. She released one hand from her hips, grabbed the dictionary, pointed out a word, and howled: "*Vora! Vora!*" The English translation said "thief."

Stunned, I initially figured they were upset about the letter requesting a traveler's discount when I obviously had money. However, then they pantomimed me drinking with the mafia in Krasnoyarsk and yelled phrases that were unintelligible except for the words *shampanskoye* and vodka. Looking down at the dictionary again, the word next to *thief* was *pickpocket*. After much discussion and cooling of tempers, it turned out Ninnell and Andrei were concerned that I would be robbed by the mafia or crew, or worse—as Ninnell's finger across her throat graphically illustrated. Ninnell screwed her eyes in mock anger, waved a finger at me, knocked her knuckles on my head, and said in English: "How you get Fiji, if lose money and passport?"

I kissed Ninnell's cheek, thanked her for being concerned, and skipped Russian lessons the next day to protest being treated like a bad boy.

45

MEETING MALGORZATA

THE DAY EXPANDED AS WE sailed north. Sunsets lasted all
night. The lulling wind began to whistle and bite. The
ever-present forest grew shorter, and groundcover became
emerald green, like California hills in winter. Vapor lurked on
the surface of murky waters, like smoke from a dampened fire.
Gray birds followed in the ship's wake, flittering ghosts in the
mist.

Each day, the villages we visited along the Yenisei changed
steadily in character—from vibrant with sawdust in the air, to
smoky, drab, and smelling of fish. Small cars packed people in
like sardines, and motorcycles with rattling sidecars buzzed along
mud roads. Frigid winters, hard work, and vodka were stamped
on leathery Asian faces that looked older and smaller. Men in
rough work pants and heavy plaid shirts wore wiry, long beards.
Mothers in flimsy print dresses pushed Forties-style baby carriages, while diminutive grandmothers wearing faded wool coats
and *platoks* (headscarves) walked hand-in-hand with little girls in
skirts with ribbons in their hair.

Their weathered plank houses with sharply pitched roofs
were reminiscent of army barracks—but with clothes hanging
on lines and fishnets on fences. Firewood was neatly stacked.
Gaggles of white geese were herded by determined matrons
and little boys brandishing switches. There was no plastic. Dogs
with eyes of wolves roamed and sometimes fought in the streets.
Each town had its own statue of a serious-looking Lenin in his
overcoat and a sprinkling of pockmarked, scraggly-bearded, blue-
faced drunks staggering the streets.

I often explored the villages alone. Sometimes I would practice songs from sheets of lyrics I took with me. I had a good voice, but not the confidence to use it. This was the time and place to gain self-belief. Needless to say, my "rehearsals" garnered strange glances.

Ninnell's Russian lessons became a daily affair, as were late-night parties with the crew and Russian women. People introduced themselves. One man pointed to my water bottle, asking, "*Voodka?*"

"*Vada*," I said laughing—because it was funny. Shit, they were thinking I was drinking vodka?

Sometimes I felt like a voyeur within my own movie, in a social life where I could only express simple phrases and emotions. What did they think about this friendly, middle-aged American hanging around with younger people? An answer came when Ruslan passed on an older woman's request that I contact her son in San Francisco. This gave me confidence—I was indeed unusual. An easygoing celebrity.

The teenage pianist practiced in the plush room while I wrote. We had an unspoken arrangement. And his darling, blond, eight-year-old brother, also a classical pianist, followed me around, occasionally laying his head on my shoulder or hugging me as I read. Not to be left out, his sister, the singer-dancer-comedian in the vaudeville genre was also my buddy.

About midway in the voyage, the tall sailor Alexi, Ruslan, and the Russian women, sans Oxanna, abducted me into Svieta and Natasha's room. "We need ask you questions!" said Svieta, dressed in a soft purple sweater, which hugged her chin and highlighted her hair and green eyes. All rooms below the main deck were carbon copies, except this one had a woman's touch—a smell of oils and colorful woolen bedcovers.

They wanted to know about Americans: their looseness, religions, drugs, movie stars, styles, cars, feminism. They wanted to know how businesses worked and what "profit" meant. Ula, puffing a cigarette and flipping through pages, could not find *business* or *profit* in her Russian dictionary. Actually describing capitalism and profit was quite difficult with people who did not think in those terms, like describing snow in the jungles of Uganda.

When they, in return, described how public ownership worked under Communism, I had to make my mind a blank slate and think reverse economics.

In answer to my questions, they told me that the average Russian woman would have four abortions, that the major conflict in Russia was between the desires of old and young, and there was frustration with past leadership regarding Russia's war with Afghanistan. Then, without a trace of embarrassment, Ula asked, "What 'fuck' mean?" She said "fuck" so blatantly that I laughed hard. After being stunned at my response, she laughed, too. I noticed my laugh had changed. Back home I made people laugh, but didn't have a good laugh myself. So I'd been practicing a natural laugh, which had begun to fit me.

After delicately explaining "fuck," I changed the subject and spoke slowly so they could stay with me. "The railroad from Moscow took three days and covered half the country. Who organized Russia to grow so large?"

"What you mean?"

"When companies in the United States grew fast, people began to understand that the faster the growth, the more organized and experienced management must be. What philosophy could conquer such a vast area and manage it for so long?"

The Russians conferred at length about this question before Svieta answered with precision and passion.

"Denis, a thousand years in past, small but strong Russian culture center around Moscow. They Muscovites! Led by emperors named tsars. They very organized people. Conquer tribes not well organized. Many tribes see Muscovite strength. Ask them to help fight neighbors. Muscovites say, okay! Then Muscovites not leave. They send own people to settle areas, marry, to ... to ... transfer religion and culture."

"Sounds like American West, except quilt not knitted through marriage.

"Administering so vast an area must have taken much talent!"

Ula checked "quilt" in her big black dictionary, nodded with understanding, then rifled through the dictionary again before speaking.

"Yes, strong leaders. But big advantage—only one church! Church organized. Much profit. Peter the Great make country modern. First, military, he build navy. Second, very important for future, he plant seed for education of masses. Lenin receive benefit of seed!"

"Why Communism?" I asked. "Americans are taught that under Communism people were zombies in an evil system."

She looked up the word "zombies" and laughed.

"It food source that hold key to my country direction," she said with zeal, "When tsar free serfs in 1850s, he make nobles sell land to local village. Village organize *commune.* Commune collect taxes, pay for justice, pay debt to nobles. Peasant must to carry passport. Later workers organize committees called *soviets.* Lenin used philosophy that already existed at source of food. Lenin great organizer—he recognize Marxism fit what already exist."

It sounded like an example of the theory of dissipative structures. An organization will grow until it can't function properly, then an explosion creates a simple but elegant improvement towards a higher order.

Revolutionary thought in Russia created socialism because royalty simply didn't have enough talent to manage growth. And Americans adopted democratic capitalism because the people who settled were predominantly adventurers and more literate. They were risk-takers. Capitalism required an educated middle class or else the money would flow to a small group knowledgeable in the language of money. It all fit! Russia's royalty-church complex lasted longer than Europe's because its society was uncomplicated—agrarian. Church and royalty kept the people in line. When societal complexity arrived, the old system gave way to one that could handle super growth with an illiterate foundation—Communism.

"Why so many statues of Lenin," I wondered, "but none of Stalin?"

Svieta fondled a dainty gold cross and chain around her neck as she conferred with Ula and Natasha. Ula and Svieta were remarkably attractive—*Cosmopolitan* magazine cover girl attractive.

"When Khrushchev take control," Svieta finally responded, "we realize how many people Stalin kill. Maybe twenty million. Many sent to Siberian towns, and gulags."

"Some say Lenin also killed many people," I stated, stretching my legs to remove stiffness that age deposits in joints. I was in heaven with such beautiful and intelligent women.

319

"Many people die in Volga during Civil War because they no have food," Ula explained, in consultation with the dictionary. "Seven million, I think. That was Stalin's region. He starve farmers to no supply food to White Army."

"Lenin must have known the type of killer Stalin was. Why did he continue with him?"

"Lenin write letter to central committee before he die," Svieta answered. "He say, 'Do not to let Stalin have power in new government.' But Stalin very clever man, I think. No one knows what happen. All papers destroyed."

"What happened to the others on Lenin's central committee?"

"Stalin kill them and set up new committee."

After a few hours, the session broke up. Svieta said: "We meet again, tomorrow!" Thus, a routine of socio-economic discussions was also established.

When the boat docked that day, we visited a small hamlet under huge white clouds hanging heavy in the sky. Fish were for sale, punctured by wooden spears and hanging from wire lines outside living quarters. At twenty-six and a universally known revolutionary, Lenin was exiled by the Tsar to a place like this.

As the days progressed, the romance with Oxanna oscillated from titillating to confusing. One "night," as the ship ploughed ever deeper into Siberia, we entered a persistent cloudbank, which hovered just above the waves. An omen? Dressed warmly in ski jackets, Oxanna and I leaned over the bow railing outside the piano room listening to the hum of the *Chkalov*'s powerful engines. Desperate to communicate orally, I had prepared a written narrative and several questions in Russian.

"Oxanna, I ... need ... to ... talk ... to ... you."

Surprised at my Russian, she reluctantly grabbed the dictionary and paged through it. Her expression had changed from carefree to intense. Laughter and music echoed from inside. I'd gotten to know Oxanna a little. Her smile camouflaged her competitiveness and self-centeredness. After five long minutes, she responded: "*Da!* About ... what?"

"For instance, what work parents do?" I asked in my prepared Russian.

She tossed her eyes impatiently into the air and shook her head, aiming a perturbed glance my way. She then peered over the railing, as if considering how much effort she was willing to put into this encounter.

It ended up being quite a bit of physical effort, as she mimed her parents' jobs. She raced the length of the deck to show her mother taught physical education and coached track. And demonstrated a stranglehold on me, which meant her father coached the international wrestling team. Great! We were getting somewhere.

"How ... many ... children ... in ... family?"

"Twenty ... four ... I ... nineteen," she said, using her fingers to help me.

Whoa! I thought, that was a big family. She was the nineteenth born? However, I'd missed some words. After several minutes of her flipping through pages, the revised translation came: "Two children. My brother twenty-four. I nineteen." She handed the dictionary back.

Jesus Christ, nineteen! I was at once shocked and proud. My travels had taught me that youth was no big deal, but nineteen! For ten minutes, I searched the dictionary to compose a new question for Oxanna in Russian: How do you feel making love to a man as old as your father?

She smiled, her cheeks a blush-red from the weather. "*Hurashou*," she said, using the Russian for "good," which I knew. She grabbed the dictionary again, as well as a pad and pen stored in my jacket. Stripped down to its basic elements, communication was, I could see, a precise science. As I pondered this, Oxanna concluded her writing: *We dance now.*

The *Chkalov* reached the Arctic Circle on the seventh day of the voyage, my birthday. At nine, the crew ferried forty hearty people to shore for a twenty-kilometer round-trip trek to a gulag. Most were in their sixties, dressed in hard-to-breathe mosquito nets that protected their faces and bodies. Natasha said Poles braved this trek because the Romanovs and Communists exiled millions of their relatives to Siberia. The Poles and Germans helped settle the land.

Svieta, Natasha, and Alexi, the six-five gentle giant, walked with me under angry skies on the grueling hike through swamp grass and forest. Ravens cawed above the muddy track forged by vehicles long since rusted into oblivion. Each member of the group trudged along looking like somber beekeepers, except for me. Hardened by Africa, I'd rejected my net and put my faith in insect repellent, natural herbal anti-insect wrist bracelets, and a black box the size of a watch that emitted a high-frequency sound designed to mimic the signal predator bats used to locate mosquitoes. A hat with earflaps, bandanna around the neck, and light-blue plastic rain cape completed my defenses. My eccentric reputation among my boat-mates had received a further boost.

Two kilometers into the hike, a sign reading *Arctic Circle* marked the location of an underground atomic bomb test site three hundred meters below the surface. Burned-out shacks, a junk heap of twisted steel, and scattered wood surrounded an innocuous hole in the earth. I milled around wondering what I was doing at a nuclear dump listening to the *tick tick* of mosquitoes pelting my plastic cape.

Back on the path, my repellant barely working, I shivered to imagine a line of political prisoners walking here. Without nets or repellent, they must have been eaten alive.

We soon came upon the first evidence of the gulag: a rusted train engine with a long smokestack in the middle of the mud. There were tracks that lead nowhere. Stalin used prisoners to build the railway along the Polar Circle, figuring it would provide refuge in case of attack from the West. The engineer must have miscalculated here. I took a picture of Svieta and Alexi on top of the engine.

At the entry to the gulag, we passed barbed wire and muddled through a series of dilapidated wooden barracks and buildings. Moss replaced stucco on the wooden latticework. The gulag was slowly becoming a wasteland of colorful shrubbery and forest, returning to nature like an ancient Mayan village.

We stared at concrete solitary confinement cells with barred windows. As if the frozen Arctic winters hadn't brought enough pain for prisoners, in summer, offenders were stripped and left unprotected for an hour or more in air thick with insects. I wondered what other atrocities the guards heaped on their prisoners. The things humans did to humans.

Crickets chirped as I stared out one of the tiny windows in the jail. I imagined a once powerful man who backed the wrong horse, a revolutionary, and a simple regular guy who believed a philosophy he'd been told, all condemned to this godforsaken place. How they must have arrived and stared forlornly out this window, like I was, at the twenty-foot notice board. A board that provided instructions that regulated life here. What must they have thought?

Amid the ruins was a theater where professional entertainers who had been sentenced for telling the wrong joke performed. Elsewhere, we saw a tile stove in one of the barracks—a camp luxury—and holes punctured in the sheet metal over the window, large enough for mosquitoes but not enough for much air or light.

Perhaps all ideologies only benefit one part of society, while the others wind up in prisons or homeless. The job of civilization has to be to minimize the fallout—not create more.

Walking past the lone watchtower, we left the ghosts in the camp and looked past wildflowers to the distant view of the tranquil Yenisei. Testaments to brutality and beauty side by side in nature.

The *Chkalov* exited the fog bank into clear and surprisingly mild weather. Perfect for my birthday party. Peeking into Alexander's room through an open window on the second deck, I saw the women, the crew, and Ruslan who wore sunglasses and a denim jacket with *US Airman* and a flying eagle stenciled across the pocket. They had already broken open a bottle of vodka and lit cigarettes. Stretching my arm through the window and dropping a bag of vegetables and two bottles of champagne on to the bed, I sparked an eruption of laughter. A feast had begun. The ladies brought bread and smoked sturgeon purchased from villagers. Alexander and Alexi supplied vodka, and the broad-faced boatswain, Vitali, beer. Magadoon, manly in shorts and a muscle shirt with horizontal black and white stripes that magnified his biceps and abs, burst in carrying a large pot and serving bowls.

He walked straight to me: "Eat, friend," he said.

"Denis, it is caviar in onions and stomach of fish," Ula informed me, pointing to the pot. "Eat fat of fish, not get drunk.

Magadoon say 'for your birthday.'" Inside the pot there must have been three pounds of cooked caviar and fish.

Alexander gave me his sailor's muscle shirt as a present, and the party commenced. We drank throughout a night colored by continuous sunset. Alexander, beer in hand, listened somberly. Natasha was ever shy. Ula watched Magadoon, who strummed his guitar and stole glimpses at Svieta. She in turn laughed and joked and tried on the guys' hats. She and Magadoon had eyes for each other. Meanwhile, Ruslan scratched a pimple and lit a joint, passing it around. Oxanna sat on the cramped bed, one hand on my leg and another on Alexander's shoulder.

Oxanna and I had been playing cat and mouse lately. When one wanted attention, the other pulled away. It didn't help that Svieta often sat with her elbow on my knee. During the socio-economic discussions with the other women, Oxanna began to hang out with the crew, especially the bronzed-faced teddy bear, Alexander, who read poetry to her.

Two nights earlier, after a day's absence, Oxanna came into my room. "Where have you been?" I quizzed, with a frosty jealous stare.

Oxanna grabbed the dictionary. In a mix of tears and frustration, she communicated that she stayed away because of her period.

Had that never occurred to me? But instead of changing the energy I wore an angry face. Sometimes I am amazed at my own stupidity. Suddenly the helplessness and tears in Oxanna's eyes turned to an angry glare. She pursed her lips, swung around, and said what sounded like "fuck off" in Russian. And slammed the door on her way out.

The *bam* brought home my foolishness, yet pride kept me from following her. I felt like a lonely schmuck, but still I wondered how she could cry so easily. Last time I cried was forty years ago when my brother punched me and chipped a tooth. And why was I jealous? I was flirting with Svieta. After reflection and self-rebuke, I resolved to change the energy and see what destiny had in store.

The next day, the boat moored at the shores of a serene village of log cabins and green pastures without fences or roads. Pigs walked freely. I picked bright yellow and purple wild flowers, presenting a bouquet to Ninnell, but saving the best flower for Oxanna along with a letter in Russian that said: "Please bring back the smile."

She did smile, stuffed the letter in her blouse pocket, and took the flower to her room. I swore to become a gentleman and regain her smile permanently, without sex if necessary. That pledge, of course, caused us both confusion and shyness. If I had been my normal, lusty self, the ensuing non-verbal miscommunication might never have occurred. But maybe destiny had this in mind. I had been trying to live entirely in the present, accepting fate instead of trying to force it.

Alexander broke into my trance by leaning over and snapping his index finger against his neck, bellowing: "Denis, drink!" The room was cozy and the people favorably familiar with each other from days of hanging out.

There was no question that alcohol pulled our gang together, with the women slugging the stuff down with an efficiency equal to the men. The clear liquid helped us fit in, and created instant camaraderie. Timid folk became back-slapping buddies. Even the Russian music was geared for drinking, encouraging guttural voices to sing easy-to-remember lyrics. "What else is there to do?" Ruslan, who was slowly developing a romantic liaison with a considerably older Polish woman, had asked. "We begin drinking at nine, ten!"

At three in the morning, the *Chkalov* reached the end of the line: Dudinka, a port city at the top of the world. Vitali climaxed the festivities by escorting the birthday boy to the ship's bow. I was by this time gallantly dressed in Alexander's black wool uniform—complete with gold buttons—shiny shoes, and cap with a patent-leather visor. Vitali had finally accepted the *Americanietz*. Against a frothy crimson horizon, he handed me ten loops of rope with a five-pound knot at the end, to be used mooring the ship. This was a consolation, since the captain had refused to let the *Americanietz* drop anchor. Using exaggerated movements mixed with laughter, Vitali motioned for me to whip the knot and trailing rope on to the second level of a rather impressive dock. The Dudinka dock functioned just three months a year, and was then folded up, lest the ice flow drag it into the Arctic Ocean.

"Like a discus thrower, not cowboy!"

Two wide receivers on the dock, when informed of the quarterback's identity, yelled *"Americanietz"* and ran for cover. I heaved. Vitali laughed. The knot barely cleared the deck railing. We high-fived and strutted back to the party. The peacocks had shown their stuff.

When someone from Krasnoyarsk asked: "How did you like Dudinka?" you were expected to say something like: "Dudinka and my mother-in-law have something in common, a rotten disposition!" A nickel-mining town of thirty thousand, it was devoid of any niceties, such as trees. However, it was quiet, except for heavy green trucks crunching gravel on dusty, work-mangled roads. And its mosquitoes were angry after being thawed from the tundra. Very angry.

I saw people on their way back to the boat flailing themselves about the head and face, like institutionalized crazies. What the fuck are they doing? I wondered. Only when I also undertook the two-mile hike into town—along a pitted gravel road by the river—did I find out. Turned out tundra mossies were smart. They waited until their victim entered a zone equidistant between the boat and town before attacking. By the time I reached town, the slightly balding spot in the back of my head had more lumps than unstirred pudding.

'Town' consisted of rows of drab rectangular concrete housing and office buildings, a green town hall with a statue of Lenin, and the city's crowning joy—an aqua and beige mural of a dedicated, dark-faced Asiatic soldier wearing a turtleneck sweater. The mural was painted on the exterior of a four-storey building. Alexander and two friends in their late twenties found me staring at it. He introduced curly-haired Sergei and a bear of a man by the name of Igor. They worked on an icebreaker and lived in Dudinka. Driving a beat-up flatbed, Sergei ferried us to his apartment building, where Ruslan and the Russian ladies waited.

The snug apartment contrasted sharply with the building's exterior and the town's general ugliness. The living room was sparsely furnished but comfortable, with varnished hardwood floors. An ironing board stood next to a glass cabinet containing china dishes, while a Turkish rug and photograph of young Sergei with his parents hung on the wall next to a picture of

Christ with a halo. The TV flickered. It was showing a foreign movie with a single Russian voice interpreting all the parts.

We ate and drank everything in Sergei's small refrigerator and cupboard—a canned ham, freshly baked bread, sausages, two chicken legs, which I carved with my Swiss Army knife, more chicken, and, of course, vodka.

Svieta and Ruslan translated throughout the evening and night, as friends trickled in to meet the American. One friend, Tara, grabbed my shoulder and led me to another building and his tiny flat to meet his "English-speaking" spouse, Natasha. A stout young woman, she welcomed this man from another world with a humble smile, but spoke fewer words of English than Tara. That would be around twenty.

I returned to Sergei's carrying a present of Russian music and the couple in tow, only to be grabbed upon entry by a chunky woman in her fifties with dirty-blond hair. She was German and unhappy. Her husband had died in February of a heart attack, and she hated Dudinka. Speaking with sad, blue eyes, she related that after the big war, Stalin had rounded up Germans and moved them to this nowhere city. Her eyes lit up when she described her son—"my joy in this land." She wanted to go back to Germany but didn't know if she ever would.

Igor and I were bosom buddies by the end of the night, neither of us speaking the other's language. I became rowdy—basically shit-faced—singing, dancing, and laughing like a Russian with an American's looseness. I exchanged items of clothing and wrestled with men and women. Generally acting like a fun-loving fool. At night's end, Igor, Alexander, and Oxanna carried me out, laid me singing and laughing in the truck, then, with the others, helped me stumble up the ship's gangplank.

As the *Chkalov* glided back towards Krasnoyarsk the next morning, I sat in the piano room listening to the boy wonder play Tchaikovsky and feeling like shit. Hair dry, knee swollen, head pounding, and mouth like flour. I sipped water, and resolved to change company—for survival purposes. Also, I needed to get my body and mind in shape for the next leg of the journey. I had gained a balanced perspective about alcohol. No doubt, people like Alexander unlocked passion that otherwise might never play out. On the flip side, they burned out by forty and made a lot of people unhappy.

As I sat writing in a soft Victorian chair, a finger touched my shoulder. I gazed upwards towards the exquisite face of a young woman of indeterminate age, and the clearest green-gray eyes I had ever seen.

"Excuse me. You are the American?" she said in a firm voice with a pleasing nasal resonance. "My name is Malgorzata. I studied English at Warsaw University. When you have the opportunity, I would like to practice my English and talk to you. Not now, I can see you are busy."

Who would *not* talk to this person? She had a comfortable demeanor and fetching smile, long, curly, blond hair the color of spring corn, light skin, high cheekbones, and pleasant lips. Her neck flowed delicately into a petite body.

"Sure! I'd love to," I responded.

We agreed to meet later, and then she turned and walked gracefully across the red carpet. The piano boy played while, pen in hand, my eyes followed her. I noted the preciseness with which she dressed and flow of her walk, while trying to assess her age, to which I had become more sensitive. Jesus! I thought, where had she been?

Alexander organized a swim with my Russian friends—except Ruslan, who'd left the ship for home in Dudinka. We climbed into a launch and visited a somber, grassy location where a tribute to Stalin was encased in a marble monument. In former times, Stalin's statue stood in front, but when the magnitude of his crimes surfaced the people pulled it down. They threw Stalin into the river, creating a danger to navigation.

We trudged along a dirty, brown beach to a suitable spot, stripped to our bathing suits, and tiptoed into the frigid river, grimacing before plunging. The cold water was surprisingly painless and seemed to get warmer the longer one persevered. Magadoon did handstands and Oxanna walked to shore rubbing goosebumps. Gone, however, was that smile meant just for me.

46

THE ARCTIC: LOVE AND ROMANCE

O N THE ELEVENTH DAY, THE *Chkalov* docked at river's
edge, the sky an angry gray. Chilly winds blew. I
climbed a grassy knoll onshore, and looked out over a
vast meadow with fresh haystacks cut like old German helmets.
Crows and starlings squawked and chirped. The father of the
three artistic children that followed me around, a stocky accordion player wearing a brown tasseled beret, tapped my shoulder
and motioned to follow him across the meadow and into the forest. Speaking Russian as we traipsed over rotting, moss-covered
tree trunks, the man indicated how the silver birch was Russia's
national tree. Without speaking my language he gave meaning to
each tree and plant. I had no idea why he showed me the forest.
But I was thankful.

Back on the beach, the Polish elders had gathered, singing
songs around a cauldron of boiling water hung from a crossbar
over a raging fire. My new friend picked up his accordion and he
began to play.

From behind the cauldron, Malgorzata, in white tennis shoes, leggings, and a black woolen sweater, made her way
through the milling crowd. Her face aglow by the fire and her
long, blond, curly hair whipped by wind, she said hello and
handed me a cup.

"A special tea," she said with tranquil dignity, "made from
herbs picked in the forest. The Polish are honoring their relatives
that died in Siberia." She was self-assured and sweet.

Had she been invisible the first ten days? Or was I blinded?
I became tongue-tied. After a pregnant silence, she wandered

off. Watching her weave through the crowd, I wondered again about her age, and about my social awkwardness. I climbed the gangplank, and observed her from the deck of the boat. She was engaged for quite a while with a man in his seventies. I was impressed by how she listened and her poise with the older man.

At the opening ceremonies of the *Miss* and *Mr. Cruise* contests later that evening, I again spotted Malgorzata, and ambled over next to her.

"Do you know what the people on stage are saying?" she asked.

"Don't have a clue, and I'm performing in *both* contests. I never know what's going on in this ship. Usually I walk blindly into an event and get snagged—the American's good at making himself look stupid. By the way, you have no idea of how liberating it feels to use the full extent of my vocabulary."

"I've witnessed your Russian," she said with a gentle giggle. "I watched from the audience of the variety show when the master of ceremonies asked you your name. You were funny. You kept saying '*Da! Da! Da!*'"

"That's what I get for avoiding Russian lessons. You speak Russian?"

"*Da.*"

Before I was summoned to perform, she leaned my way and interpreted the current action on stage. Her perfect translation was refreshing. In *Miss Cruise* I dressed up as the drunken boyfriend of a pretty Russian woman with bad teeth. My acting debut was received with some fanfare. In between acts, Malgorzata casually mentioned a massage she had recently received from the ship's masseuse, and recommended her. Later, the gaunt giant Alexi became *Mr. Cruise,* with help from a sterling performance from yours truly as the drunken present he brought home to mother. I attributed this success to an American ability to ad-lib, or possibly a genetic Irish fondness for drunken, foolish behavior. They gave me a prize.

Later, as we sat in a cubbyhole cut into the wall of the second deck, Malgorzata filled me in on her life. She had recently graduated with a Master's degree from Warsaw University and worked in advertising. Though she was raised in a happy family, her father now faced the loss of his job—fallout from Poland's conversion to a market economy. Like many younger people in Poland, she had to pick up a portion of the financial load at home.

I remained in character as a divorcee, as the conversation moved to dominance in relationships, but for the first time the blank slate approach felt deceptive.

"I don't see a problem with dominance," she said, in a comfortable voice. "I think someone naturally adjusts to living with a dominant person. From a woman's perspective, I would rather the man be dominant. I am always the strong one.

"I had to break up with my boyfriend because I could not rely on him. I like a strong and dependable man. This is it! What about you?"

"I'm your dominant guy, a legacy from my grandmother. She died a few months ago."

"I am so sorry."

"It's okay, she lived a good life. Taught me how to use body language to convey inner strength. I've only known what it feels to be dominated one time."

"What happened?"

"I worked for one of the early computer companies, like Apple. The CEO and I disagreed on how to finance the company's growth. He owned sixty-five percent of the business, and venture capitalists—umm, they are people who raise large sums of money to invest in high-risk companies—owned most of the rest along with management. He had designs on being among the super wealthy, didn't want to sell any more of his stock to raise money. We got in a heated discussion over raising money at a party. He blew up, yelled in my face. I was stunned."

"What did you do?" She leaned forward. Such small hands.

"I went home and thought long and hard about whether I wanted to work for him. This company was what they call 'on the leading edge,' which means it pushed the very limits of known technology. The financial backers were powerful, and I owned enough stock ... Do you understand stock?"

"Yes, I think so. I have studied this term in school. It is a share of ownership in a company, is it not?"

"Exactly! Anyway, if the company was successful, I would fulfill a very old vision of being financially independent.

"A couple of days later, we were playing tennis after work. He was still angry. He smashed the balls, aiming at me. The game of tennis got lost in a barrage of battered balls."

"Oh my goodness!" She pronounced it *goo-di-ness*. "Egos are so important to men! What happened?"

"Well, I was the more accurate player so he slowed down, but in my mind I had already resigned the job and was in the process of reclaiming ego, as you say. So I started to increase the intensity of my shots at him. He yelled 'stop!' then walked to the net for a powwow—"

"I know that word. My English thesis was on the Native American."

She listened so intently, so interested. It was a pleasure telling the story.

"Then what happened?" she asked.

"We were able to talk it out."

"Did you become friends?"

"We are now. But, at the time, I didn't want to be friends until I had enough money so that no one could pull my strings."

"Why did you risk being fired? In Poland, jobs do not come easily."

"It was the principle of the matter. One of the responsibilities of a chief financial officer, which is what I was, is to guard against running out of money."

"And now? What are your principles?"

"Now I don't have principles."

There was a brief silence before we both erupted in laughter.

"Why did you come to the Arctic?" I asked.

Malgorzata's cousin had seen an article about a Siberian cruise in the newspaper and asked her to join him. However, a couple of days before leaving, she was rushed to the hospital with food poisoning. Her cousin took her tottering from the hospital. "We took a bus into Belarus to meet the plane. The pilot wanted more money, so we waited for thirty-six hours in a dreary hotel until negotiations finished. I was so sick and nervous about the plane. Thank goodness for my cousin. Just as we decided to go home, they agreed on price. My first plane! But then my illness kept me a recluse on the ship."

"That's why I didn't notice you!"

"The trip sounded so adventurous," she continued, ignoring my comment. "I want an exciting life. This is it! One must start."

Just then a Polish couple strode by. The woman leaned over and spoke Polish to Malgorzata. When they left, she revealed the secret. "She said they would protect me from the Russian women, because I've taken you from them." Malgorzata giggled at this and added that she had already been approached by one of the woman she saw me with.

She left to go to the bathroom. It was three in the morning.

Oh no, I thought. I didn't want to neglect the Russian women. They had been so good to me.

When she returned, she tapped her fingers on her teeth: "How old are you?"

"Forty-one." A twinge of guilt came, but like a fly it buzzed around briefly before choosing to go elsewhere. No guilt. I was who I became.

She laughed. I've been found out, I thought.

"What are you laughing at?"

"I don't know," she said, wrinkling her brow, and shaking her head slowly. "You look younger."

"That will get you everywhere."

"My pleasure!"

"Let's see. You've been working for a year. That must put you somewhere around twenty-three." A lot older than nineteen, I persuaded myself.

She nodded, and then looked around. "Are you tired?"

"No. Are you?"

"No! Then why go to bed? Are you going to find the masseuse?"

"I already did a couple of days ago. She gave my muscles a workout."

That was one way of describing my naked torso—freezing from an open porthole—being pounded raw by a burly woman. I continued, trying not to appear disdainful.

"Some years back, I learned a more soothing technique at a place called Esalen in California. I could give you a massage sometime if you want?"

We left it non-committal and continued exploring each other's life with an easy intimacy. At seven, we shook hands goodnight by the wooden banister leading up to her quarters on the second deck, in the high-rent district. I couldn't help thinking that young women were in long supply lately.

The morning found the *Chkalov* docked at yet another nondescript Siberian town. Cars, motorcycles, buses, and kiosks filled the streets. I'd been told seven out of eight Russian adults, of both sexes, smoked. I believed it. The kiosks sold cigarettes with names such as More, Sprint, and American Full Flavor, along with fish, canned goods, cheap clothing, and textiles for home sewing. Homebrew was available—if the customer brought their own container. Outdoor markets, patronized by senior citizens, displayed stacks of vegetables with defects in neat piles next to newspaper for wrapping. They used wooden pegs for calculators. The only lines I noticed were for fresh bread.

Walking down a sandy street lined with weathered cottages with gray-blue shutters and misshapen roofs, I passed a diminutive middle-aged woman carrying two pails of water. The street ended abruptly at a deep gully in which a chocolate-colored stream flowed lazily between banks of crabgrass and wildflowers. Under blustery clouds, gaggles of milk-white geese trudged up the bank chattering like bowlegged explorers. I wanted to lie under a tree at the water's edge and talk philosophy with Malgorzata.

I crossed to the other side of town to try to find her. An old man in a dirty brimmed cap gripped two bottles with dirt-encrusted fingers. A smile ripped across his furrowed face as he yelled *"Voodka!"* and climbed into the crammed back seat of a car. He put one bottle in a red plastic pail on the floor, uncapped the other, and passed it around to three other laborers.

By an old church, I came across a flow of people from the boat. I soon caught a glimpse of Malgorzata's trussed hair and attractive tush. She stood at a vegetable stall talking to a short, middle-aged man with soft, brown hair and a serious face, distinguished by a long, drooping Cossack mustache. He was listening intently to her.

She noticed me and finished the conversation. He glanced over at me, and then departed. When I approached her mood was comfortable. She said the man was her cousin. We walked to the gully, conversing like old friends. She stooped over to smell the wildflowers and pick a blade of grass to munch.

"I would like very much to take this massage you offered," she said nonchalantly. "And I think after dinner would be nice."

Just after dinner, I was in my cabin ripping the underwear off the portholes, gathering clothes draped on the chair and bunk-bed, and stashing the whole wad in the closet. The room smelled strongly of a man's odor when Malgorzata shyly entered around eight. We faced each other in the cramped space of the small quarters, said our hellos, and got down to business.

"Umm," I said, feeling composed, nervous, and brazen at the same time. "You'll have to take off your blouse."

"I do! Why?" She looked startled.

"I use massage oil," I said, with entirely honorable intentions. "When the boat masseuse gave you a massage, did you take off your blouse?"

"Well … yes." She surveyed the room, turned to face the bunks, and unbuttoned her blouse, letting it sink to the floor. She was, I noted, one of the few women onboard who didn't wear a cross around her neck.

"The bra, too. I need a smooth surface."

While she nervously unhooked her bra, I saw the curvature of her breasts, a small birthmark. I smiled inside. Women had such power and control during sexual discovery. I handed her a piece of dark chocolate and a sheet to cover up, and pointed to the bottom bunk.

"Do you want the back, or a full-body massage?"

"Well, I don't know," she stammered. "Perhaps the back."

I sat beside her on the edge of the bed.

"What are you doing?"

"I need to be comfortable."

"I see. Can we talk?"

"I'd rather not. Just relax, listen to the sound of water outside, and feel the flow of the strokes."

My hands entered her aura slowly, respectfully, and then touched her body. She stiffened. She felt petite and tight under my hands as they explored the intricate connections and tensions between muscles and bones. I breathed, trying to synchronize with her body, and in time she relaxed.

I massaged her feet and the numerous nerve endings that link to the body's vital functions. She turned her head and looked down the bed in a drowsy meditative state. "Would you sing to me?"

The request was a surprise. I had been practicing singing, trying to get back a voice that had rusted over the years. But why did she ask?

My first song was a Beatles' melody, then soulfully, a favorite tune of my dad's:

Too-ra-loo-ra-loo-ral, Too-ra-loo-ra-li,
Too-ra-loo-ra-loo-ral, That's an Irish lul-la-by

Then I sang *Summertime*. Her feet took an hour. Near the end, she looked down at me with an endorphin-induced smile, a smile all the more alluring in the dim lighting of the room. My own endorphins stirred.

I leaned forward from my position at the bottom of the bed and softly kissed her lips. Nothing! Not a quiver of an invitation did those lips reveal. She was in absolute control. I retreated, confused, and resumed massaging her feet.

Another fifteen minutes passed and again she sat up with radiant, inviting eyes. Unable to resist, I again leaned forward and kissed her. Tight lips, but this time the barest hint of invitation.

I kissed her a third time. She sucked me into the warmth of her mouth with such hunger my mind went blank. That hunger, building since we first met, had reached the pinnacle. In contrast to the lust Oxanna filled me with, the passion of Malgorzata's kiss tapped a need for an intimacy that I had lacked for quite some time. It brought me down on her—and into her psyche.

I had missed the physical and mental contact of a loving woman lately. The slowly undulating skin on skin. The gentle caresses. The penetration of her soul. The feel of her movement and mine in response. Our hands exploring every peak and valley of each other's body. The hot blood surging. The moans. The give and take. This fire was of a younger time, one untouched by the rigors of everyday life.

"Who are you?" she whispered in her throaty voice, looking into my eyes, perspiring, and breathing heavily. The question suggested destiny—as if she had been waiting for me.

"Just a traveler," I said, coming to grips with who I had become, as if for the first time. So simple a statement! So free.

"Who are you?" she asked again.

"A traveler." Inwardly, perhaps, I was still asking the same question myself.

Our intimacy might have lasted for an eternity. Afterwards, head resting on my chest, Malgorzata said she had never talked with a man for as long as she had with me the night before.

I asked her why she didn't respond to the first kiss.

"It's not proper to appear so easy," she replied and laughed. "I knew you would kiss me again."

"When did you first know I would kiss you?"

She snuggled closer, rearranging the blanket.

"Last night, you gave me that look men give women."

"What look?"

"A woman knows when she sees it. I cannot explain … I was intimidated when I first saw you in the piano room. I liked your eyes. But really! I had to get to know you after the geese."

"The geese?"

"Yes, you were singing from a sheet of paper in a village on the way to Dudinka. My cousin and I followed you. You were walking down a small, dusty road in that loose American way, wearing colorful pants and a blue-laced shirt with red swirling patterns. A woman notices a man who dresses differently. Then you stopped to talk to geese, and we were laughing. You were so American."

"Oh, I remember the geese. No kidding! You were there? I remember passing a guy from the boat, but I don't remember seeing you. Why is that? Anyway, I was learning a song when I stopped to look at these geese drinking and gurgling in a mud puddle. This big guy bossed everyone around. When I turned to leave, he walked towards me with a beady-eyed look that said he was going to kick my butt. Did you see it?"

"Yes, that was part of our laughter. What is 'butt'?"

I pointed.

"I turned around and asked the goose what I did wrong. He stopped advancing. Then when I turned to leave again, he came after me. Same look! We had words. I told him I meant no harm and that he shouldn't be so pushy."

She laughed.

"My cousin said: 'Go talk to him. It is not often in life a person meets a man in such clothes who speaks to geese.' So this is it! He gave me courage."

The next day, Malgosia (the diminutive of her name) introduced me to her cousin in their second-deck cabin. The room had class: mahogany closeting, a sink, comfortable beds, and a large table by the window overlooking the Yenisei. Anjay, a thirty-seven-year-old Krakow journalist specializing in Russian culture and politics, stroked his Cossack mustache.

I never appreciated interpreters until this day. However, as Anjay and I spoke through her, Malgosia used facial expressions to convey content, humor, and charm. She translated subtleties in each language and quickly spotted linguistic traps between Anjay and me, laughing as they developed. So easily and attractively did she laugh, that I wanted to say something funny just to see her translate. "Ha, ha! You want me to say *that*?" she would often retort.

Maintaining a serious face and eyes, Anjay listened to every word, and spoke without wasting any of his own. But he was quick to smile and just as quick with an intelligent, witty comment. His fondness for his cousin was evident in the deference he paid her, and the easiness with which they communicated. I suspected Malgosia's comfort with older men had a lot to do with her cousin.

What did I think of Russia, Anjay asked through Malgosia, while we sat sharing a bottle of champagne, which she had been saving for a special occasion.

"Tell Anjay, Malgosia, that I like the people. Those I have met are educated and have a vigorous sense of humor. The country seems largely undeveloped with a cheap, educated work force, which should eventually be attractive to Western technology. Granted, the economic problems are gigantic, but I'm optimistic. Tell him I believe Russia has been fortunate to have had two great leaders back to back."

Anjay shifted in his chair, glanced solemnly at me through cupped hands. Looking out the window at the Yenisei and the birch trees along the riverbank, he discoursed earnestly.

"Spoken like a true Westerner. They often don't understand these people, and how much money it will take to fix this country. I agree with you about Gorbachev, but not about Yeltsin. The money that Yeltsin has raised from the West is nothing. Russia's problems are staggering. Their nuclear plants and environmental problems alone are bombs waiting to detonate.

"It will take fifty years to turn this country around. They do not have fifty years. Russia is an imperialistic society and will revert back to Communism. We will not be allowed to ride the *Chkalov* to Dudinka ten years from now."

"Tell Anjay, Malgosia, that maybe he is correct. Russia may not make the transition. However, there is such evolutionary momentum here. In a relatively short time, fifty years, Communism created an educated middle class. Why? One very plausible answer is that a large middle class is the prime ingredient for democracy, the next improvement towards a higher order." I was again thinking of the theory of dissipative structures.

"Doesn't it seem to you that Communism was an evolutionary step for a powerful society to catch up to those more advanced?"

"What do you define as evolution?"

"Organization."

"Then ants will inherit the earth." He smiled.

Everyone erupted into laughter.

"He says you are observant," Malgosia continued for her cousin. "It is even possible that Russia will create a hybrid form of capitalism, where workers own the assets along with investors. But, he says to tell you this: Russia's push to a market economy is going too fast. This IMF of yours, these bankers, how do they know what they are doing? They want an economy patterned after US materialism, but the US is saturated with debt. Why prescribe for Russia the same pill?

"Gorbachev wanted Russia to go slow, like Germany after the big war. Control the stock market, the central bank, imports. Collect taxes. Beware my friend! Russia is dangerous! The last time Russia patterned their economy after the West, they dumped the bankers and went on their own."

"You, too, are observant," I exclaimed. "Maybe the forces of change will be too fast. But Russia can do amazing things, don't you think? Why not be optimistic, pay them to disarm and form a society with the benefits of capitalism and democracy?"

"If you want to be optimistic look to Russia's east, here in Siberia. They have the work ethic and strength of will. And Russia does have the unfair advantage of a highly educated, low-wage workforce. But be careful of the Big Bear! She will go back to old habits when short of food."

47

HERO OF THE SOVIET UNION

PLANNED TO CATCH THE THREE o'clock train for Moscow when the *Chkalov* docked in Krasnoyarsk the next day. As part of the goodbye process, Malgosia and I climbed to the third-deck cabin belonging to Ninnell and Andrei Pavlovich. Ninnell gave me their Moscow address and telephone number, handwritten on a business card. The print on the card, in both English and Russian, read:

Andrei P. Katishev,
Member of Presidium, Soviet Committee for Peace,
Disarmament and Ecological Security at Seas and Oceans.
Rear admiral (Retired). Hero of Soviet Union.

To my query, Malgosia translated that Andrei became a hero as the first captain to maneuver a submarine under the polar ice-caps and plant the Russian flag. Andrei looked at me with his normal authoritarian face.

"You brave man," he said in English.

"Why?" I asked him through Malgosia.

"Because I would be much afraid to travel across the United States without knowing the language."

I couldn't believe it. This guy navigated under ice, and he called *me* brave for having a great time. One man's meat is another man's poison.

We shook hands warmly. Ninnell pointed a finger at me, eyes bulging somberly behind the wide rims of her glasses, and using Malgosia she said: "Be careful of the crew. Last year, a poor unfortunate drank with them. They spiked his drink, robbed him, passport and all, and threw him unconscious into the river."

"Malgosia, please tell this to Ninnell, word for word: 'I have a beautiful Polish woman who is going to make sure I follow those directions.'"

"I cannot tell her that!"

"Word for word!"

She blushed as she spoke in Russian. But the words had their desired effect and the stern faces of Andrei and Ninnell transformed to laughter.

Goodbyes completed, and out of earshot, Malgosia threatened: "I am not going to let you drink with the crew, you know!"

"I'll need one or two toasts to avoid insult. And, by the way, I asked the Russian women if they could show me their town and take me to the train station tomorrow."

"You what? Tomorrow is our last day! A Polish bus is touring the town and I thought you would go with me."

"I have to go with them. These women treated me special, and I've hardly spoken to them since I met you."

Just then Magadoon and Vitali grabbed me for a farewell shot of vodka. The crew had gathered in Alexander's third-deck cabin, but without Alexander. The captain had unceremoniously dumped him for getting drunk and cavorting with passengers. Malgosia followed along, into the smoky room. One drink, then Alexi hugged me and Magadoon said he'd see me in the United States.

That last night, Malgosia and I made love in my room. The sound of water marked perhaps what would be our last night together. I told her I loved her.

Suddenly distant, she asked soberly, "Why?"

"Because that's the way I feel." She remained listless. Then she pulled me tightly to her. Both of us knew this love had little chance of survival.

The next ten hours passed romantically and frantically. Around four in the morning, Malgosia asked if I wanted to take the plane back to Moscow with the Polish. A chill crept up my spine. Their pilot was moonlighting in a giant jet! Part of me was up for the experience, but, besides the danger, another reservation was that

Sasha would be waiting for my train in Moscow, and there was no way to contact him if for some reason the pilot caused trouble again. Sasha would arrive at half past five in the morning from his dacha, twelve hours by train from the city. His sole reason for returning was to pick me up—Irina and their son were staying on for another week.

Malgosia spoke to Andrei Pavlovich to confirm that I could fly at no charge. However, her cousin reminded us about the shaky nature of the pilot and uncertain departure. If I intended to be in Moscow at a fixed time, I was taking a big gamble, he thought. Malgosia was adamant that I fly, but accepted a compromise. If my train arrived on time, I would get on it. If not, I would fly.

Soon it was time to leave. I stood next to the gangplank saying goodbye to Malgosia. Her tour bus, loaded with Poles and spewing diesel, waited thirty feet away. It was ten to twelve. The Russian women were due at twelve sharp to show off their city. Vitali, drunk, with tears streaming down his face, was writing my address on his palm while the captain glared from the bridge. Malgosia was visibly annoyed at Vitali for monopolizing the moment. After he left, she stood hands on hips, eyes deep into mine.

"Miss the train!" she commanded.

"Malgosia," I implored, "I'd love nothing more, believe me! But if that train comes in on time, I just know I'll get on it. I'm a traveler."

She kissed me deeply as the occupants of the bus cheered. "Miss the train!" she repeated, before turning to go.

Just after her bus pulled out of sight, the Russian women emerged from inside the *Chkalov*. Close call! Ula and Natasha wore long, formal dresses and black, double-breasted jackets, and Svieta a tight, gray flannel, knee-length skirt, her flaming hair dominant. "Oxanna not make it," Ula said. "You understand."

In a flurry, they showed me their city, and then deposited me at the train station. The Moscow train arrived on time. Part of me had hoped it would be hours late. Yet there was also the thought that fate had saved me from an involvement that would cause great pain. Before stepping on to the train, I gave Svieta a sealed letter with a $50 bill inside, to be opened after I boarded. It read:

To Oxanna, Svieta, Ula, and Natasha. For being so hospitable, please put on your makeup and best clothes and go party.

I watched from the train window as the three women walked down the platform opening the envelope. When they looked inside they jumped in the air, holding each other like lottery winners. Fifty dollars went a long way in Siberia.

48

BACHELORS!

THE TRAIN HADN'T CLEARED THE station when my three fellow travelers, all women in their mid-forties, began unzipping bags. First, white napkins, then a thermos of hot water to be mixed with raspberry preserve, then the food. I waited for the tap on the shoulder. It came. "Oh, I couldn't! Well, maybe just a taste!"

The sweetness of this beginning almost scrubbed away the sense of loss. The words *Miss the train! Miss the train!* beat in unison with the *ka-chunk* of wheels on track. It seemed a lifetime ago that I left Sasha in Moscow. Relationships made and left, then alone again.

I wrote Malgosia a letter telling her my journey was about becoming another person. In other times, I was forty-eight and married, with two daughters older than she. When I was "divorced" I didn't have to answer questions about why I didn't bring my wife along. No restrictions, no biases. Otherwise, we might never have shared what we did, I said, and hoped the experience was as much fun for her as for me. She helped me renew a passion. Though we knew each other for such a short time, I believed destiny brought us together for a reason.

As the miles passed, I wondered if we would ever meet. Coincidently, if there is such a thing as coincidence, I was reading a book of short stories by Chekhov.

"Needless, petty and deceptive were the things that keep people from loving each other," his character spoke. "They ask themselves where this affair will lead me. In judgments about love, start with something higher than happiness or unhappiness, virtue and sin, or make no judgments at all."

For a thousand miles these words of Chekhov became intermingled with *Miss the train.*

I started my journey a man in control of his destiny, and now I felt destiny was in control of me. Was that the difference between the controller and the traveler?

Sasha met me at the vast Moscow station still looking like Abraham Lincoln in jeans. We trundled over to the Western mini-market, and dropped a bottle of good French wine in the basket along with fixings for another spaghetti dinner—Sasha's choice and my treat. At his flat, Sasha heated up mushrooms Irina picked and cooked at their dacha, adding them to the sauce I was making. He poured wine into two glasses and toasted "to friends." After a refill, I asked Sasha if Russia would revert back or move forward.

"Young are future! For too long people not visit other countries. Young want what is new, and old die! Five years ago, I never hear of dollar. Now change come like flies to rotten meat. There is no stopping!"

Sasha sipped the French wine gently, and then held the glass forward, beaming. "This," he said, "better than vodka!"

What's next?

BOOK 2
BREAKING FREE—THE TRAVELER

B OOK 2, BREAKING FREE–THE TRAVELER continues zesty travel adventures through Europe (Poland, Greece, Turkey), and distant lands of Asia (India, Nepal, Thailand, Vietnam), Indonesia, Australia, and New Zealand.

Denis has three major tests of his *traveler* character, as he flows with the wind and follows his heart. The traveler expands discussions on relationships and visions, and relishes smart conversations, intimacy, adventure and funny situations. It took until the tundra in Russia to embrace a traveler personality and let go of his controlling nature. Now freedom of having little control is intoxicating. Denis has six more months to travel the rest of the world, test his new personality, and achieve a vision he carried through life—of a great family and enough money so that nobody can pull his strings.

The book continues the writer's personal life and its turmoil. The love story with Malgosia becomes more complicated as reunion with his wife and daughters nears. Malgosia's last kiss in Siberia still burns intensely. But now he begins to consider consequences.

He formulates new values and learns how change is accomplished through visions. A changed man, he reunites with his family in New Zealand and returns home hoping he is equipped to balance the challenges that dominate his life—family, money and personal freedom. The reader closes the book with a new perspective on the world, a fresh means for enacting personal change, and curious about whether Denis will fit into the life he left behind.

Excerpt from Book 2
Breaking Free—The Traveler

The author and longtime friend Frank Zolfo (the Big Z) take their first elephant trip through the jungle in Thailand, winding up in a small primitive village where the Z gets his first taste of a natural way of life.

BIG Z TRAVELS LIGHT

NEXT, WE HAD TO MOUNT our elephant. We climbed steps to a platform made out of hewn trees. At the top, a handler instructed us to walk on to the massive, wrinkled head of an Indian elephant with a sawed-off tusk, then along its back to a bamboo cradle. This looked far more dangerous than the bridge. Traversing those few steps from the platform across the leathery head of the beast was like balancing fifteen feet up on Jabba the Hutt. Attempting to ignore the height, I stepped along with my arms out. What did the elephant make of it? Finally, I could gingerly turn around and plop into the cradle next to Frank, who somehow had maneuvered the distance with his swollen leg. Sitting side by side, we laughed nervously, legs dangling from the cradle on to the elephant's back.

The beast set off into the jungle—delicately, like a ballerina, tip-toeing down a red-clay path no wider than the length of a child's arm. High in the air, we clung to each other, staring at the middle branches of trees and looking down at the path. It was like being on a moving four-story bridge. The elephant's eyes were small, unlike those of horses. For some reason, that made a difference, made me feel more trusting. When the dips were particularly treacherous, Frank and I yelled and screamed like kids on a roller coaster, clutching the rickety cradle and each other. We shouted our fears and wild instructions to the elephant and the guide riding on its neck. My New York accent, which had lain buried under layers of Northern California propriety, blasted its way out to mingle with the Big Z's in a coordinated opera of profanity.

Frank knew how to say "fuck" naturally, with perfect inflection and tone. He wielded it like an artist wields his favorite brush. You had to have New York-Irish or Italian blood to use the word properly. It was definitely nurture over nature. The fetching flexibility of the word was lost in the gentility of California. Fuck cut through the bullshit. It created meaningful dialogue between Frank and me, helped us relate and identify with each other, to get in touch with our feelings.

As we shouted, the twelve-year-old guide took a different approach and Frank got his first taste of how another society treats animals. The boy beat the head of this noble beast with a wooden truncheon, until blood trickled down its forehead and into its eye. I yelled at him to stop, and he did. Elephants were beasts of burden, and dogs and cats a barely tolerated evil. Remembering the magnificence of elephants in Africa, I couldn't help but think how we had enslaved so many millions of animals on the principle that they were inferior. Our egos must need this distinction.

Two and a half hours into the jungle, the caravan halted at a clearing. We then trekked by foot another two hours, emerging into a primitive settlement of thatched huts. Chickens and small pigs meandered about the garbage. Jungle John escorted his troop to an elongated hut made entirely of bamboo. Colored gray-white like aged hair, the thatched roof came halfway to the ground. A weathered picnic table sat awkwardly outside. Inside was dark and humid with a hard dirt floor. Thick woven bamboo mats covered the wooden-slat bunks. Clearly not incorporated into the village, this hut marked us as outsiders.

Frank, however, thought the place was "fuckin' great." Discarding his cane for the first time, he limped along on a pre-dinner excursion, discovering that men worked in the fields until dusk. He saw women with babies strapped to their backs balancing buckets on both ends of a pole running across their shoulders. With joy, he listened to the sound of music coming from a strange-looking bamboo pipe, sniffed the aroma of cooking herbs, and observed dirty kids laughing as they kicked tin cans and threw kittens into the air (or at trees). This was his first sense of the old way.

"People go to bed when the sun goes down, and get up when it rises!" Frank exclaimed with amazement. I'd had that exact thought in a little village in Zimbabwe at the start of my journey. His enthusiasm was renewing my own sense of seeing, tasting, and feeling.

After dinner, two long-haired, somber young men walking barefoot entered the hut. One of them carried a long opium pipe and asked for volunteers. Angelo, the Italian in our group, quickly offered to be first. The New York Italian meanwhile paced up and down the dirt floor puffing furiously on a cigarette, struggling with his conscience. The rest of us waited our turn with the pipe.

The villager with the pipe had a characteristically sparse mustache and wore blue sweats with a yellow line down the sides and a smudged white T-shirt. He gestured at Frank to be next to sample nirvana. "No way," said the Z, speaking to the group. "I just don't feel right about drugs. But I don't mind if you guys try."

In case anyone else succumbed to guilt, the young tribesmen told us of the positive medicinal effects of opium. Their solemn countenances attested to the fact that opium sales were serious income for this hamlet. While drug sales were illegal in Thailand, that stricture did not apply to the hill tribes.

From a process perspective, smoking opium started with a bamboo mat, which served as a workbench, and tools: a candle, a long needle that looked like a hatpin from the Thirties, a lighter, and the pipe, consisting of a foot-and-a-half-long stem connected to a singed green, metal container. Slouching forward, the young villager mixed the poppy with aspirin granules for bulk and consistency, then, using the long needle, shoved the resulting black gunk in the pipe. To smoke, you lay prone and inhaled while he applied the candle flame. The black mass undulated and bubbled to the dancing flame as you puffed away.

I didn't find the opium overpowering, more it felt like the lingering lethargy of lying on a beach in a daydream, watching sunlight flicker off waves. Afterwards still in that state, I wandered around the hamlet. Opium was right in these hills—a place devoid of television, movies, video games, city activity. Here was only nature and basic life activities.

    ...

CPSIA information can be obtained at www.ICGtesting.com
Printed in the USA
LVOW10s0517140913

352202LV00004B/126/P